Women and Political Conflict

Women and Political Conflict

Portraits of Struggle in Times of Crisis

Edited by
Rosemary Ridd
and
Helen Callaway

NEW YORK UNIVERSITY PRESS
Washington Square, New York

First published 1987 in the U.S.A. by
New York University Press
Washington Square
New York, N.Y. 10003

Photoset in Times by
CAS Typesetters, Southampton

Printed in Great Britain

Library of Congress Cataloging-in-Publication Data

Women and political conflict.

Based on a seminar convened by Rosemary Ridd in Trinity term 1981 at Queen Elizabeth House, Oxford, under the auspices of the Oxford University Women's Studies Committee.
Includes bibliographies and index.
Contents: Powers of the powerless/Rosemary Ridd—War in Cyprus: patriarchy and the Penelope myth/Maria Roussou—Women, the damned of the Iranian revolution/Homa Nategh—[etc.]
1. Women in politics. 2. Power (Social sciences)
3. Women—Social conditions. I. Ridd, Rosemary.
II. Callaway, Helen. III. University of Oxford. Women's Studies Committee.
HQ1236.W634 1987 320'.088042 86-12817
ISBN 0-8147-7398-2
ISBN 0-8147-7399-0 (pbk.)

Contents

Acknowledgements

The impetus for this collection of essays came from a seminar series convened by Rosemary Ridd in Trinity Term 1981 at Queen Elizabeth House, Oxford. These seminars were held under the auspices of the Oxford University Women's Studies Committee. Five of the eight papers have been revised for publication here together with three additional chapters, those by Homa Nategh, Moiram Ali and Rosemary Sayigh and Julie Peteet. The editors wish to thank the Oxford University Women's Studies Committee for its financial support, Jo Garcia for her translation from the French of Homa Nategh's chapter, and also Wade Goria and Selwyn Gross for their comments and expert advice in the editing of two of the chapters.

ROSEMARY RIDD
HELEN CALLAWAY

Notes on the Contributors

Moiram Ali now works for Third World First as a fieldworker with responsibility for anti-racism. She has a degree in sociology with education from the University of York.

Alison M. Bowes is Lecturer in Social Anthropology at the University of Stirling. Her publications include 'Strangers in the kibbutz' in *Man*, 1981, and 'The Organisation of Labour in an Israeli Kibbutz' in Long (ed.), *Family and Work in Rural Societies*.

Helen Callaway is Deputy Director of the Centre for Cross-Cultural Research on Women at Queen Elizabeth House, Oxford. She is a social anthropologist who did fieldwork in Nigeria, and has numerous publications relating to women, and her book on European colonial women in Nigeria is in preparation for the St Antony's/Macmillan series.

Lynda Edgerton is a political scientist, a graduate of Queen's College, Belfast, who now lectures at Belfast College of Technology. She left school at the age of 15 to work in a scissors factory in Sheffield. In 1969, an unemployed single parent of two children, she moved to Belfast, where she became a founder member of the Northern Ireland Women's Rights Group, an active member of the Civil Rights movement and a member of the Communist Party.

Clare Krojzl trained in Oriental studies and social anthropology, did her doctoral research on the social institutions of Turkish migrant workers in West Berlin. She now lives in Czechoslovakia.

Maryon McDonald is Lecturer in Social Anthropology at Brunel University, a former editor of the *Journal of the Anthropological Society of Oxford* and research fellow at the Université de Haut Bretagne, Rennes, 1978–9, and Girton College, Cambridge, 1983–5.

Homa Nategh is a leading member of the radical Iranian Writers' Association, author of *Djamāl-ed-Din Assad-Ābādi dit Afghāni*, Paris 1969, and numerous other publications on late nineteenth-century Iranian history, and is an editor of *Zamān-e Now* (The New Age). She was formerly Professor of History at Tehran University and now lives in exile in Paris.

Julie Peteet is an American social anthropologist who did her doctoral research among Palestinians in Chatila camp, Beirut, 1980–2. She now teaches at Georgetown University.

Rosemary Ridd is a social anthropologist and member of Wolfson College, Oxford. Her doctoral research on an inner-city area in South Africa where women had a dominant role in the community as a response to racial oppression (summarised in Ardener (ed.), *Women and Space*) prompted the questions raised in this volume. She is interested in inter-religious dialogue and has written, *inter alia*, on South African Muslims in Weekes (ed.), *Muslim Peoples: A World Ethnographic Survey*.

Maria Roussou is a Greek Cypriot educationalist resident in Britain. She wrote her doctoral thesis on women's issues in Cyprus for the University of London and has been employed as the Greek Co-ordinator of the Schools Council Mother Tongue Project in London.

1 Powers of the Powerless[1]

ROSEMARY RIDD

What happens to women in periods of political conflict and how do women express themselves politically at such times? In this collection of essays we consider how women's experience of public strife conforms to or differs from that of men and how women perceive their interests in the context of a struggle in which their society is engaged.

In times of conflict, when an entire community is directly affected by public or institutionalised political goals, the lives of men as well as women become more politically focused; but for women this experience can be the more intense when they encounter what is conventionally deemed to be the male domain. Some of these studies show women as the victims of powerlessness as they become more heavily controlled by bureaucratic procedures and societal conventions designed to keep them out of public political affairs; others bring out the ways in which women deploy their own powers in public service as they gain greater freedom of expression in the course of conflict.

Women's powers, men's power

We begin with three propositions. The first is that institutionalised power is for the most part controlled by men, and that where women enter the public domain they generally do so within a male-ordered framework. There has been much discussion in feminist circles since 1974, when Michelle Rosaldo published her 'Theoretical Overview' where she distinguishes between women's 'domestic orientation' to a lifestyle devoted to the home and family relations, and men's 'public orientation' to a lifestyle concerned with extra-domestic matters of economic, political and military import. Rosaldo argues that this social dichotomy is commonly treated as a 'natural' function of the physical differences between men and women although it is in reality no more than a man-made device.

It has been shown, in the context of Western Europe in particular, that the distinction between public and private has become blurred over the past decade by the trend among women increasingly to seek work outside the home. In broad terms, however, the dichotomy remains. Women's employment is often considered as a secondary activity, as witnessed by the large numbers of women in part-time and low paid jobs. And very often where women do take up careers they must work their way up through male structures, along the kind of path Max Atkinson (1984, pp. 119–21) traced out in his analysis of Mrs Thatcher's rise to power. It is not our intention to argue that women *should* necessarily break into the public domain but to recognise that where women do step outside their allotted domestic sphere they enter a dominantly male terrain, just as those intrepid men who choose to be 'househusbands' or full-time childminders are faced with the conventions of the female domestic orientation.

In our second proposition we join various other feminist writers in arguing that the distinction between domestic and public orientations should be strictly correlated with non-political and political spheres of activity. In recent years attention has been drawn to the political significance of housework (e.g. Malos, 1980), motherhood (e.g. Lewis, 1980) and abortion (e.g. Jaggar, 1976), and to the intrusion of public decision-making into women's domestic orientation (e.g. Randall, 1982, pp. 108–15). The essays contained in this volume present solid evidence that women are not without power in their non-public roles and nor are they non-political beings.

Rosaldo herself refers to powers that women may exercise in the domestic sphere in terms of their influence over their family members and, in some cases, their control over their grown-up sons. But she depoliticises such power by arguing that women possess this when they act on their own behest but they lack the authority to legitimate their actions in society. In this volume, however, it is more appropriate to think in terms of *women's powers* and *men's power*: women's powers as being more diffuse and individualised outside the bureaucratic structures of society; men's power as being more co-ordinated and structured within an institutionalised framework.

The pervasiveness of men's institutional power to penetrate beyond recognised political organisations into the whole public sphere of life is suggested in a seminal essay on power by Steven Lukes (1974). To the first dimension of overt political action, to which many commentators confine themselves, Lukes adds a second dimension, that of power as a more covert coercive force, and then goes further to consider a third dimension where power is used to control people by taking no apparent action at all but allowing people to misunderstand where their interests lie and so to acquiesce in their own subordination. In this volume we shall see examples of how power is exercised within a wide institutional framework, through religious and industrial as well as specifically political agencies, and how women in particular are vulnerable to institutional power because they are strangers to it. But we shall see also how some women make use of their own political powers through the strength and agility they derive from being at least partially removed from the bureaucratic structures of society.

In times of conflict

We come now to the third proposition; that when a community is involved in open conflict and all resources are directed towards countering an external threat and meeting a common goal, there is likely to be some fluidity in the social ordering unless steps are taken to prevent this. It is a curious paradox that conflict, however much it may be outwardly directed towards bringing about change in society, can be at the same time an inherently conservative agent. The sense of insecurity that accompanies such disturbances reflects strongly upon women, particularly where they are represented as the custodians of a society's cultural values which, like its art treasures, are in constant need of protection and especially when that society comes under attack. Thus we may find at these times a tension existing between women who find new opportunities to express themselves politically and men who step up their efforts to control women and try to reinforce the boundary that separates the domestic from the public sphere.

Western media sometimes reflect this tension in their coverage of political conflict by interpreting women's action as being purely supportive of men's struggle (as they tended to do with the part played by women in the British miners' strike of 1984 to 1985) or by treating women's contribution in terms of their accepting a temporary role change to meet a crisis. Cinematic presentations of British women in the Second World War, wearing military uniform or managing heavy factory machinery and driving ambulances, used these conventionally unfeminine stances to suggest women's special sacrifice to the war effort. At the end of the war women were expected to return to the home and, for middle class married women in particular, it became again not quite respectable to go out to work. *Tenko*, Lavinia Warner's television series for the BBC, reveals many of the frustrations of British women who, once released from Japanese prisoner-of-war camps, were expected to revert to conventionally passive feminine roles and to leave the public affairs to men. Where women do assert themselves in some political role *as women* they must be well received, even honoured, as were the Women for Peace in Northern Ireland, if they are seen to hold steadfast to their conventional domestic roles, but once they focus their action outside the home they become liable to rough treatment from society. The suspicion of Greenham Common women towards the media reflects their deep mistrust of journalists who accuse them of abrogating their responsibilities as mothers, the very responsibilities as it happens that most concern them in their fight against American nuclear bases in Britain.

Where, however, women do not appear to step out of their domestic orientation in times of conflict, we may glimpse instances of their political powers, sometimes in covert, sometimes in symbolic forms. Women seen as political innocents can on occasion use this immunity to take initiatives and responsibilities of a covert political nature. Conditions of guerrilla war provide a number of examples of women employed as couriers because they are less likely than men to be body-searched. During the early days of the Algerian war, women smuggled weapons under their long robes until this ploy was discovered by the French. Also, Brian Lapping (1985, p. 335) reports that EOKA, the Greek Cypriot guerrilla army, used women as couriers in the 1950s, and that the two who attended Colonel George Grivas when he concealed himself in a house near Limassol were the only persons entrusted with the knowledge of his whereabouts.

Women's powers can take on various symbolic forms. A society may use the power of women, for example, to represent to the outside world its determination on all-out struggle in which 'even' women, and children, play their part. This principle has been used effectively in Muslim, especially Shi'ite, communities where women in chadors are photographed by the Western press, fists clenched and shouting for Ayatollah Khomeini in the streets of Tehran or holding aloft Kalashnikov rifles in Beirut and southern Lebanon. Here the seemingly conflicting notions of the protected female and the militant woman are juxtaposed to maximum effect. Women can also represent the heightened sentiments of society in times of conflict, particularly when mourning the dead. Israeli women have also been shown on British television screens in the 1980s weeping over the bodies of soldiers who sacrificed their lives at the war front. Such funerals, like those for victims of sectarian killings in Northern Ireland, became politically charged, with women consciously or unconsciously most cogently expressing the mood of the people.

It may be argued that such powers, covert or symbolic, are inextricably bound up in women's powerlessness, where women are subject either to the control or manipulation of their activities by men or to the form in which society represents them. In Britain in 1982, for example, widows and mothers of the nation's dead were presented by those who upheld the fighting as women who had made sacrifice in a just war in the Falklands and at the same time by the opponents of the war to publicise the unnecessary anguish brought about by a misguided cause in the South Atlantic. But there is also evidence of ways in which women assert themselves politically through their domestic orientation, and indeed such powers can be the most pronounced through women's capacity to embody the culture and essence of their people. Something of this power was seen in Argentina among the mothers of the *Plazo de Mayo* as they paraded before the presidential palace to demand that their government account for the disappearance of their sons in that country's 'dirty war'. More dramatic still was the power of Jewish motherhood when in 1985 three women successfully pressed Defence Minister Rabin and the Israeli Cabinet for the release of over a thousand Palestinian prisoners in exchange for their three sons being held by the PLO.

Some glimpses of the part women play in a period of conflict can be gleaned from Philip Hallie's (1979) absorbing study of Le Chambon, a small Huguenot community, in its resistance to the Vichy regime in wartime France. Hallie argues that the study of power need not stop with the powerful but should also take account of the response of the weak who stood up to Marshal Pétain's government and who had their own modest achievements which were in danger of going unrecorded. He described Le Chambon's war effort in sheltering a stream of Jews fleeing the Nazis as a 'kitchen struggle'. Here it seems there is much scope for examining the political role of women within the community.

But even in these conditions the study is focused on male resistance organisation, and while it becomes clear that women also took political initiatives, women are still presented in a wholly supportive role. The author looks at the struggle through the institutional framework of the village as a conflict centred on the pastor, Andre Trocmé, and his wife: the Protestant temple and the presbytery. Trocmé is the hero of the book, the one who rallied the people from the temple pulpit, held meetings in the presbytery, trudged through waist-deep snow to keep in regular contact with his *responsables*, risked his life by refusing to sign the oath of allegiance to the Vichy regime, and together with other local spokesmen was arrested and taken to a detention camp from which he was lucky to return at the end of the war.

Within this chronicle there are glimpses of another story, that of the women of Le Chambon. It was Mme Magda Trocmé who was confronted on her doorstep with the first Jewish refugee to come to Le Chambon, and who, in taking the stranger into her home, initiated a chain of activity which was to occupy the village for the rest of the war. It was she who went to the mayor's office to obtain papers for that refugee and, upon encountering non-co-operation, recognised that she must rely on her own initiative to get what she required. (The village authorities were prepared to defend their own people but they would not take risks to help outsiders.) So it was Mme Trocmé who reluctantly recognised the need to compromise on hard-held Protestant principles for practical ends; to lie if need be, to counterfeit identity documents and, most difficult of all, to teach her children about these deceptions. Mme Trocmé's network of 'the houses' in which Jews were secreted became one of silent action in which women moved with the minimum of discussion, recognising that in sharing information they also passed on the heavy burden of responsibility for human lives.

Hallie's study is well worth reading as a faithful record of the way the people of Le Chambon themselves appear to have perceived the framework of their resistance in the Second World War. But it may leave the feminist reader, at least, with the tantalising desire to know more about the women's 'kitchen struggle'. In a study that attempts to break away from the conventional approach to power by looking at localised response to governmental control, it would have been most instructive to have gone one stage further, beyond the institutionalised response of the men's network, to the informal, silent network of the women. This is the approach we set out to take in this volume.

It is important to note at this juncture that in looking at changes which occur in times of conflict we do not imply adherence to the functionalist view of society in which disturbances are treated as though they are abnormal and isolated events in an otherwise untroubled and unchanging world. The seeds of strife are continuously present and where conflict does break into the open we should recognise this as being a consequence of events in supposedly 'normal' and peaceful times. Wars, for example, which may seem at the time to be bounded by specific declarations to mark the beginning and end of hostilities, become in the long term part of a succession of events between antagonists. Likewise, industrial action does not occur out of the blue, but represents the breakdown of relations between workforce and management, relations which the observer may follow over a much longer time span.

Most of the studies presented here take cognisance of a period of heightened tension in the context of a broader period of conflict. Because the scope is so wide, the topics selected for investigation are restricted in time and space to contemporary Western Europe and the Middle East. The types of political conflict, however, are diverse: war in Cyprus, Islamic revolution in Iran, the National question in Northern Ireland, industrial action in Britain, the Palestinian struggle for survival in refugee camps in Lebanon, ideological conflict within an Israeli kibbutz, the Breton separatist issue in France, and the Turkish migrants' fight to retain an ethnic identity in West Berlin.

Living with conflict

The spotlight turns here on to women in the mainstream of society, ordinary women whose lives become enmeshed in a political conflict that involves the whole community. This collection is not intended as an addition to the important corpus of material already published on those more exceptional women who devote their lives to a political cause, eschewing family and domestic life for this purpose. Rather than concentrating their attention on women as cadres for the PLO or the IRA or as soldiers in the Israeli army, for example, the contributors have set out to give the reader some sense of what living with conflict really means to women with family responsibilities and what happens to them when they become caught up in political issues that concern everyone in the community.

Living with conflict is also a statement on the contributors to this volume, each of whom writes from personal involvement in the community under discussion and, in most cases, from personal observations of the conflict, to back up the information they derive from interviews and published sources. The contributors fall into three main categories. Homa Nategh and Maria Roussou write of their own Iranian and Greek Cypriot societies, which both were forced to leave as a result of the conflict which they now analyse. Nategh is one of a number of academics in Tehran who, as she states in her chapter, welcomed the revolution in 1979 but was later to share in the general disillusionment of the people.

Lynda Edgerton and Rosemary Sayigh are English women, one a political scientist of Protestant background who went to live in a mainly Catholic suburb of Belfast in 1969 at the time when the Civil Rights Movement was gaining momentum, the other a social anthropologist who has lived for three decades in the southern suburbs of Beirut. 'Having been involved in the working class struggle in my home town of Sheffield', Edgerton writes:

> it was natural for me to be interested in the struggle for civil rights in Belfast. Working class people experience similar living and working conditions in both these towns but the Northern Ireland of 1969 was also very different from the British mainland. For the first time I saw police with guns, and on demonstrations we were surrounded by jeeps and armoured cars. Here I found myself

> involved in a campaign for basic democratic rights, like one person one vote, which were taken for granted in the rest of the United Kingdom. For fifty years the Stormont government had been allowed to exact a succession of repressive laws and policies which were directed at the Catholic Republican sector of the working class and those sectors of the Protestant working class which did not subscribe to Unionism and Orangism. (Personal communication, 1985)

Sayigh, the mother of Palestinian children, tells of how her writing arose out of her observations during regular family occasions:

> I first became interested in Palestinian women during visits to relatives of my husband in Debayak camp where I was struck by the absence of the 'harassed housewife' type. In spite of large households, poverty, insecurity and heavy workloads, they betrayed none of the personality disorders that I associated with a life confined to domesticity. Chaos reigned from dawn to dusk, there was never a moment of peace or relaxation; there were always a hundred calls on their attention, yet they never lost track of what they were doing, never for a second lost control of themselves or their domain (lost their tempers, yes of course, but that's a different thing). I never heard one of them say, as English women do when indulging in a good grumble, 'I can't bear it. . . .' So although I became aware of their oppression as women, I responded first to their strength, second to their objective situation. (Personal communication, 1985)

The other five contributors write as temporary sojourners and participant observers who set out specifically to study a community other than their own. For most of them, successful research necessitated their identifying themselves with their informants. Moiram Ali found her sympathies with the miners' cause were important in gaining the confidence of the women and for encouraging them to speak frankly of their experience, revealing their own dilemmas behind the resolute public face. Likewise the fact that Julie Peteet (an American social anthropologist) was known to support the Palestinian cause helped her to gain an entreé to the Beirut camps and introductions to women living there through female PLO cadres. Such connections were vital for establishing a level of trust with housewives beyond the conventions of superficial conversation. For Alison Bowes, it was not necessary to take a militant stand on Israeli issues, but she writes as one who lived and worked on the kibbutz which she pseudonomyously calls Goshen. Out of this experience she dispels the popular myth of gender equality in the kibbutzim and challenges the pronouncements of writers like Tiger and Shepher on the kibbutz women's 'natural' female role.

Such studies offer the reader insight into women's thoughts and feelings which often elude reporters who must rely on a question and answer format. But the counterweight to this privileged insider view is the particular responsibility the writer has to the community she studies and to her informants who may risk much danger in sharing information with her. Sensitivity to this danger then calls for some commitment to the community on the part of the writer and, in many cases, makes it unfeasible and inappropriate for her to become involved with people on more than one side in an issue.

The writer as an outsider seeking to be objective may learn on the job the hazards of research in circumstances of high tension. Clare Krojzl, an English woman, had to dissociate herself from Germans, with whom she was sometimes confused, if she were to gain the confidence of the Turkish migrants in Berlin. She also came up against German suspicion towards outsiders who posed a potential threat to German paternalistic perceptions of the Turkish community's needs. Krojzl writes:

> Early in my fieldwork I met a [German] journalist who gave me the address of one or two women's refuges in Berlin. As I knew that anything up to fifty per cent of the intake of these refuges was accounted for by Turkish nationals, I was eager to make contact. I wrote a long letter, explaining who I was and offering to give any assistance I could in exchange for being allowed to speak with Turkish women staying there, to obtain material for my research. I received no reply, so after a few days I telephoned and explained my position again. This time I was invited to go to the refuge the following day.
>
> On arrival I again explained who I was and gave the name of the woman who had invited me. The response I received [from the German organisers] after what I believed to have been a

> cautious and appropriate introduction, was hostile out of all proportion. I was shouted at and abused, and almost thrown out of the house as a suspicious character and intruder. The following day my original contact at the refuge, who had not been there at the appointed time, telephoned, and she insulted me with accusations of attempting to infiltrate the refuge for my own ends.
>
> This experience proved to be the most dramatic example of 'racial paternalism' of German towards Turk that I encountered, but the fundamental attitude behind it caused me to question the political framework in which the problem of Turkish women could be articulated. (Personal communication, 1985)

Maryon McDonald, writing on Brittany, also uncovered an unanticipated facet of conflict through her own entanglement in it. After staying a year with Breton separatist militants in Rennes, she moved inland to live among Breton peasant farmers and the 'real' Breton culture that the militants were devoted to defending. But here she encountered an ageing population (with younger people leaving for the towns) who seemed to denigrate what the militants esteemed and who saw *their* ideals in Parisian refinement. In this case the social anthropologist herself added a new dimension to the situation. McDonald's revelations about Breton peasant attitudes threatened to be more damaging to the militants' cause than the muted voice of the peasants themselves. As a result of her research, she found herself fiercely denounced by her earlier informants, and for a while the conflict became publicly focused as one between herself and the Breton militant world.

In Western Europe and the Middle East

Out of the diversity of this collection of studies a pattern emerges of conflicts which, with two exceptions (the Breton peasants and Turkish migrants), are led and organised by men within an institutional framework. The strength and purpose of the contenders' challenge to power varies greatly. In the Iranian situation at its more virulent, the opposition was strong enough to topple and replace a government. The challenge of the British miners' strike was more restricted, being focused on a particular issue, namely pit closures. In so far as it was directed towards undermining the Conservative government, its participants wanted to see the government replaced not by their own organisation but by a party more in sympathy with their particular interests as striking miners. In its more reduced form, the response to power among kibbutzniks and among Turkish migrants in West Berlin is one of people desiring to influence a government rather than to challenge its authority.

To understand the position of women and the part they play in these conflicts, however, these chapters may be read in two ways. The title of this Introduction contains the key words for these different perspectives: *powerlessness* and *powers*. Read in one way, the studies demonstrate the powerlessness of women within the structure of public political life. In this context, whether or not they are allowed actively to participate in the conflict, women are shown to be subject to male institutionalised power which attempts to contain them within the domestic sphere of life. From a second perspective, however, the reader may pick out various and diverse strands of women's own political powers such as may be derived from their 'domestic orientation'.

This does not mean that these chapters are written to bring out a balance between powerlessness and women's powers. On the contrary, each of the authors places her emphasis where she sees fit within the context of her study. Thus in the chapters on Cyprus and Iran situations are presented in which any powers that women may possess become submerged beneath the repressive forces of religious and political institutions. In regard to Breton peasant farmers and Turks living in West Berlin, however, the authors consider more specifically the resilience of women and their capacity for exercising non-bureaucratic powers within the context of communities in which there is little public voice.

Powerlessness and power

The concept of political powerlessness is one that refers specifically to public life in relation to institutionalised power. In common parlance, 'powerlessness' is used to refer to people, whether they be elderly, unemployed or those in an un-unionised or poorly unionised labour force, who do not possess sufficient power to be heard or to have their grievances attended to unless others speak on their behalf. Governments too become powerless on occasion when their normal ability to act is curbed by the power of antagonists, whether they be warring factions, as in Lebanon, or guerrilla fighters taking hostages and demanding terms. *The Guardian* (21 November 1985) referred to riots brought about when powerless people, 'feeling themselves oppressed and seeing no effective response to their grievances, despair of progress and physically defy the world which denies them what they want.'

It is significant in this context that a penetrating study of power and powerlessness by John Gaventa (1981) should be concerned specifically with the condition of a group of men. The implication, it seems, is that it is the men who have been deprived of their normal position within the public sphere, while women lie outside its scope. Gaventa's study, following Lukes on power, analyses the powerlessness of some Appalachian hill farmers at the turn of the last century when the Anglo-American Mining Corporation took over their valley, bought their land at nominal rates, turned them into cheap labour on the mines and derided them as 'hillbillies'. Within thirty years these people's rural valley had been transformed into a busy industrial complex with outsiders flocking in to share the new wealth being generated. Gaventa explains the powerlessness of these mineworkers in terms of two factors; first, 'the shaping of their wants and values' by the industrialists through the artificial excitement of the emerging industrial environment, so that the mineworkers came wrongly to identify their interests with those of the corporation that exploited them. And second, through the weakness of political organisation to represent the mineworkers' interests. The author traces the road away from powerlessness as these men gradually became politically conscious of their position and as they began to develop trade union organisation.

Where feminist writers have helped to explain women's powerlessness, however, there is no such Gaventa-type road forward. Elizabeth Janeway (1980) discusses women's acquiescence in their own subordination in terms of their socialisation as a persistent obstacle. Margaret Stacey and Marion Price (1981) trace women's present circumstances in Western Europe through the rise of capitalism during Medieval times when men but not women found new opportunities opening up outside the home. Vicky Randall (1982) argues that even where feminism has made forward strides in forming women's political consciousness, women still face covert institutionalised barriers where, for example, political writing is drafted primarily for male readership.

As studies of women's powerlessness, these chapters can be broadly divided into two groups. The first group, comprising the chapters on Cyprus, Iran, Northern Ireland and the British miners' strike, focus on situations in which women are suddenly exposed to the public political sphere at a time of crisis. In the second group, on Palestinian refugee camps, the kibbutz, Brittany and West Berlin, the authors examine the part that women have played over an extended period of conflict, where women's position has become more regularised.

While Cyprus, Iran, Northern Ireland and British mining communities represent a markedly diverse set of social environments, the authors of each of these studies present very similar patterns in which women, with little or no experience of public affairs, find themselves caught up in a conflict and men, with power at their disposal, sense a danger in losing control over women and take steps strenuously to enforce the conceptual divide between public and private domains. While women gained new political awareness through this encounter, they learnt more about their position through the very efforts that were made to keep them out of public affairs or to control their participation.

In Cyprus this pattern is starkly revealed in a patriarchal social system maintained by the Greek Orthodox Church and the state which keeps women in the home under the male protection of father or husband. Peter Loizos (1975) has shown elsewhere that even at the level of 'parish pump politics' women are strictly excluded from public life.) The six-weeks of war in 1974 represented a culmination of the anti-colonial struggle which turned into inter-communal strife. But although there had long been fear of a Turkish invasion, it was not until Greek and Turkish-Cypriot families began to move apart shortly before the war, that women were directly confronted with men's political issues. Men became heroes of war, women its victims. The reason, Roussou demonstrates, is that the war so disturbed the order of patriarchal control as to leave women sullied by rape and devoid of male protectors as widows and wives of missing persons. So they became outcasts to their own people and 'object lessons' to other women never to deviate from the social position that has been set for them.

Although in Iran, women in chadors were in the forefront of the crowds shouting that 'the Shah must go', Nategh argues that they were acting as nothing more than the marionettes of the mullahs. They were particularly vulnerable to such manipulation for, while the Shah had liberalised women's position somewhat, they had still remained largely outside the public sphere, lacking the education and employment experience to give them any basis for independence. Under such conditions, Iranian women surrendered themselves to the mullahs' teachings of the Ayatollah as the awaited mahdi. But hope turned to disillusion as the revolution was to bring such repression on women as to turn them into non-persons, deprived of human as well as political rights. Nategh, like Roussou, shows how women, through the intensification of their suffering under patriarchy, come to recognise the entrenched nature of their subordination, a position which hitherto they had been more inclined to accept as being in the natural order of things.

In Northern Ireland and in British mining communities we are looking at women's position not so much in relation to state control as in relation to male-dominated organisations which confront the state. Here womens' participation in the struggle is allowed, even welcomed, but with provisos: that it is temporary, supportive (rather than assertive) and that it remains supplementary to women's principal domestic responsibilities. In other words, while women's support was needed in an all-out political effort, this should not be allowed to lead to any permanent alteration in gender relations. Against this background, Edgerton and Ali show how women's involvement in conflict brought them new political experience within the public sphere and the desire to break free from those restrictions which hinder their full participation with men in the world outside the home. Both authors end by relating how women resign themselves to the status quo. In Northern Ireland they see no choice; in the mining communities it is an uneven choice between the working class world they know and middle class feminist ideals which are alien to them.

In Northern Ireland, although, as Edgerton says, women 'are no strangers to social and political action', they are again shown to be excluded from direct participation in politics by the teachings of both the Roman Catholic Church and the Protestant churches and by social pressures which keep them in the home. This position began to change with the intensification of the 'troubles' in the late 1960s and with the introduction of internment in 1971. The first brought public politics over the threshold, as when the Falls Road curfew restricted women's access to essential food supplies and brought them out on to the street, for the first time in public protest. With men in Long Kesh and many more in hiding, women also assumed organisational responsibilities hitherto reserved for men. But new political skills were gained not without cost, as women found themselves directing their energies into organisations to protect themselves against a new wave of violence within the home.

The sudden exposure of women to political action is graphically presented in Ali's chapter on the miners' strike. There were some women with previous experience of political protest, but many more with no such background who became immediately and intensely involved in a strike in an exclusively male industry. These women also encountered difficulty with husbands but there is a buoyancy in this account that suggests that women did gain strength through organisation, in the support groups, that enabled them to achieve something even if it was, as Ali says, more an accommodation between men and women than an overhaul in gender relations.

In the second group of chapters, the authors dwell less on the introduction of women to political action as on the patterns of their participation in conflict that have emerged over time. The chapters on Palestinian and kibbutz women can be studied together, not simply because they stand on opposing sides of a common dispute but more importantly because of the contrast that exists between them in women's relationship to institutionalised power.

In the Palestinian case, Sayigh and Peteet show that women cannot help but be politically committed, not only because they have been uprooted from their homeland, but also because of the continuing catastrophes which place their lives in a state of utmost insecurity. The authors describe this state as that of being 'between two fires': with the Israeli army determined to keep all PLO supporters at bay and the Arab host countries anxious to be rid of them. Peteet discusses the importance to the Resistance Movement of recruiting women into active political roles. She concentrates her attention on the period from 1970 to 1982 when this programme was gaining ground in Lebanon, with the PLO headquarters then based in Beirut. Young unmarried women were recruited as cadres and some of the traditional Palestinian values were being eroded to allow women also to work outside the home.

Peteet suggests that such changes as were taking place in the

Beirut camps of Chatila and Sabra were gradual and constituted no more than a modification of women's clearly defined domestic orientation. The concept of honour is so vital to the Palestinian people that the Resistance Movement argued for some relaxation by popularising the slogan 'Land before Honour'. Secondly, the use of women in formal political activities was temporary and contingent on their freedom from family responsibilities. Once married, women cadres were expected to return to the home and devote themselves to motherhood. And third, it is significant that women's activities as cadres appear to be primarily concerned with raising the consciousness of other women. There is no suggestion in this chapter than women constitute any threat to male control in the organisation of Palestinian resistance.

Bowes's study of Goshen critically examines the popular idea of the Kibbutz Movement as an instrument for breaking with the conventional distinction between the male public orientation and female domestic orientation. In the pioneer days, she shows that there was not so much an erasure of the dividing line between these orientations as an underplaying of domestic functions. Bowes writes of the 'asymmetrical egalitarianism' of this time when women shared in the manual work of setting up the kibbutzim and little attention was given to domestic comfort. So when men still became dominant, woman had no base from which to defend their interests. Women's 'return to familism' in the 1960s came too late, for they had already shaped their aspirations within male structures so that women's traditional roles were diminished.

Instead of 'public' and 'domestic' there developed in the kibbutz a parallel distinction between 'productive work', deemed to be men's work in which women participated, and 'maintenance work' which was unesteemed and left mainly to women. The macho image that Bowes encountered among male kibbutzim during her fieldwork was all part of the frontier spirit on which the kibbutz was built. Perhaps it was also associated with the political marginalisation of the kibbutz movement in relation to government policy making, especially since the 1967 war when the kibbutzim lost their function of defending the West Bank, and the male pioneers were left to recoup their pride in their physical strength as against government administration and female maintenance work.

In the final two chapters, on Breton peasant and Turkish migrant women, we end this volume with a twist in the conventional pattern of gender relations, with studies in which men do not have an active political role. Had Maryon McDonald concentrated her study on the separatist militants she might have presented the conventional pattern of male dominance within an organised political movement. But her study of the peasant community provides an illuminating diversion into informal and almost imperceptible political response. The author shows peasant women caught up in a web of external coercive forces, each promoting their own set of political and cultural values, and how these women quietly weave their own way through this convoluted network, picking out the values they find appropriate to the circumstances.

In the old days they were caught between church and state; the one fostering notions of wholesome, rustic Bretonism in the region, the other intent on creating a sense of French national identity centred on Paris. Although this rigid centrist policy was relaxed in the mid-twentieth century when planners like Jean Gravier (1947) expressed concern over what he called 'Paris and the French desert', the state was to become once again embroiled in conflict, this time with Breton separatists who demanded political as well as cultural devolution. With sensitivity to detail, McDonald uses the language issue of French versus Breton to show how peasant women manipulate the values of the different political groups for their own purposes; French is used to convey a sense of Parisian refinement when entertaining one's guests, Breton for the practicalities of making one's living from the land.

The study of Turkish migrant women addresses itself directly to a community which is, in institutional terms, politically powerless. Although the Turks are the most numerous of the 'guest worker' (*Gastarbeiter*) groups, they represent a very small proportion of the West German population scattered over the major industrial towns. In West Berlin, when Krojzl worked there, they numbered 120 000, or 6 per cent of the population. With strong German prejudices against them for their un-German ways, their poverty and their lack of formal education, Turkish migrants have little opportunity to be heard in public let alone to have their grievances redressed. The position of the women is even less secure than that of their husbands for they are officially treated as dependants and do not have *Arbeiter* status.

Krojzl identifies the issue as one between German policy, that of restricting the entry of Turkish (and other non-EEC) immigrants into the country and integrating those with residence rights into the German host community, and the Turkish response which is to defend their ethnic identity. Berlin co-operates with German policy by dispersing Turkish families from boroughs of high concentration, while liberal-minded Germans, who think they are defending the Turks against the prevailing prejudices, try to help them acculturate themselves into the German way of life. But from the Turkish perspective, their integration into the host population threatens to depersonalise them and to dispose of them as a problem by filtering them into the lowest level of German society. It is the women who take the main initiative in 'refusing to be invisible'. By wearing Islamic dress, sending their children to Qur'anic schools and by taking positive steps to establish social networks among themselves, they promote their own cultural distinctiveness.

Such initiatives raise an interesting theoretical argument for, although women are shown to be in a weaker position than the men, they still find the inner resources to express their political will. The men are the more directly confronted with their own powerlessness because in Germany they are unable to compete effectively in the public sphere. Krojzl describes older men as being forced into passivity and obedience to their employers and younger men as unemployed, dilatory and associated with drug trafficking and other criminal activities.

Power relations

The study of Turkish migrants leads us away from conventional notions of the exercise of power as something that has to be seen within a formal institutional framework. In many of these chapters the reader is also likely to find a variety of informal powers that women have at their disposal outside the public orientation, powers that, in consequence of this, often go unrecognised.

In Anthony Giddens's analysis of power there is no such state as one of powerlessness. Giddens (1979, p. 6) writes of 'power relations' as 'regularised relations between autonomy and dependence'. 'Power relations', he continues, 'are always two-way; that is to say, however, subordinate an actor may be in a social relationship, the very fact of involvement in that relationship gives him or her a certain amount of power over the other. Those in subordinate positions in social systems are frequently adept at converting whatever resources they possess into some degree of control over the conditions of reproduction in those social systems.'

The exercise of power in this broader context is clearly appropriate to both public and domestic orientations in society and can be seen to cross between them, although the public institutionalised form remains ever dominant. Nor should our notions of power be restricted to its direct or immediate use, but rather it should take account of the element of threat or potential for use. Even in slavery, for example, people may be said to possess the potential power for rebellion, else why should their owners make any effort to restrain them? For centuries, Aristophanes's play, *Lysistrata*, has stood for women's ultimate power to control men by refusing to have sexual intercourse with them; in that particular instance forcing the men to bring to an end a protracted war. The withdrawal of domestic labour likewise represents a form of power available to women, one that was used in Iceland as a symbolic gesture in 1975 and 1985 to mark the beginning and end of the United Nations International Women's Decade, when women called a 24-hour national strike as both housewives and paid employees.

In regard to the studies in this volume, it has already been noted that much variation exists in the degree to which the authors attach significance to women's informal powers. The emphasis that McDonald and Krojzl give to the powers of Breton peasant and Turkish migrant women respectively may be in part due to a social anthropological training which equips them with a keen eye for levels of informal activity and symbolic meanings that lie behind a community's public face. At the same time we, as readers, may appreciate how women's response to a conflict situation may become the more significant in the absence of formal political activity in the community.

These two points notwithstanding, the political manoeuvrability of both groups of women is remarkable in its own right. In both these cases women are shown manipulating the cultural attributes of their respective communities to political effect. In the Breton peasant case, women display a mastery over the Breton world as the very embodiment of its indigenous culture. McDonald stands the conventional view of political action on its head as she shows how the young militants need the seemingly non-political peasant women, with their 'real' Breton culture, more than the peasants need the militants. Among the Turkish migrants, on the other hand, we focus attention on women who produce their own idea of 'Turkishness' to suit political ends and create a cultural distinctiveness which is more a way of being Turkish in Germany than of being Turkish in secularised Turkey.

For Palestinian women, Sayigh and Peteet make plain that the division between public and private spheres does not mean division between political and non-political activity. Since women's 'uprooting' in the late 1940s and early 1950s, every household activity has taken on political significance. Peteet refers to the idea of the housewife as a 'struggler' whose every effort to maintain domestic routine against the odds is treated as her contribution to the Palestinian cause, and she takes the reader through the daily life of an 'active housewife' who combines motherhood with attending seminars and discussion groups. The very act of childbearing is loaded with political significance when a woman sees herself possessing a 'military womb' for producing the next generation of fighters. Palestinian women, unlike Greek Cypriots, do not lose their place in the community when they lose their husbands. Palestinian widows are given respect, and wives of missing persons have ambiguous status only to foreign relief organisations. A woman's primary social and political status remains vested in motherhood. Sayigh shows how women without men have the capacity for 'coping with chaos' and rebuilding their shattered homes as a base from which to continue their political struggle.

Women's ingenuity and resourcefulness are again brought out in Ali's chapter on the British mining communities during the 1984–85 strike. In this context, Ali shows how women sometimes have more opportunity than men to act effectively when they are unfettered by bureaucracy. This chapter is rich in anecdotes about women who amazed themselves with new found abilities for public speaking and fund raising abroad when they made use of opportunities for political action that were available to few men other than the more senior officials of the NUM. Ali's observations also bring to our attention wider issues about the nature of women's powers acting outside and around unwieldy bureaucratic operations.

The chapters on the kibbutz, Northern Ireland, Cyprus and Iran, however, act as sober reminders that women, whatever powers they have, are ultimately subject to male institutional power. This position is perhaps most poignantly expressed in Bowes's chapter on Goshen where officially women are given full rights in their participation in political affairs and where public and private spheres of activity are ideologically collapsed into a unitary communal system. Practice differs from ideology, and the situation becomes doubly difficult for women who find themselves fighting a system which purports to uphold gender equality and which in reality controls them by assigning to them the low regarded maintenance work.

The powers of women in the Northern Ireland context are illustrated in Edgerton's chapter as strengths coming out of their weakness, the powers of the weak. She refers, for example, to role reversal whereby it is women who see their men friends home because it is safer for women to be out on the street alone in sensitive areas, and to women who become public spokespersons when journalists and television reporters come into these areas looking for human interest stories. Here again it is often safer for women to be seen and quoted as 'political innocents'.

Maria Roussou writes of the model of the Virgin Mary and other female saints that is set before Greek Cypriot women by the Orthodox Church. In some societies such a model can offer women a form of power through sexual purity, and while this may also be true in Cyprus, what is important here, as Roussou demonstrates, is the way this model has been used to suppress women, to exclude them from all forms of public political life, and to keep them under the control of their fathers and husbands. While these women were given no opportunity to participate in the formal structures of political power, Roussou's chapter implies that they embody a form of symbolic power through maintaining the ideals of chastity and motherhood. Such power is suggested by the rape of so many Greek Cypriot women by the soldiers of the invading Turkish army. This cannot be seen simply as a series of acts of individual aggression, but must be interpreted as political action through which the aggressor was attacking the honour of Greek Cypriot men and, through this, breaking the continuity of the social order which it was the women's responsibility to uphold.

Such power as Greek Cypriot women possessed is shown therefore to have been largely symbolic. Roussou ends her chapter by introducing a different form of political power that emerged as these women began to recognise their longstanding subordination to patriarchy. This was their capacity as victims to use outside agencies on their behalf. In reporting their grievous experiences of the war to representatives of international organisations like the Red Cross and the European Commission for Human Rights, these women could not hope to gain redress, but they were nevertheless taking direct action as an expression of a new political awareness of their own condition.

In Iran, the dire position of women again makes it more important to explain their powerlessness in the public political sphere than to dwell on women's informal political powers. But such powers are still implied in Nategh's account as a plausible reason for the severity of the regime's repression of women under *shari'a* law. Women who attended the mullahs' lectures and entertained them in their homes for religious functions became numbered among their chief disciples. However misguided they may have been, Iranian women exercised political power in promoting the cause of the Islamic revolution in their social circles. Indeed, Nategh shows how the repression of women intensified as they began to see how the revolution had rebounded against them. The chapter ends with a bleak picture of Iran embroiled in its desperate war with Iraq and women in Tehran queueing in the streets for hours to buy household provisions. Here in these queues women, whose voice has been eliminated from all public life, joke wryly about their intolerable state of affairs and engage in informal association which, however ineffective it may be, is nonetheless political.

Rosaldo's conceptual distinction between domestic and public orientations remains a useful model for understanding gender relations. This has been shown here to be particularly true when examining situations of political conflict where the line that divides the two spheres threatens to become blurred and where, as we have seen, strenuous efforts are made to restore it. But these chapters also suggest that such a division should not be correlated with non-political and political spheres of activity but rather with informal and formal spheres. The question may now be considered as to whether the raising of women's informal political powers to public awareness might reduce their effectiveness, for the evidence suggests that much of their strength lies in their diffuseness, intangibility, elusiveness and freedom from formal structures.

Note

1. A number of people, through the interest they have kindly shown in this book and through their inspiration and encouragement, have contributed to the development of this Introduction. In particular I would like to thank members of an informal Oxford women's social anthropology seminar, convened by Shirley Ardener, who gave me a forum for discussion at an early stage, and Ghazala Bhatti, Helen Callaway, Marieke Clarke and Anne Griffiths who later read and commented on the chapter.

References

Atkinson, Max (1984) *Our Masters' Voices. The Language and Body Language of Politics* (London and New York: Methuen).

Gaventa, John (1980) *Power and Powerlessness. Quiescence and Rebellion in an Appalachian Valley* (Oxford: Clarendon Press).

Giddens, Anthony (1979) *Central Problems in Social Theory* (London: Macmillan).

Gravier, Jean François (1947) *Paris et le désert Français: décentralisation équipment et population etc.* (Paris).

Hallie, Philip (1979) *Lest Innocent Blood be Shed* (London: Michael Joseph).

Jaggar, Alison (1976) 'Abortion and a Woman's Right to Decide', in Gould, Carol and Wartofsky, Marx (eds.) *Women and Philosophy. Towards a Theory of Liberation* (New York: G. P. Putnam).

Janeway, Elizabeth (1980) *Powers of the Weak* (New York: Knopf).

Lapping, Brian (1985) *End of Empire* (London: Granada).

Lewis, Jane (1980) *The Politics of Motherhood. Child and Maternal Welfare in England, 1900–1939* (London: Croom Helm).

Loizos, Peter (1975) *The Greek Gift: Politics in a Greek Cypriot Village* (Oxford: Basil Blackwell).

Lukes, Steven (1974) *Power: A Radical View* (London: Macmillan).

Malos, Ellen (ed.) (1980) *The Politics of Housework* (London: Allison & Busby).

Randall, Vicky (1982) *Women and Politics* (London: Macmillan).

Rosaldo, Michelle (1974) 'Women, Culture and Society: A Theoretical Overview' in Rosaldo, Michelle and Lamphere, Louise (eds), *Women, Culture and Society* (Stanford: University of Stanford Press).

Stacey, Margaret and Price, Marion (eds) (1981) *Women, Power and Politics* (London: Tavistock).

2 War in Cyprus: Patriarchy and the Penelope Myth

MARIA ROUSSOU

> 'My daughter', scolded her husband's grandmother, 'Penelope waited for Odysseus for twenty years. Have you lost your patience after only five?'

In the summer of 1974, the Turkish army invaded Cyprus. Among politicians there had been fears of this eventuality for some years (Hunt, 1975), but the experience was nonetheless abrupt and devastating. Under the Makarios regime, the Turkish Cypriot population was becoming restive as its representatives in government were edged out of cabinet decision-making. Archbishop Makarios himself was under pressure from both Greek Cypriot and from Greece to wrest more control of the island for the Greek Cypriot majority. On 15 July, he was temporarily ousted in a coup engineered by the Greek military junta, and Nicos Sampson, a tough EOKA guerrilla fighter, became Head of State. Five days later, Turkey responded with an invading force of an estimated 40 000 troops which landed on the coast of Kyrenia in the north of Cyprus.

Along with Greece and Britain, Turkey was a guarantor of the island's independence and, acting without reference to the other two powers, invoked this status as a pretext for action: 'We came as peacemakers to save the sovereignty and territorial integrity of Cyprus.' This was the public declaration justifying military invasion. But having achieved its avowed purpose of overthrowing the dictator, the Turkish army did not withdraw from Cyprus. Instead, it advanced south, driving Greek Cypriots from their homes and ultimately establishing Turkish control over the territory of nearly forty per cent of the island, north of the Atilla line.

Greek Cypriots living in this northern section fled for their lives – on foot, in cars, in tractors, or by whatever means of transport they could find. Over 200 000 became refugees. The 20 000 left behind – mainly women, children and the elderly – found themselves 'enclaved' (the official term used by the Greek Cypriot government to describe those Greek Cypriots who remained or were forced to remain in the Turkish-controlled area) at the mercy of the Turkish soldiers.

One evening five years later, I sat with Maria, a young Greek Cypriot woman, on the veranda of her home in Nicosia. The tranquil atmosphere seemed far removed from the war, but her words show how much it remained with her:

> Where are they now? What can we do after five years of waiting for them? They are not coming back, are they? I was married for only two months before the war started. He had to join the army to 'save the country'. The country wasn't saved, and he's lost. . . .

Maria is one of over three hundred Greek Cypriot women whose husbands did not return from the war but were never listed as dead. Wives of these missing men are informally called 'false widows' (*pseftohires*). They are expected to wait for their husbands to come home, even though for many it is a lost hope.

One of the consequences of the 1974 war was the creation of categories of 'problem' women: raped, refugees, enclaved, war widows, wives of missing persons. While women were not directly involved in fighting and, compared with the men, few were killed, some were subjected to the violence of the enemy who attacked women 'belonging' to other men, women who thereby lost the purity and innocence considered in their cultural values to be the essence of their womanhood. Many lost their homes and many, too, were deprived of the male protection on which they were totally dependent.

Even during peacetime in Cyprus, women who lose their husbands, fathers, brothers, or other male kin protectors, find life difficult. The women who suffered directly during the 1974 war are now, more than a decade later, suffering in different ways. Those who were physically violated are rejected by their own people, since they are no longer 'pure'. Those who were widowed are expected to remain in mourning for the rest of their lives. But the 'false widows' are in the most difficult position: just as, in the Homeric poem, Penelope patiently tended her loom for the twenty years it took Odysseus to make his way home from the Trojan war, they are expected to wait indefinitely for the return of their men. Indeed, the story of Penelope has been revived among the Greek population in Cyprus to bring home to the 'false widows' their duty to wait quietly for their missing husbands and thus maintain the cultural standards set by Penelope thousands of years ago. Where these women cannot live alone, they seek the protection of their relatives, but some of them receive little understanding or help from them or old friends. The state, too, has been slow to support them.

The plight of these wives of missing persons forms the starting point of this chapter. Although the problems of this group are particularly severe, I argue that even in normal times in Cyprus cultural conventions restrict the patterns of women's lives. My thesis is that Greek Cypriot society requires certain forms of social control or moral regulation of women in order to maintain existing power structures. Cypriot women are brought up to depend upon male 'protection'; they are seen as pure and innocent, therefore to be kept away from the ugliness of public affairs. Women's compliance in this need for 'protection' entails their acceptance of a socially subordinate position.

The difficulties of these 'false widows' reveal the ideologies and practices that sustain women in their subordinate position. In the aftermath of the 1974 war, the Greek Cypriot women who had suffered during that war were used as an example to maintain control over all women. They served as an object lesson to all other women in the message communicated and occasionally made explicit: 'If you do not appreciate and assent to what you have now, with your husband or father protector to take care of you, look what will happen to you'. These unfortunate women had done nothing to bring their fate upon themselves, but were deliberately defined outside the boundaries of active social life to show the value of life under existing structures of male power. If they were to be 'rehabilitated' and their position redefined, this would involve a serious disruption of the patriarchal order. In short, the 1974 war brought to the surface problems derived from the patriarchal ideologies of state and church – ideologies firmly set against social change.

History of patriarchy and conflict

When the Republic of Cyprus was created in 1960, its sovereignty had to be guaranteed by three interested parties: Greece, Turkey and Britain. Unlike most former British colonies, Cyprus was not regaining for its people a self-determination lost during British rule: the history of the island had been one of successive military conquests and foreign domination over the last 2000 years, a history of men in action as invaders and rulers. And for the women of both the Greek and Turkish-speaking populations that settled there, patriarchy was entrenched through their own community structures in the Greek Orthodox Church and Islamic institutions respectively.

The third largest island in the Mediterranean (with an area of 3 572 square miles, just a little larger than Ulster), Cyprus lies only 40 miles south of Turkey and about 500 miles to the east of mainland Greece, at the junction of three continents. It is the strategic importance attached to this position that has made it so vulnerable to empire-builders, although, as Brian Lapping (1985, p. 311) points out, 'Cyprus has always proved a strategic disappointment' to those who have sought to control the island.

Greek, Turkish and British cultures have each left their imprint, the first two representing the major population groupings. The official census of 1973 gives the total population as 634 000, divided as follows: Greek Cypriots 77 per cent; Turkish Cypriots 18.3 per cent; other minorities (including Maronites, Armenians and Latins) 4.7 per cent. But after the war and the partition of Cyprus, the Turkish-speaking population increased from 115 758 in 1974 to 150 000 by 1980 as a result of the Turkish government's settlement policy in the occupied section of the island.[1]

Although the prehistory of the island goes back as far as the beginning of the sixth millenium, it was not until the second millenium that Achaean Greeks founded city kingdoms there on the Mycenaean model and introduced the Greek language, religion and way of life. The wealth of the island, derived from its copper mines and forests, made it the object of successive conquests until eventually it was incorporated into the Roman Empire. With the transfer of the capital of that empire from Rome to Constantinople, in AD 330, and the adoption of Christianity as the official religion, Cyprus shared in the fortunes of the rest of the Greek Orthodox world. Further conquests placed it in the hands of Richard *Coeur de Lion* of England, the Knights Templar, the Lusignans, and the Republic of Venice. Then, in 1571 it was taken by the Ottoman Turks, the ancestors of the present Turkish Cypriot population. The Ottoman occupation lasted until 1878, when fear of Russian expansion led the Sultan to hand over the administration of Cyprus to Great Britain in return for British support in the event of a Russian attack.

The British administered the island in the name of the Sultan until 1914, when they annexed it upon the entry of the Ottoman Empire into the Great War on the side of the Central Powers. Cyprus was finally declared a Crown Colony in 1925. Britain used Cyprus as a military base to protect its route to India and the Far East via Suez; by the Second World War the island was considered indispensable to the protection of British interests abroad. In 1954, as the empire receded, Britain said, 'Never', to independence for Cyprus. The House of Commons burst into uproar but, more important, this one word triggered off the independence struggle, with five years of guerrilla activity from EOKA (The National Organisation of Cypriot Fighters) and a severe clampdown by the British authorities.

In all the years of British rule, *enosis*, union with Greece, had been preached by the Greek Orthodox church and taught in Greek-medium schools. The expectation of this eventual outcome for Cyprus was now dashed. EOKA stepped up its action, with Colonel George Grivas coordinating guerrilla operations in the mountains and Archbishop Makarios stretching out negotiations with the British.

By 1957, Britain was prepared to give independence to Cyprus, retaining two naval bases, because military technology now enabled it to operate effectively from these bases without maintaining the rest of the island. By this time it had stocked the police force with loyal Turkish Cypriots, who had thus become EOKA targets and had alerted Turkey to the dangers of *enosis*. Britain left Cyprus in 1960, as it had left Palestine in 1948, with the havoc of inter-communal violence impending.

Archbishop Makarios, the Ethnarch of the Greek Cypriot people, now became President of the new Republic of Cyprus. But the anti-colonial struggle unleashed in 1955 had ended in the Zurich–London agreements in 1959 with a constitution virtually imposed upon the people of Cyprus and including features leading towards the subsequent partition of the island (Polyviou, 1975; Hunt, 1982). Greek Cypriots considered that their Turkish compatriots had been given too much representation in government in proportion to their number. And for Turkish Cypriots the fear of *enosis* continued, for although it was formally rejected by the Makarios government, the idea remained active in the minds of former EOKA members. The Greek and Turkish Cypriot armies fought each other sporadically from 1963 until 1967, when Ankara sent an ultimatum to Athens threatening to invade the island unless these clashes ceased – a graphic illustration of the role of the mainland governments in Cypriot affairs. The dictatorship that had recently seized power in Athens responded by bringing pressure on the Greek Cypriot forces through the Makarios government, and the fighting stopped.

Opposition to the government line among EOKA supporters increased and, in 1971, George Grivas returned to Cyprus secretly to create the second fighting force for *enosis*, EOKA B. Even the three bishops in Cyprus, though they did not actively support EOKA B, adopted the extreme nationalist stance and opposed Makarios. In Greece, the right-wing junta actively supported Grivas. The climax came on 15 July 1974, with the military coup aimed at assassinating Makarios and finally solving the 'Cyprus problem'. The result of this action was to provoke the Turkish invasion of the island, leading to the occupation of the northern part of Cyprus by Turkish troops from the mainland.

Women as reproducers of society

Writing of women in Israel, Nira Yuval-Davis (1979) argues that women are very important for the nation by reproducing the collective in the 'legitimate manner' and thus ensuring the continuity of its specific character and belief; they are used and controlled by the collective while being excluded from important positions and decision making. She observes that in all countries formerly under Ottoman occupation there is a particularly close cooperation between the state and the religious authority: between Judaism and the State of Israel, for example; between Islam and the various states of the Arab world; and between the autocephalus

Orthodox Church of Cyprus and the newly established Cypriot state.

A prominent feature of such a relationship is that religious laws coexist with secular laws in some areas and supersede them in others. Family law tends to be left to the religious authorities. Even those countries that have modernised their legal system, modelling it on those of the West, have incorporated religious laws in the area of family law, particularly pertaining to marriage and divorce. In Cyprus, all matters related to marriage and family cycle rituals have been left to the church, with the exception of questions relating to the custody of children and family property in the hands of the state. These laws exercise rigid control over women, the 'reproducers', so as to enable the Greek Cypriot society, the 'collective', to replicate itself in the traditional ways which exclude women from equal participation in social and political life.

Cypriot women are encouraged to follow the example of the *Panagia*, the mother of Christ, and other female saints such as Helen and Marina, who symbolise women as chaste, loving, and invariably sacrificing themselves to their husbands, their children, to God and society. The reverence attached to the Virgin Mary serves as an instrument for the inculcation in women of humility, patience and subservience. She is the archetypal mother created and sustained for centuries by the church (cf. Warner, 1976). Teaching resignation as a paramount female virtue, the church in Cyprus has always found it easy to cultivate this attitude, especially among the less educated section of the population.

During the Ottoman occupation of Cyprus, and later the British, Orthodoxy was fused with Greek nationalism into a formidable ideology. Over the centuries the church acquired a prominent and revered position, respected by politicians and laity alike. Since statements emanating from the hierarchy on social and moral issues are rarely ignored, the church holds considerable influence in swaying attitudes in favour of or against social reform. It is important to note that most of the Greek Cypriot population does not resent this kind of hegemonic power, but accepts it as an established part of life. The relation between church and state in modern Cyprus is apparently peaceful and mutually supportive, ensuring the credibility of both in periods of crisis.

The church nowadays exerts its influence in the political arena while standing discreetly in the background. It is confident in its firm grip on the island, having become the largest landlord on Cyprus as well as the centre of nationalist activity (Sant Cassia, 1981). During the period from 1960 to 1977, the church's position was strengthened as a result of the double role of Makarios as head of state and head of the church. The hierarchy successfully supervised the evolution of the nation state with considerable flexibility, diplomacy and determination.

War and its aftermath for women

During the fighting in 1974, over three thousand Greek Cypriots lost their lives. Of these, four hundred Greek women were killed and a further 152 listed as missing. The Red Cross has estimated that one in every 150 married women lost a husband, while one in every hundred has a son or daughter missing. Given the importance of the extended family in Cypriot society and the value given to sharing problems among family members, it is clear that most Cypriot women experienced bereavement within their own families. Of the women whose husbands were missing or dead, an estimated 25 per cent had dependent children under the age of eighteen. Many of these women lived in tents for two years or more.

Greek women living in the north of the island were raped by Turkish soldiers during the invasion, in some cases repeatedly. These women suffered the worst possible humiliation – 'worse than death' – of having been sexually abused by the enemy. The Report of the Commission of the Council of Europe on Human Rights in Cyprus 1974 attests: 'The evidence concerning allegations of rape is voluminous' (1976, p. 120). The text states:

> The applicant Government [Cyprus] complained of 'wholesale and repeated rapes of women of all ages from 12 to 71, sometimes to such an extent that the victims suffered haemorrhages or became mental wrecks. In some areas enforced prostitution was practised, all women and girls of a village being collected and put into separate rooms in empty houses, where they were raped repeatedly by the Turkish troops.' In certain cases, 'members of the same family were repeatedly raped, some of them in front of their own children. In other cases, women were brutally raped in public. Rapes were on many occasions accompanied by brutal-

ities such as violent biting of the victims, to the extent of severe wounding, hitting their heads on the floor and wringing their throats to the point of suffocation.' In some cases, 'attempts to rape were followed by the stabbing or killing of the victim. Victims of rape included pregnant and mentally retarded women'. (*Ibid.*)

One woman related her experience:

> I saw him (the Turkish soldier) still over me and I noticed others showing that they approved of what he had done to me. . . . Then he took my watch and engagement ring. Immediately afterwards another threw me to the ground and started to undress me, with the same intention as the first . . . I staggered in the direction of the other women, and caught up with them. I saw a two year old boy and took him in my arms, even though I was losing my strength, hoping this would save my life. While I was holding the little boy, some Turks surrounded us again, and one of them started pulling me. . . . As we were walking towards Six Mile Beach, we found some charcoal and I used it to make my face black, to look old, hoping to avoid being raped again. (*Ibid.*)

The detailed evidence includes the following statements:

> – a man (whose name was stated) reported his wife had been stabbed in the neck whilst resisting rape and his granddaughter aged six had been stabbed and killed by Turkish soldiers attempting to rape.
> – a girl of 15½ years who had been raped, was delivered to the Red Cross.
> – the witness had to take care of 38 women released from the Voni and Gypsou Camps, all of whom had been raped, some of them in front of their husbands and children; others had been raped repeatedly, or put in the houses frequented by the Turkish soldiers. The women were taken to Akrotiri hospital in the sovereign base where they were treated. Three of them were found to be pregnant. (*Ibid.*, p. 123)

In terms of numbers, the European Commission took into account 'written statements of 41 alleged victims of rape, of four alleged eye-witnesses of rape, and 24 hearsay witnesses of rape' (*ibid.*). Those Cypriot women who survived these dreadful experiences, particularly those who did not become pregnant, hid their 'painful secret' deep within themselves and tried to start a new life. It was difficult to trace these women who were scattered throughout the south of the island. Although the whole question received extensive press coverage, this gave no numbers, names or detailed descriptions.

This press interest, in fact, brought into the open the hitherto taboo issue of Cypriot women and sexuality. Cypriot men showed their obsession with the code of honour and shame by expressing, both verbally and through the press, that their women had been made impure by the enemy. They were concerned with the presence of enemy blood in 'their' women and the consequent impurity of 'their' nation. The strong feeling came through that these children should not be born. In consequence, the abortion law was changed overnight and the rape victims were provided with terminations through the Red Cross and the health authorities at the British bases.

The girls and women who had been raped, and who made their statements as soon as they arrived at the Red Cross, tried at the same time to convey and to conceal the unbearable memories that kept unfolding before them. There was more suffering to come, however, and this time it was inflicted by their own men.

The Nicosia press reported in November 1974 that some of the husbands and fiancés of rape victims had applied to the church for divorce or for dissolution of the engagement contract. These initial reports aroused much public discussion. Subsequent articles and letters provide ample evidence of men who did not want to take back their wives. Typical of the views expressed: 'They just do not want them,' or, 'It's not easy for a man to be attracted to his wife again if he knows what has happened.' Most people in such a male-oriented culture 'understood' the men's view and excused them. Nobody spoke for the women. Nobody considered their psychological needs for love and acceptance. Those who were the abused victims of the male invaders were now to be rejected by their supposed male protectors.

As the only institution with the legal power to grant a divorce, the church was involved. Even in the case of engaged couples, where the priest had blessed the rings and signed a dowry contract, it was necessary to seek the approval of the church in order not to proceed with the marriage, since vows had been exchanged and the engagement had received the blessing of a church ceremony.

Of the Greek refugee population of 200 000 scattered over the south of the island, almost half are women. The military occupation by a conquering nation led to social reform in allowing women to involve themselves more in activities outside the home: work in factories, participation in political life such as demonstations and other gatherings. Close contacts in everyday matters developed between refugee and non-refugee women, affecting both groups in their attitudes towards each other. The experience of war politicised some women, first by making them aware that their passive stance towards the political problems of Cyprus was as harmful as that of those who acted wrongly and brought the enemy to the island, then by making them realise that violence and war created more problems for women than for men and that the men did not care about solving women's problems. As a 65 year old woman, resettled at Horio, put it:

> We left these things (politics and war) to the men, and we had faith in them. They were our husbands, who talked for hours in the coffee shops about this or that politician, about the English, the Americans and the Turks. . . . We just used to listen to them and hope for the best. . . . They made a mess. We women shouldn't leave everything to them. Men don't give birth and don't care much about killing people. We know now what peace is and what war is.

The dowry system plays an important role in Cypriot society. In most cases the wife brings to the marriage a house, or a plot of land, as her economic contribution to the newly established household. The Cypriot women refugees have lost these houses and with them the thing they valued most: their homes. The majority of those who came from rural areas also lost the land bequeathed them by their fathers, land on which they had worked for years to make productive. Their flight from the bombing and the fighting was so sudden that none was able to take even their moveable possessions. Deprived overnight of their entire material world, they also have to adjust to the new social environment and the new people in the neighbourhood or refugee camp where they were resettled.

Some of the population, however – mainly women, children and the elderly – were unable to flee and, at the end of the invasion, found themselves cut off in the occupied areas. These Greek Cypriots, as noted above, are officially referred to as 'enclaved'. Women in this group, particularly those whose husbands were serving in the army across the divide, often had to care for their children and elderly parents, as well as cope with the occupying forces. Many were under the added psychological stress of not knowing whether their husbands were dead or alive. No research could be carried out in the occupied area; thus no evidence is available on the social degradation to which they were subjected.

Although it is true that more men were killed during the war than women and that men lost more property and money because they owned more, the consequences of the war were borne more heavily by women than by men. For almost every man lost, a dependent woman – a wife, sister or mother – has been left behind without male protection in a society that makes integration very difficult for the woman who does not have a man through whom her place in the social world is defined.

The social negation of 'false widows'

Five years after the Turkish invasion, the fate of 2197 Greek Cypriot men (including both military and civilian) still remained unknown. Photographs and other documentation in the hands of the Red Cross and the UN affords irrefutable evidence that at least some of these were captured by the Turkish forces, not only during the hostilities, but also afterwards. The official Turkish attitude is that they have given back all the declared prisoners and that no Greek Cypriot is detained as an undeclared prisoner of war. Having repulsed a number of initiatives between 1974 and 1979, the Turkish side still refused to allow any investigation by the Red Cross or UN forces. A UN resolution, expressing regret that two previous resolutions had not been implemented, called for immediate establishment of an investigative body which would function impartially, effectively and speedily. Although a commission was eventually set up, it was unable to carry out its purpose. Talks between the two interested parties held in May 1979 with the mediation of the UN Secretary General resulted in a report stating that one of the parties was not prepared to appoint representatives to the investigative body. The talks thus came to a standstill and the thousands of relatives of missing persons even today do not know whether they are dead or alive.

In 1979, as part of a wider study on the position of women in Cyprus, I interviewed 27 women married and three engaged to missing persons at some length and a wide range of subjects including family history, marriage, child-bearing, their experiences of the war, economic position, health, involvement with the social services, their aspirations for the future, relations with the church and official government bodies. The sample consisted of women of various ages, but slightly over three quarters of these women were between 21 and 40, since this group faces greater social problems because they are of an age when remarriage might be considered a possibility. The sample also covered a range of educational levels (from illiterate to university graduates); jobs (housewives and women in full-time and part-time employment); and domestic situations (women living alone, with parents, with in-laws, or with other relatives).

Five years after the end of the war, the experiences of these women were still vividly alive in their memories. They all complained of sleepless nights reflecting on their cruel fate. They clearly felt a sense of permanent loss and uncertainty about the future, living as they do in a social limbo. Anna, a 28 year old university graduate with no children, told of feeling ill:

> I went to the doctor with various symptoms, and I often needed tablets for loss of appetite, to make me sleep, for my nerves, for my stomach and so on. I wasn't very keen on taking the tablets but I saw it as the only solution left to me. I feel like a volcano erupting from time to time.

And Nitsa, aged 24, said:

> I'm suffering from depression, tension and nerves. Before, I was a calm and sociable character. Now I don't want to mix with people. I feel as if my bleeding wound is wide open to them.

Two of the university graduates, discussing the political situation in Cyprus and internationally, concluded that they and the other wives of missing persons were the most oppressed group in Cypriot society. All the women expressed distress at the way they were treated by the special committees that had been set up and by government authorities in general. In the first years after the war, all of them had devoted much time to the appropriate committee for missing persons, participating in demonstrations and all-night prayers, but they have now lost hope after so many disappointments and do not even open the newsletter published by this committee.

They felt let down, too, by the welfare services. Of the 30 women interviewed, 25 claimed that they had been disappointed on their first visit and did not want to see the welfare officers. According to Roula, a 27-year-old mother of a girl aged five and a half, the social worker was interested more in finding out about her economic position than her emotional condition or her relationship with her relatives. Another of these women stated: 'We needed them in our loneliness to speak to about our problems and to advise us on serious matters, not to comment on how few possessions we had.' This questioning on their economic status was so insistent that many of the women asked: 'Were the Social Services so keen to reduce the £12 a month we were given by the government?'

In the period immediately after the war, the families of missing persons were not regarded by the government as families that had lost their male breadwinner forever; therefore, they were not given a monthly pension. Marina, 29 years old, had this experience:

> Soon after the war the social worker visited us in my parents' home and asked about my economic problems. Two months passed and then they decided to give us free tinned milk for the child and a few pounds in cash for my immediate needs.

Two thirds of those interviewed had been compelled, mainly for socio-economic reasons, to move into their parents' home or into a refugee camp close to their next of kin. Katina, aged 26, told me:

> I stayed close to my family. My grief was so great that I couldn't move from my chair next to the radio. I used to cry all day. My mother took over all responsibility for the baby, who was then two months old. All my relatives helped me but, of course, nobody could understand my loneliness, nobody could identify with all my problems. Living in a small village with so much

> gossiping around, my parents became stricter and stricter towards me.

Many of the women could not go out to work because they had babies or young children or because they were physically and emotionally drained. The resulting psychological and economic dependence on relatives had an adverse effect on their powers of decision making and their freedom of movement. The father usually became even stricter with his daughter than he had been before her marriage. He now felt doubly responsible for her honour and wished to protect her from other males who might treat her offensively. The daughter was expected to behave correctly and to respect the 'name' of her parents, her husband and her children. In short, she had to keep herself in isolation. As one said, 'People soon gossip about the wife of a man who is away from home.'

Five of the women interviewed complained bitterly about bad relations with their fathers, leading to trouble at home, nervous tension in the children and a generally unhappy atmosphere. They felt strong social pressure and regarded themselves as imprisoned in their own homes by their own relatives. A 29-year-old mother said:

> When my husband was lost. I worked in my parents' home, sewing. It was a very difficult time for me because I was imprisoned day and night with the same people talking about my problem over and over again. I fought a real battle to persuade my parents to let me go out and work in a factory.

In some cases, these women reported supportive and harmonious relations with affines. Helena, who was 35 years old and had two children, lived a long distance from her husband's parents:

> I have a very good relationship with my mother- and father-in-law. They live in Larnaca in a house let to them by their brother from Australia. They are refugees too. They love my two children and visit us every Sunday. Sometimes they take them out. I look forward to their company.

But others told of problems with affines who regard their young daughter-in-law as their property and want to control her. Margarita, a woman of 35 originally trapped in the Turkish-controlled area and now a refugee in the south, told me her story:

> Soon after we were released by the Turks and became refugees, we were given second-hand clothes by the Red Cross. A red skirt happened to be my size, so I put it on because I had nothing better to wear, and went to Nicosia, where one of my husband's sisters had a clothes shop. I had only one pound in cash on me and I intended to buy a cheap dress in a dark colour. My sister-in-law embarrassed me with her comments on the colour of the skirt. She said that I ought to be ashamed to walk around without wearing dark colours because my husband was away. 'Do you want to attract the attention of other men? That's what people are saying. Red is only for the insane.' My in-laws don't think about me or my two children any more, except to criticise. The old saying is true in my case: 'The ox has died, so our cooperation is over.'

In some cases, the woman's relations with her affines were the source of her most upsetting problems. In the absence of the husband, who was the link between them, relations deteriorated and the wife lost the support of her kin, especially when her own family lived at a distance. Some of these women had to fight against the traditional image of the dependent wife and assert themselves in order to get control of the family and establish that they were the rightful legal representatives of their husbands.

Legal issues formed the basis for many problems. Since their husbands had not been declared dead or lost forever, they did not enjoy the rights of a widow with regard to the property of the children or the husband. If the husband had a bank account in his name, the wife could not make any withdrawals, however great the needs of herself or her children. If the family car was in the husband's name, the wife could not sell or exchange it without a lengthy court procedure. Five of the women who decided to go to the district courts felt guilty. Myrto put it like this:

> I feel that I have done, or am doing, something wrong in having to deal with judges and the courts. I have to depend on the court's humanitarian feelings to allow me to sell the old car and buy a new one, which is in the interests of the family.

Some women commented that special provisions should have been made in the case of the wives of missing persons to establish these women as the legal representatives of the families.

In one case, the wife found herself in a serious conflict between her affines and her own family over the property of her lost husband:

> About a year after he was lost, and my father-in-law and I had enquired everywhere, my relationship with his family started to deteriorate. My dowry had just been built on my husband's land and I moved in near my in-laws. I've been here for four years now, but they've turned against me and say that I usurped the land and that I'm not their own any more. My mother- and sister-in-law insult me and my parents whenever we meet.

The subject of divorce and the possibility of a second marriage was naturally very sensitive. Even when the woman being interviewed trusted me completely, she found it hard to discuss her real needs and feelings. One 24-year-old woman who had been engaged to a missing person confessed:

> My parents put pressure on me to get engaged again, but I know how hard it will be for me to get any proposals. I think that I'll need a matchmaker to make the arrangements for me. I can't look for a husband myself, and although my parents want me to get married soon, they can't help through their network.

Of the women interviewed, I was sure that most had not had any sexual relationship since they were parted from their husbands. I could not, of course, enquire about extramarital affairs as this would have caused great offence. Some of these women, especially those without children, were considering a second marriage, but were waiting for action from the church or state to grant them all a divorce, or to issue a declaration to the effect that after five years without the return of their husbands they were free of their first marriage. They felt that with a group ruling they could take steps to get married for the second time without feeling guilty. Alexandra, aged 29, said:

> If I go as an individual to ask for a divorce so that I can remarry, my in-laws and my husband's friends will be outraged that I have forgotten him so easily. The church objects and, if I do manage to get a divorce in the end, it will be on my conscience that I caused trouble by marrying again for selfish reasons. And how will this second husband behave towards me and my children? How will his parents treat me since, in crude terms, they will regard me as a 'second-hand' woman?

A representative of the church, who wished to remain anonymous, told me that only a few divorces had been granted and these in cases where the woman was already living with another man and had children from this union. Neither the church nor the state are prepared openly to assist the women on this matter but, on the contrary, allow restrictive attitudes towards them to persist, making it unlikely that they will be married again. To re-define these women as 'widows' and allow them back into the social world would seem to undermine the existing male-oriented social patterns. A young woman gave her view: 'Even if I were only engaged and he was lost, I would never consider marrying someone else. I would always remember him as my man husband. But I don't blame other young women who have different characters and want to remarry.' Another told me: 'Yes, I'll support them in every way, They must get a divorce and remarry. It's a pity for them to spend all their lives in misery.'

Two-thirds of the women interviewed referred to the role played by the church in their lives during the early days of their problems. For the women who did not work, visits to monasteries and churches and involvement in charitable work or the rituals of the Orthodox church formed the only publicity acceptable social outlet. Some of the young wives became involved in religious activities not because they felt the need, but because they felt obliged to accompany their mothers or mothers-in-laws to church ceremonies and all-night vigils. In this there was at least the solace that the tiredness induced by long hours of prayer would help them to sleep. Very few of these young women took their religion seriously; from deep in their hearts they complained that God did not help them. Disillusion and disbelief in God succeeded the illusory comfort offered them by the church and religious ritual.

Penelope in the present

The problems faced by the wives of missing persons are caused by the absence of their husbands, whose presence would give them a place in the social structure. The fact that their difficulties derive from being defined outside the boundaries of the social world, almost as non-persons, suggests that the normal state of affairs for women is acceptable; but, in fact, the common situation of women also involves pain and denial, albeit to a lesser degree. A mere restoration of the accepted forms is not the solution. The lack of the husband-protector, under the specific conditions of the aftermath of 1974, calls attention to a general series of constraints upon women in normal times. And it becomes more clearly apparent that the concepts of honour and prestige are really the bars of a prison for women. This does not, of course, make the sufferings of the wives of missing persons any less real. The point is that as yet no identity has been made available to them in their society. They are denied re-entry into social life.

A second important point to emerge is that religion forms part of the secular identity, whether personal or collective: being a Greek Orthodox Cypriot woman involves behaving in a certain manner and failure to do so risks ostracism from the community. Religion and ritual establish certain values and examples for the way women live. Women act as a kind of moral litmus test of the authenticity of a culture: customs, folklore, religion and rituals are all condensed in the prescription of how women should be as an expression of 'our way of life' or 'the way of life of the nation'. In other words, in Cyprus, women express the social values. To challenge the dense substratum of norms is almost to challenge the very notion of being human and to become monstrous, unreal, animal-like. The rarer alternative is to become an angel, holy, godlike and special: hence the Penelope myth.

Note

1. The number counted by Turkish authorities in October 1974 and signed by the Minister of Interior and Justice, Mr Ahmet Sami.

References and further reading

Alastos, Doros (1975) *Cyprus in History* (London: Zeno).

Attalides, Michael (1981) *Social Change and Urbanization in Cyprus* (Nicosia: Social Research Centre).

Campbell, John K. (1964) *Honour, Family and Patronage* (Oxford: Clarendon Press).

Council of Europe (1976) 'European Commission on Human Rights Report: Cyprus vs. Turkey', Application No. 6780/74 and 6950/75.

Hunt, Sir David (1975) *On the Spot* (London: Trigraph).

Hunt, Sir David (ed.) (1982) *Footprints in Cyprus. An Illustrated History* (London: Trigraph).

Lapping, Brian (1985) *End of Empire* (London: Granada).

Loizos, Peter (1972) 'Aspects of Pluralism in Cyprus', *New Community*, vol. 1, no. 4, pp. 298–304.

Loizos, Peter (1975) *The Greek Gift: Politics in a Cypriot Village* (Oxford: Basil Blackwell).

Loizos, Peter (1981) *The Heart Grown Bitter. A Chronicle of Cypriot War Refugees* (Cambridge: Cambridge University Press).

Peristiany, John (1974) 'Honour and Shame in a Cypriot Highland Village', in *Honour and Shame: the Values of Mediterranean Society* (Chicago: University of Chicago Press).

Polyviou, Polyvios (1975) *Cyprus, the Tragedy and the Challenge* (London: Jonn Swain and Son).

Sant Cassia, Paul (1981) 'Patterns of Politics and Kinship in a Greek Cypriot (1920–80)', unpublished PhD dissertion, Department of Anthropology, Cambridge.

Stravrinides, Zenon (1976) *The Cyprus Conflict. National Identity and Satehood* (Nicosia).

Warner, Marina (1976) *Alone of All her Sex. The Myth and the Cult of the Virgin Mary* (London: Weidenfeld & Nicolson).

Yuval-Davis, Nira (1980) 'The Bearers of the Collective: Women and Religious Legislation in Israel' *Feminist Review* no. 4, pp. 15–27.

3 Women: the Damned of the Iranian Revolution

HOMA NATEGH

Oh, Allah, in loving You
We trust that You will protect our children
And not have them slain.
(Slogan of Iranian women)

What happens to women in a harsh and uncompromising Islamic nation when a modernising dictator is replaced by a religious despot? How do women feel, especially those from the strictest religious families, when repression is carried out in the name of Islam itself? Why are Iranian women, who took part in such massive numbers in the revolution, now becoming society's most powerful opposition to the regime which they welcomed with so much rejoicing in 1979?

To answer these questions, we must review the economic and social situation in which these women now find themselves and consider the laws and institutions which threaten not only their personal interests and civic rights but even their security at the heart of the family and society. First, however, we shall examine the contradictions between popular beliefs and religious dogma.

The Islam of the people and the Islam of those in power

Today even the leaders of the fundamentalist Muslim Brotherhoods of Egypt and Syria who strongly supported Iran's Islamic revolution, are unanimous in stressing that 'there is an essential difference at a basic religious level between Sunni and Shi'ite Muslims'

(Luizard, 1983, p. 172). Indeed, the survival of the revolution in Iran depends on its adherence to the country's own religious tradition which is independent of, and often at odds with, the teachings of the Prophet Muhammad and the Qur'an. In other words, the Iranian revolution which claims to be Islamic cannot easily be exported to any other Muslim or Arab country.

It is important to remember that the spoken and written language of Iran is not Arabic but Farsi. As Muslims are explicitly forbidden to read or recite the Qur'an in any language other than Arabic, its content is poorly understood by much of the population, 50 per cent of whom are illiterate. Even the Islamic Parliament states, 'In most of our villages the peasants are ignorant of the basic tenets of Islam. . . . They do not know the meaning of prayer and fasting' ('Discussion in Parliament', *Keyhan*, 25 January 1984).

And yet the people remain religious in their own way as Shi'ites. Shi'ism itself, the official religion of Iran, has for many centuries been considered a 'heresy of Islam', because it is based on that which the Qur'an prohibits the most – the cult of saints. It generates a passion for the martyred Imams who fought for the survival of the religion in the early days of Islam. Its messianism, borrowed from other religions in Iran (Mithraism, Manicheism and Zoroastrianism), holds that the world filled with shadows and tyrannical powers will not see light and joy until the appearance of the twelfth Imam, the absent Mahdi.

In Shi'ite Iran, even the Prophet Muhammad must take second place when Imams are commemorated. During the month of *Muharram*, for instance, when the rest of the Muslim world celebrates the Islamic new year, Shi'ites wear black to mourn the third Imam, Hussein, who was killed on 10 *Muharram* by agents of Yazid, the Sunni Caliph. Sunnis reject all these traditions and insist that the salvation of Muslims depends only on the correct observance of Qur'anic laws.

The Shi'ite apocalyptic belief in the coming of the Mahdi has permitted at various times, particularly during national crisis, the appearance of appropriate saviours, each bearing a different message. As a result, Iran has become a country of multiple sects. In the nineteenth century alone, Babism, Azalism, Sheikhism and Bahaism appeared, all founded on messianism and each influencing the others. From 1975, during the last years of the Shah's reign, when repression and inflation were at their height, the credulous population again succumbed to 'the expectation' of a new messiah. Old traditions resurfaced: small pieces of paper appeared on the branches of ancient trees or beside old wells announcing the arrival of the Mahdi. Evening prayers repeated the plea: 'Oh master of time, hasten your coming. The world is losing its way. Come with full speed.' Festivals and meetings took place honouring the advent of the messiah. There were even letters of invitation circulated in European languages, one of which said (in English): 'Come you will have also some tea and sweets.'

It was in this context that, in 1978, Khomeini appeared as the bearer of a great message: '*The Shah must go*'. This was the will of a people who, in their ignorance, had come to see the Shah as the incarnation of evil and the banished Ayatollah as the embodiment of goodness. They began to identify the face of Khomeini in the moon or to find one of his hairs between the pages of the Qur'an. While the streets were empty under martial law, the mosques were filled with believers eager to learn what the future had in store.

Throughout this burlesque, women acted as bewitched heroines. They proved themselves more susceptible to religious fervour: always a refuge for those no longer protected by law and society. Sustained by false hopes, they generously passed on what had been told them, as for example: 'On the day the Shah departs, Khomeini will order that every family be given a free daily allowance of twenty litres of petrol and a kilo of rice.'

From the start, women were mobilised into action from the mosques. Nearly every day during the months before the Shah was deposed, groups of over a hundred women dressed in black chadors could be seen wailing messianic slogans, 'Beloved Khomeini, hasten your coming to save us.' It is not surprising, then, that women played such a massive part in the religious demonstrations during the February 1979 revolution and were the ones to shout the most reactionary slogans, going so far as to say, 'Khomeini, order me to shed the blood of others.' This religious fanaticism shown by women during the revolution demonstrates at the same time the low educational level and the weak social conscience acquired during the Shah's regime.

In 1979, women made up 16 million of the total population of Iran; only just over a million had paid employment (407 200 in the cities and 752 000 in the country areas). Illiteracy among women was high, with 55 per cent of those in urban centres and 87 per cent in rural areas unable to read or write. The number of women with higher education barely exceeded 8000, not enough to lead a progressive movement during the course of the revolution. These figures show that the majority of women, especially in the cities, were 'good housewives', with little education and no place in the productive sector outside the home. Besides remaining the foremost pupils and spiritual clients of the clergy, women were also their financial supporters, not only by their direct payments (in relation to some vow or other), but by the celebration of the various family or religious celebrations during the year which required the presence of the mullah.

For urban working-class women, the mosque was the place to spend their time, meet others and make plans. The mullahs taught them to love and respect the monarch as 'the shadow of Allah on earth'. Even Khomeini, in his letters to the Shah, advised believers to 'obey the monarch as the defender of Islam and the territorial integrity of Iran' (Davani, 1964). And again: 'The clergy has never opposed the monarchy; on the contrary, we have supported it and built it up in the course of history' (Khomeini, 1940). In the same way, he had actively participated in the 1953 Anglo-American counter-coup against Mossadegh and in favour of the Shah. Later calling this 'a blow in the name of Islam against Mossadegh' (television interview, 22 June 1980), he had announced in 1952 that the nationalisation of oil was against Islam's respect for private property. It is enough to look at the Iranian newspapers of the day to see the photographs of clergy leading a demonstration of prostitutes in favour of the Shah. In spite of all these memories and contradictions, women hoping for a better future once more followed the ayatollahs on a new path and a new struggle.

The more affluent women had acquired certain economic and family freedoms under the Shah: the right to vote and to be elected (in 1963), the right to abortion and divorce. Similarly, the 'Family Protection Law' passed in 1968 protected women against polygamy and temporary marriage. In relation to employment legislation, the two sexes were considered equal. But among the poor, where women were almost completely dependent on their husbands, the right to divorce had little meaning; these women campaigned for legislation to prevent their husbands from putting them aside. The Women's Organisation of Iran, set up by the Shah's sister, drew its members mainly from those in administrative posts and did little to promote the social advancement of women. The authorities looked upon this association as 'the right arm of the regime' and its members were encouraged to display their approval of the government. In November 1976, for example, they demonstrated as 'mothers of families' against student protesters.

Women, therefore, were absent from the strikes of workers and students which led up to the revolution; their role was in religious demonstrations. The mullahs knew better than any political party how to indoctrinate and politicise them.

Lost illusions

> *Oh, Allah, we have had enough of your Imam;*
> *Send us his assassin now.*
> (Popular slogan in Iran today)

Disenchantment set in very quickly for those who had held the most hope. From its inception, the Islamic government began its assault on women. In March 1979 the 'Family Protection Law' was repealed. Civil tribunals were replaced by Islamic tribunals which reestablished polygamy and withdrew women's right to divorce their husbands. Men were now able to have not only the four wives legitimised by the Qur'an but also an unlimited number of 'temporary wives' in accordance with Shi'ite tradition.

Temporary marriage, today being promoted by the authorities in mosques and schools, is no more than legalised prostitution. It permits a man to contract a marriage with a single woman for the limited time of an hour, or a month, or whatever. But the children born of such contracts have no rights of citizenship unless the father accepts and claims paternity; this depends on his humanity and generosity. If he refuses, in a country where abortion is now forbidden, not only is the infant considered to be illegitimate but the mother risks her life as an adulteress. This type of marriage, which seriously weakens the security of women at the heart of the family and of society, serves the interests of the regime. It allows the 'legal rape' of young girls in prison, for instance, and the disposal of war widows to soldiers.

As early as the spring of 1979, the age at which girls could marry was lowered to nine years. On this subject Khomeini wrote, 'Happy the father who has his daughter married before she reaches puberty' (1979, Problem 2459); all the same, he goes on to advise husbands to 'rape' their little wives. By such devices the ayatollahs sanctioned the removal of young girls from all cultural and social activity. They were prepared to put to death one half of the population for the better control of the other. By reestablishing the marriage of minors, they hoped to win the approval of poor families who were happy to have one less mouth to feed.

But they miscalculated. Women who have been subservient and docile themselves do not wish their daughters to be repressed in the same way. Here, for example, is how one working woman rejected the homilies of the preachers:

> I will never allow my children to be as downtrodden as I have been. My youngest daughter is eleven. She's top of her class. I'm prepared to work all my life so that she can continue her education. . . . Allah is as close to me as he is to the mullahs. He gave life to me and to my children for our delight and not for sacrifice at the feet of others. . . . Even if they take away my job, I will borrow the money so that my daughter can have her school pinafore and notebooks. (Nategh, 1980 p. 15)

Before the theocratic regime came to power, women were unaware of the 'beautiful' image that Islam conferred on them. They had to learn, and quickly, that the Qur'an depicts women as 'unhealthy beings' with 'crippled souls' who lack 'healthy reason', resemble 'lunatics and children' and are 'unworthy of all confidence'. The words of Muhammad were likewise evoked to relegate woman to 'an object of pleasure' with no rights over her own person. She is the 'prisoner' and 'absolute property' of man, who can dispose of her as he wills. The Qur'an recommends that good husbands should 'beat' their wives from time to time so they do not 'corrupt' pious men. Khomeini himself directed, 'A man must punish his disobedient wife'; if good advice is not enough, he should 'banish her from the marriage bed' and 'use corporal punishment' (1979, Problems 2030–31). But these teachings go further to say that a man can put aside his wife wherever and however he wants to, even in her absence and without warning her. From the day that the good Muslim no longer requires her to submit to his needs, she must consider herself 'put aside'. In addition, as Khomeini has explained,

'Islam does not recognise a woman's right to divorce, but if at her request her husband agrees to divorce her, the wife must pay whatever compensation he may demand' (1979).

It goes without saying that the Constitution of the Islamic Republic in 1979 has taken away all the rights previously granted to women. At the same time, it proclaims their 'illustrious role' in Islamic society as the 'gentle mother' and 'faithful wife'. Khomeini has addressed women: 'You are the pillars of the nation. Your job, the most noble of tasks, is to bring up children' (speech 7 March 1979). The two token women elected to Parliament certainly did not take the floor except to reinforce the Constitution and send women back to the home.

But how did women who had already tasted economic independence and those whose families who could not survive on one salary, respond to this legislation? Had the essential role of women in agricultural and peasant economic life already been forgotten? The cultivation of rice and tea, for example, was carried out by a female workforce, as was carpet weaving. Women also held an important place in teaching and public service occupations. Here, again, is the judgement on Islamic law by a woman of the people:

> Me, I did not vote. They told us to 'vote for Islam', as if we were unbelievers before. They told us, 'Vote for us. We represent the Qur'an.' I cannot read and I can judge them only by their actions. I am afraid to vote for inflation and war. (Nategh, 1980, pp. 14–15)

Such was the growing discontent and disillusionment that in 1980 the government introduced a new penal law, the *lex talionis* (or law of retribution), without publishing the text in the official press. Even after the law was partially in force, its contents were being circulated to the authorities as a 'confidential document'. The *lex talionis* not only disinherits and debases woman, but dehumanises her in the full sense of the word. In effect, it denies her any rights as a mother, a wife, or even as a human being (Tabari and Yeganeh, 1982, pp. 93–98). The law announces openly and without reservation that Islam considers a woman to be 'half a man'. Thus her judgement, her testimony and her being cannot be considered those of a whole person. For this reason, she has 'no rights' over her children.

In consequence, a woman who is attacked or raped cannot bring any charge against those who have wronged her because her testimony will not be heard; if she is arrested, she cannot prove her innocence. In the case of even a minor dispute, a 'just' man can accuse her of any crime whatsoever, classifying her as an 'unsound person'. (Article 29 of *lex talionis* states, 'The confession of a lunatic, an intoxicated person or a minor. . . . will not be admissible.') Nor is she able to defend her children, for they are considered the 'property' of her husband. As witness to this, a man who kills his own child is not liable to punishment (Chapter 2, Article 16). A man can easily condemn his wife or daughter to death by claiming, for example, to have caught her in an act of adultery. In this situation, he can kill her himself. The law, however, recommends that he hand her over to the Islamic tribunal who will arrange a public death for her, since the penalty for adultery is death by stoning. The faithful are invited to come and stone her bound body, with 'small stones so that death will be slow'. The first such executions after the revolution took place at Kerman, where one of the condemned women took forty-five minutes to die.

When a condemned woman is pregnant, she must give birth before she is executed (Article 50). In Mashad, one woman was executed after the delivery of her child because she had sheltered the parents of Massoud Rajavi, the leader of the *Mojahedin*.

Nor are young girls protected from the penal code, even though Islam forbids the execution of virgins and holds that they go straight to paradise when they die. They are raped by the Guardians of the Revolution (the *Pasdars*) before being put to death. Khomeini justifies this by asserting that counter-revolutionaries are the 'spoils of war'. And indeed Ayatollah Montazeri has pronounced: 'It is not seemly to send young virgins to their death, they go to paradise. . . The *Pasdars* of the prisons must marry them by religious rites before putting them to death' (statement, 29 March 1981). In the face of strong protests from parents who daily receive the mutilated and tortured bodies of their children, the regime defended itself in a radio broadcast: 'We are accused of being torturers, but torture is the best way to cure wrongdoers. Sick people don't like injections but doctors use them as a means of treatment.' People are tortured and raped, including young girls who, after being judged innocent and released from prison, sometimes killed themselves. In a suicide note to her parents, one young girl wrote, 'I can no longer live with the shame of having been raped by the Guardians of the Revolution' (quoted from 'The text of a testimony' in Farsi in *Enghelab-e-Eslami*, 22 February 1984, p. 2).

Where women are concerned, the Islamic tribunals do not even have to justify themselves. The *lex talionis* states that a man who kills a non-Muslim woman will not be punished. If he wilfully murders a Muslim woman, however, he will be sentenced, but before he receives punishment the woman's family must pay the murderer half the blood price of a man, in order that he be considered the killer of a whole human being (Article 5). It is clear that while a rich family can transform the corpse into that of a human being, the poor must suffer this fierce and inhuman destiny.

Repression in Iran has now gone too far for the government to draw back or for the people to hide their hatred. Even the General Prosecutor of the Tribunals acknowledges this. In reply to those who complained of repressive measures, he stated during Wednesday prayers: 'We cannot allow ourselves any liberalisation. If these people became free, we should be submitted to that which we have made them undergo' (Moussavi Ardebili, sermon, April 1984).

Moral conflict

> *Liberty is neither Western nor Eastern;*
> *It is human.*
> (Slogan of demonstrators, 8 March 1979)

The Islamic regime is intolerant towards art, literature, sport and all forms of entertainment. It uses the presence of women as a reason for banning cinema, theatre and music. A woman is forbidden to sing; her voice could excite good Muslim men. She is forbidden to dance; her body could evoke erotic pleasure in a spectator. She may not appear bare-headed; her hair might dazzle the faithful. In a word, her presence, as the Qur'an affirms, 'corrupts' believers. As early as 1963, Khomeini criticised the Shah for giving women the right to vote. He wrote, 'Woman is an influence for depravity. It is enough for her to set foot in a public building for the place to be transformed into a place of prostitution' (Letter to Alam, the Prime Minister, November 1963; quoted in Davani, 1964, p. 80).

New artistic and cultural activities must conform to religious teachings. In a book for writers and artists published under official control, the authorities set out rules relating to women (Makhmalbaf, 1980). In general, the part of a woman should be played by a man. Showing a woman in 'close-up' makes the scene 'indecent' and should be avoided. But there are exceptions where the presence of a woman in a scene would not be considered an outrage to modesty and would even serve to mobilise the people for Islam. Appropriate roles, for example, include 'a pious and patriotic mother, veiled in her black chador on her way to hand over her recalcitrant children to the Islamic Tribunal', or 'the courageous mother, leaning on the tomb but refusing to cry over the death of her counter-revolutionary son', or a woman 'praying and thanking Allah for having allowed her to offer martyrs to the revolution'.

But the authorities have sorely misjudged popular moral attitudes. Drama forms an inherent part of Shi'ite life. The foundation of Iranian religious belief, as Ernest Renan emphasises, is based on 'myth'. Even the lives of the martyred Imams have been made into a passion play (*ta'ziyeh*) for public performance. Furthermore, popular theatre and cinema provide the main recreation for Iranian families. Each Thursday night the whole family, with babes in arms and snacks of watermelon seeds in their bags, fill the long queues for the cinema ticket offices. The themes of these Persian films are always the same: scenes of family life enlivened by quarrels, songs and belly dancing.

In this life of privation and renunciation, the poor still suffer the most. A mother of four gives her view: 'I have no garden where my children can play and they have no toys. Their only entertainment used to be the cinema and television. The mullahs look down on our amusements because they do not work and have no need for leisure. Cinema and television are for us workers. I was just as poor under the Shah, but sometimes my children had meals, without meat, watching a cartoon on a neighbour's television and they were happy. Today they refuse the same meal in tears' (Nategh, 1980, pp. 16–17). Television now has nothing but sermons in black and white: black turbans and white beards.

Here again government policy has run into a serious obstacle. The rich can easily get hold of video films ranging from pornography to music hall programmes. For the poor, a black market of popular songs flourishes in every street. In the same kiosks displaying the Qur'an and tapes of religious talks, they can buy cassettes of banned songs – which even find their way to Europe. Popular entertainment has been removed from the public sphere to the home. Faced with such a reaction, the regime has had to step back and Khomeini ordered the *Pasdars* in the course of a radio broadcast: 'Turn a blind eye to what people do in private and at home. Do not transgress on family intimacy.'

In a regime which is day by day losing popular support (three million votes in 1984 as against fifteen million in 1979), the family becomes secretive, turning in on itself and away from the Islamic 'community'. Despite Khomeini's instructions, the government cannot avoid invading family privacy. The authorities, therefore, place emphasis on another of their Imam's directives made in an address to the people on 22 June 1980:

> Spy on each other. The thirty-six million people of Iran must consider themselves all the watchdogs of Islam. Families should be kept under surveillance mainly through the schools. Children who have not yet learned to lie can be pressed to answer questions such as, 'Do your parents engage in political activity?', 'Do they play cards?' 'Does your mother wear her chador in front of guests?' and 'Does she fast?'. ('Report on schools', in *Enghelab-e-Eslami*, 2 March 1984, p. 2)

It goes without saying that the reactions of the authorities depend on the children's answers. Parents are thus obliged to teach their children to lie convincingly. (While I was in hiding from April to November 1980, my seven-year-old daughter was interrogated about my hiding place.)

Paradoxically, the ayatollahs are afraid of the chador which they themselves imposed, as the General Prosecutor of the Tribunals (*Sane'i*) has publicly admitted. In a warning to the *Pasdars*, he said, 'You should be aware that women counter-revolutionaries hide under their chadors . . . They use chadors to transport explosives and to pass as believers' (television speech, March 1981). We should remember that although the chador was banned in 1935 by Reza Shah, the father of the deposed Shah, it never completely disappeared. Without having any ideological significance, it became customary dress for the urban poor. Easy to wear, it hid their poverty and reduced signs of social inequality. On the other hand, it was unknown among the nomads and in most of the countryside.

During the last years of the Shah's regime, the chador reappeared in student circles as a sign of protest against westernisation and imperialism.

After the Islamic government was set up, Khomeini took advantage of the huge involvement of women in the revolution and retained 'Islamic habit'. On International Women's Day (6 March) in 1979, he recommended, without insisting on it, that the chador should be worn by all good Muslim women. Twenty-five thousand women demonstrated against this for several days. Most participants were students, civil servants, nurses and the like, but also a number of veiled women. These, when questioned by journalists, answered, 'I am here to support my daughter' or, 'I want my daughter to have a better life than I have had.' (A documentary film of this demonstration is available at the MLF, *Mouvement de libération féminine*, in Paris; this provides the source for these quotations). For various reasons, the movement failed. In particular, it was not supported by any opposition parties. Those on the left went so far as to condemn the demonstrators for 'serving the interests of the bourgeoisie and of imperialism' because, for the working class, the chador was only 'a secondary question'. Academics, myself included, made errors no less serious by interpreting the movement as being royalist inspired (Homa Nategh, 'On the women's demonstration', conference at Tehran University, 11 March 1979).

All these mistaken judgements encouraged the regime and, in the summer of 1981, the wearing of Islamic habit became compulsory. A second demonstration was organised but had no support, even from feminist groups which were each affiliated to a political party. In this way, intellectuals and opposition groups played along with the regime in the constraints placed on women only shortly before they in their turn became the objects of massive repression. Apart from the chador, Islamic dress consists of a headscarf which completely covers the hair, long sleeves, and thick stockings. Grey, black and dark blue are the only authorised colours. Mixed groups in schools, stadiums and beaches were forbidden. A man cannot help a woman to carry her shopping unless he can prove he is her father, husband or son. When a woman is arrested for an infringement of Islamic dress or for letting passers by glimpse the ends of her hair, prison guards release her after punishment with a notice around her neck which reads: 'I swear that I have been a prostitute all my life. I repent and promise never to return to it' ('Letter to the women of Iran', in *Iranshahr*, 2 March 1984). On this subject, the General Prosecutor has stated, 'There is no trial or judgement for unveiled women who are arrested. Everyone knows what punishment is due'. Addressing the Guardians of the Revolution, he adds, 'If by some misfortune your glance should fall on such a woman, wash your eyes as soon as possible' ('The Sermon of Sane'i', in *Keyhan*, 21 March 1984).

Women have begun to rebel against this humiliation. The same women who surprised the world by their massive involvement in the religious demonstrations during the revolution are today the most open enemies of the regime. They use every opportunity to dress up, wear make-up and even take off their headscarves. But women's opposition shows itself above all in their daily protests against the war with Iraq and the resulting economic recession. This has forced the Islamic Parliament to confirm: 'Everywhere families are complaining. The people are so worn out they cannot go on' ('Discussion in Parliament', *Keyhan*, 25 March 1984).

Women faced with war and economic crisis

> *Imam Khomeini, it is you who have*
> *Defiled the revolution.*
> (Slogan on a wall)

The war with Iraq – with its half a million 'martyrs' and its economic, political and religious consequences – has contributed even more than the revolution or any political party to Iranian women's political awakening. That is to say, it is in the domain of everyday reality that women's attitudes now help to unmask the nature of the Islamic Republic and symbolise the fall in popular morale.

Scepticism grows when the mullahs' sermons about the war and its 'martyrs' conflict with popular beliefs and religious traditions. By calling the Iraqi Sunni leader 'Yazid the renegade', the Iranian government not only insults Saddam Hussein, it also offends its own large Sunni minority, especially Kurds and Turkomans. Within the Shi'ite majority, dissension has arisen between the people and the clergy about the concept of martyrdom. Although believers must always wear mourning for two months (*Muharram* and *Safar*) to commemorate the martyred Imams – the ceremonies being opened with the tears of Khomeini himself, and the victims of the war are considered to be martyrs – a contradiction arises in the prohibition of families from wearing mourning for their lost relatives. On the contrary, the mother or widow must 'congratulate herself and rejoice' for having offered one of her own to Islam. Aware that disorder can spread, the *Pasdars* regularly disperse meetings of families in mourning. In the daily newspapers, statements appear: 'I am certain that our parents, who so cherish their sons, will celebrate with smiles on their faces the day we offer our lives to God' ('The testaments of soldiers', in *Sorouche*, 8 September 1981, p. 59). What is the origin of these predictable testaments? This leads to the question which families pose: if it is just to mourn for martyrs, why not for their own sons?

The war has also poisoned family relationships and led to serious differences between parents and their sons. Without making any direct reference to the age for military service, the authorities have officially announced, 'Children do not need their parents' permission to enlist and go to the front'. This decree has had serious consequences. So now, after a minor tiff, the child leaves the family home in search of adventure without so much as a word to his parents. Furthermore, all schoolboy volunteers are exempted from the end of year exams and receive the school certificate without having attended the lessons. Children between ten and twelve, who have never handled weapons, thus enlist for the 'holy' war. The government exploits the situation to turn family members against each other.

Everyone knows that young schoolboys leave for good and that the survivors on the wrong side of the border (numbering 5000) are no longer wanted by a regime which makes no concessions to the enemy for handing back prisoners. Some mothers hide their children and the number of volunteers has fallen considerably.

In the devastated frontier towns, 'it is not unusual to see mothers resorting to prostitution to provide for the needs of their families' ('A letter from the women of Iran', *Iranshahr*, 2 March 1984). Others leave in search of shelter and work. It is extremely difficult, of course, for a woman on her own to find accommodation. In Iran an unmarried woman is considered improper; the government has frequently advised against letting to unmarried women. The solution is to give herself as a temporary wife to a *Pasdar*. The example was set by the widow of the Prime Minister (Redjai) assassinated by the *Mojahedin*. She accepted the hand of a *Pasdar* and invited others to follow her, but few of these men are prepared to accept a woman with several children.

These women refugees without protection fill the streets of Isfahan, Shiraz and Tehran, whose population have grown enormously. Furthermore, several demonstrations have arisen spontaneously by survivors of the war, who have introduced the slogan of 'Peace'. It goes without saying that each of these demonstrations becomes the occasion for arrests, violent attacks and that the families of the war victims have come to be treated as 'counter-revolutionaries in the pay of Saddam'. The daily press, nevertheless, continues to report sharp criticisms against the government by the victims of the war. As an example: 'For four years you have done nothing but waste the country's money without doing anything to help our devastated towns or their inhabitants.'

The war has economic and political repercussions as well: unemployment, inflation and especially food shortages, with long queues of women waiting outside foodshops. These queues, as Persians say, have become a sort of 'women's political party'. Gathering in numbers of four or five hundred and waiting together for five or six hours in the hope of getting a kilo of meat or a litre of milk, these women get rid of the false hopes of the early days of the revolution. Not only is nothing given away as they had been led to expect, but prices have risen excessively.

In the queues, which the *Pasdars* keep under strict surveillance for fear they might degenerate into demonstrations, women daily observe that the wives of the clergy and even of the *Pasdars* are never in line. These women obtain all they need and more. Everyone knows that Ahmad Khomeini (the son of the Imam) and Sadegh Taba Tabai (arrested in West Germany for drug trafficking in 1982), between them, control the market in fish, poultry and caviar ('The Monopolists', *Enghelab-e-Eslami*, 13 June 1984). While the mosques are becoming empty of worshippers, they are openly filling up with goods for distribution on the black market. In this way, the rich buy directly and at high prices from the agents of the religious authorities. Some women, at the end of their tether, collaborate with these 'holy' entrepreneurs and their markets. Jokes from the queues are very revealing about the judgement these women confer on their benefactors. One example goes: 'A woman is crying bitterly in a queue. Someone asks her the reason of her sorrow. She replies, "Yesterday my husband was kind enough to take my place in the queue, but mistaking the queue, he stood with those waiting for execution".'

The Islamic Republic has freed women of their hopes and their illusions. As the main victims of the revolution, they have little more to lose. Now they are free to begin again from nothing. In the contemporary history of Iran, this is perhaps the first time that women, in protesting against social conditions, are rebelling against their own position.

References

Davani, A. (1964) 'The Two Months of Struggle of the Clergy in 1963' (Ghôm, Iran: Islamic Publishers).

Kasravi, A. (1982) *Le Shi'isme* (Paris: Shahbaz).

Khomeini, Rouhollah (1940) 'The Explanation of Mysteries' (*Kashf ol-Asrar*) (Ghôm: W.D.).

Khomeini, Rouhollah (1979) 'The Explanation of Problems' (*Towzin ol-Masa'el*) (Tehran: Jilamie Publications).

Luizard, F. (1983) 'Les Frères Musulmans et le Moyen Orient', *Esprit*, May–June.

Makhmalbaf, Mohsen (1980) 'Art and Artistic Activity in the Islamic Republic' (Teheran: Ershad).

Mourad, A. (1982) *Les Frères Musulmans* (Teheran: Rahai Publications).

Nategh, Homa (1980) 'Entretien avec une femme ouvrière' *Fasli dar Gol-e Sorkh*, no. 6.

Nategh, Homa (1984) 'Le Grand Enfermement' in *Terre des Femmes* (Paris: Maspero-Découverte).

Nedaye-Hagh (1979) *The Speeches of Khomeini 1978–1979*. Muslim Students' Publication.

Tabari, Azar and Yeganeh, Nahid (eds.) (1982) *In the Shadow of Islam. The Women's Movement in Iran* (London: Zed Press).

4 Public Protest, Domestic Acquiescence: Women in Northern Ireland

LYNDA EDGERTON

Women in Northern Ireland are no strangers to social and political action, but their efforts have been directed almost wholly to civil rights rather than to women's issues. At the beginning of this century James Connolly described the Northern Ireland woman as 'the slave of a slave' (1981, p. 10). This graphic phrase is no less fitting today. Given the bitter political divisions of Northern Ireland, its depressed socio-economic conditions and the powerfully conservative influence of the dominant churches, it is little wonder that women have remained in a relative backwater of feminism. Striving to survive in difficult circumstances is not the most conducive forum for women's debate about alternatives that may appear either abstract or totally out of reach for the majority of the working class; more than that, many women have been encouraged to reject such alternatives as alien.

Women in Northern Ireland tend to marry young, start their families soon afterwards and remain restricted by strong family networks. They are not helped to examine in any critical way their domestic role in the home, or indeed their relationship to their husbands and families; rather, they are socialised into a strong maternal role directed to 'keeping the family together', 'making ends meet' and servicing political campaigns largely determined by men. This situation has changed little in recent years despite the shattering of many old moulds in Northern Ireland.

The social construction of gender

Catholic and Protestant churches alike lay down strict codes of social and moral behaviour, more rigidly adhered to in Northern Ireland than in England. Moreover, in a country where religious and political beliefs are almost synonymous, deviating from the accepted tenets of behaviour may be regarded as betrayal of one's community. This is especially true of the working-class areas. The influence of the church begins at an early age and continues within the education system; by the time of adolescence both boys and girls are well set in their ideas of gender roles. For Catholic women, as Hugh Brody points out, the options are motherhood or perpetual virginity: 'Roman Catholicism emphasises the authority of the father and the gentleness of the mother. It dignifies the celibate and the virgin. It symbolises motherhood as sacrifice and suffering in the greatest of its causes' (1973, p. 175). Protestantism places greater emphasis on the mutual support husband and wife should bring to each other within a similar frame of female subordination: 'the man was obliged to provide guidance in all things to his wife, and his wife was bound to obey' (Hamilton, 1978, p. 58).

The strength of religious conservatism in family life is reflected in the widespread Protestant and Catholic opposition to the 1967 Abortion Act (still not in force), divorce laws and the 1982 Homosexuality Order. The Ulster Unionists at Stormont had the power to introduce the 1967 Abortion Act, but failed to do so. While the Presbyterian Assembly does not oppose abortion in extreme medical cases, the Catholic Church remains unrelenting on this issue. Similarly, legal change on homosexuality was introduced in Northern Ireland only after a successful case at the European Court of Human Rights found the British Government guilty of contravening human rights. Opposition came from both sides, but it was Ian Paisley's Democratic Unionist Party which mounted the vociferous 'Save Ulster from Sodomy' campaign with posters, leaflets and public statements.

Both communities also show active resistance to any adequate form of sex education in the schools. It is not only in rural areas that young girls give birth to babies and then abandon them, but also in the cities of Derry and Belfast. (Note the case of Ann Lovatt, aged 15, who died in a church grotto in County Monaghan after delivering her own baby.) In addition, over two thousand women and girls travel to the United Kingdom each year to obtain abortions, an indication both of the shame of the single mother and the lack of education relating to sexual responsibilities.

The education system reinforces the concept that a woman's place is in the home. Books, curricula, and teachers all act to promote this idea in a cumulative process. Research in a number of schools in the Belfast area (Edgerton and Brown, 1983) shows that, despite the Sex Discrimination (NI) Order 1976, both single-sex and co-educational schools offer boys courses with a strong vocational bias leading ultimately to a job while offering girls non-vocational courses geared to the home. For example, in co-educational secondary schools it is compulsory for boys to do craft subjects like woodwork, technical drawing and metalwork, while girls have to take domestic science, needlework and childcare. The fact that the projected image of women in the 'hidden curriculum' within the schools does not ring true with the reality of women mounting pickets, or protesting about plastic bullets, does not necessarily mean that traditional stereotypes will be effectively challenged.

The concept of women as individuals in their own right holds little credence in this society. Given the chronic nature of the economic, political and social problems in Northern Ireland, it is difficult for working-class women to devote time and attention to personal development. The struggle to survive is difficult enough, as Eileen Evason (1976) shows with cumulative evidence of widespread poverty in the Province. Moreover, the situation will never change without an acknowledgement that women are doubly exploited: first, for their labour value by the economic system; and second, in the domestic sphere of the home. As Lenin pointed out many years ago: 'Laws are not enough, and we cannot under any circumstances be satisfied with what we say in our laws. . . . Public dining rooms, crêches, kindergartens – these are the simple everyday means which assume nothing pompous, grandiloquent or solemn, but which can in fact emancipate women, which can in fact lessen and abolish their inferiority to men in regard to their role in social production and in social life' (1950, pp. 52, 56). Alongside legal changes and the provision of facilities, a wide range of attitudes have to be confronted and changed. For this challenging task, women in Northern Ireland need all the confidence gained through their experience over the last turbulent decades. They also need the support of a strong and coherent women's movement.

Acting for civil rights

The late sixties and early seventies opened up a broad front of social and civil liberties agitation. NICRA (the Northern Ireland Civil

Rights Association), was formed in 1967 by representatives from a broad political spectrum to demand greater democracy and an end to sectarian politics. By 1969, NICRA had become a mass movement and women, as well as men, swelled the streets in protests and marches.

Action specifically organised by women, as women, however, did not become noticeable until the Falls Road Curfew in July 1970. By this time, the pressure of political events had escalated to a pitch of hostility between the Catholic population and the British soldiers patrolling the streets. The curfew, confining residents of Belfast's Falls Road area to their homes, went into effect on July 3 and was lifted two days later. Since food vans had been prevented by the army from entering the curfew zone, essentials such as fresh milk and bread were short. This situation sparked off one of the first all-women demonstrations, described in a Central Citizens' Defence Committee publication:

> The Upper Falls women (outside the curfew area) banded together to break the blockade and take bread and milk and other necessities to the people who had suffered so much . . . The long column marched down the Falls Road, turned right at Leeson Street and then was to have swung left to a distribution centre in Raglan Street. However, by this time most of the food and milk had already been given away to the women and children who had come to greet them. Word got back to Andersonstown, Turf Lodge, Ballymurphy and other areas. (1970, p. 21)

By that evening, three thousand women had gathered and again they marched and broke the curfew. It was never reinstated. This remarkable demonstration was undoubtedly inspired not only by a sense of community solidarity, but also the feeling of women sharing with other women who were being prevented from providing for their families. Working-class women readily identified themselves with this concern. The added element of defying the British Army may have been little more than an additional incentive to protest in public.

'Armoured cars and tanks and guns – came to take away our sons'

The introduction in August 1971 of internment without legal charge or trial highlighted the political contradictions in the Northern Irish state and heightened the level of conflict. Statistics issued by the Civil Rights Office based upon Royal Ulster Constabulary returns show that the number of deaths for the period four months before internment was four army men and four civilians; during the four months following internment, the number rose to 30 army, 11 RUC and UDR, and 73 civilians. While these figures do not conclusively prove that internment without trial was the cause of the increased violence, much evidence suggests that this was indeed the case.

On 9 August 1971, over 500 Catholic men and boys were arrested; approximately 300 of these were interned without trial. (In 1972, Catholic women were interned as well; it was not until 1973 that Protestant men were also interned.) Many other men went 'on the run': they left their homes to go across the border or to live with people less known to the security forces. Often those who remained at home feared interrogation by the police and the army and were reluctant to become involved in political activity. This virtual paralysis, however, did not apply to women. It was precisely at this time that women in working-class Catholic areas – especially in Newry, Belfast and Derry – became very active in the Civil Rights campaign.

One of their first responses to internment was to devise a warning system against army raids – 'bin lid bashing'. When troops entered an area, local women would begin banging their bin lids on the pavement; the noise would carry throughout the area and alert others to follow suit. On the Derrbeg estate in Newry, the women were labelled 'the petticoat brigade'. This warning system had its origins in an earlier period when women in working-class communities heralded the presence of Housing Trust inspectors, who had the power to inspect homes for cleanliness before families would be considered suitable applicants for Housing Trust accommodation. At the sound of the bin lids, scores of women would emerge armed with dusters and mops for a hasty spring clean. After internment, however, the warnings served a more serious purpose.

Women also demonstrated their contempt for the police and soldiers by extreme verbal abuse. They became active as vigilantes and provided shelter and protection for 'wanted' men. Young girls were cast in the unaccustomed role of escorting their boyfriends home, since a boy walking the streets alone at night was much more likely to be 'lifted' by the army than one who was with a girl. Of the approximately fourteen women to be interned, two were mothers with young children.

An important development was the new role of women organisers. When NICRA adopted the strategy of setting up local branches and committees, these were composed mainly of women. Despite this, if one or two men expressed an interest, they were not only welcomed with open arms, but were likely to fill the most prominent roles in the Civil Rights Association itself. Eventually a number of women were co-opted to the Executive Committee of NICRA, an improvement on the situation in 1967, when only one of the thirteen places on the Executive was filled by a woman – the formidable Betty Sinclair, a Communist and Secretary of the Belfast Trades Council. It is true that individual women, most notably Bernadette Devlin, became public figures associated with the civil rights struggle, but they were exceptions.

Women were influential mostly at the community level. At a public meeting composed mainly of women in Lurgan, County Armagh, the demand was made to withhold all payments of rent and rates to government (including gas and electricity) as a protest against internment. Again, it was they who ensured that the Rent and Rates Strike was a success – with more than 30 000 households on strike at the height of the campaign. In later years, women were also to bear the main financial burden of these campaigns; their family budgets were drastically reduced by the Payment for Debt Act 1971, which stated that wages and state benefits could be withheld from persons on rent and rates strike. Family allowances were first to be confiscated. This Act was described by the Child Poverty Action Group as 'one of the most vicious pieces of legislation to be passed this century'. It was later extended and applied to people in debt for rent, rates, gas and electricity throughout the province. Long after the strike which brought the legislation, the Payment for Debt Act continues to force many families in Northern Ireland below the official poverty line.

In the campaign against internment without trial, the pace of events and the intransigence of government authorities forced women into an increasingly active public role. Apart from maintaining NICRA itself an organisation, large demonstrations were arranged as local direct action. As an example of the latter, the Ormeau Road branch of the Civil Rights Association blocked the roads in their area. Later they joined forces with women from other parts of Belfast and had a sit-down protest at the junction of the Falls and Springfield Road about 200 yards from Springfield Road

Police Station, which also 'houses' the British Army. On protests such as this, many of the women for the first time came face to face with authority in stark political conflict. It was here that they also challenged the army and undoubtedly felt a certain degree of collective power in doing so. To sit in one place while army Saracen cars drive up close, at very fast speeds, requires determination. This is what happened, however, and not merely in isolated cases. The women sensed victory at being able to stop traffic, confront the army and capture public attention. They were motivated, of course, by a strong sense of injustice. One women said, 'I was never one for striking out against the government, but I did then and I would now, it (internment) made me very bitter against the state.'

Such action was not confined to the Nationalist Republican areas. The UDA News (Ulster Defence Association) reported on traffic diversions in East and North Belfast:

> What are the reasons for these diversions? Bomb scares? Rioters? Assemblies? Not on your sweet life. Something more effective, difficult to handle, extremely dangerous, and highly explosive. Something to make the toughest para or policeman shiver in their size 12s. The womenfolk of (Loyalist) Belfast are in action. The girls are out in force with their posters, flags, prams, and shopping bags. They form large circles and walk about in the centre of the road for up to an hour at a time occupying the road from footpath to footpath, so that traffic cannot pass. (May 1972, p. 4)

The fact that women became more politically active did not necessarily imply a change in their perceptions about their own position in society; their activities outside the home grew out of their concern for their menfolk and families. The 'security forces' were seen as a threat to working-class homes; beside the arrests and internment, there was the constant annoyance of army raids, houses being ransacked and children harassed. In short, the traditional maternal role as guardian of the family was being confronted by external, alien elements. Little wonder that working-class women in besieged Nationalist areas were spurred to action.

A wife aged 20, with three small children, told me how she had become actively involved with the Civil Rights Association:

> Before Jimmy was interned we had only been married about three years, and we were just involved in the family and that's all. We had no time for other people's problems. We had two small children and one due, and our wee house, this is all we were interested in. I had heard of civil rights marches, but it wasn't until Jimmy was interned that I got interested, His mother had joined the CRA and she went on demonstrations with me. After about two months I joined the 'Women against Internment Committee' and used to go to these meetings once a week.

Similarly, another wife, who was 24 when her husband was interned and had two small children, pointed out:

> I didn't have much choice but to demonstrate. We were all in it together, they (friends, relatives and neighbours) would have thought I didn't care about my husband. And there was the army to remind me night and day, you couldn't forget that they had taken him away and that the government were to blame for the Troubles.

A 22-year-old housewife with three children described her involvement:

> I'd taken part in some CRA demonstrations before, so you can be sure I wasn't going to stop then. It was a struggle though, because if I wasn't going on some protest, I was at a meeting or going to visit him in Long Kesh (internment camp). I sometimes took the kids, although my sister would often mind them for me.

Another wife also highlighted the difficulty of combining political action with her family responsibilities. When asked if she attended demonstrations, she replied:

> Yes, but not as many as I would have liked to go to. The kids were getting knocked about a bit (they had to be left with other people), and so I didn't like leaving them. Anyway I went to Dublin to demonstrate, I probably wouldn't have done this if he had not been interned.

New experiences

The responses of these women may be taken as fairly representative of the majority of working-class women in Republican areas whose families were directly affected by internment. They felt that it was an extension of their family duty to protest in public about the imprisonment and ill treatment of fathers, husbands, brothers and sons. In the process, however, they were exposed to a wide range of new experiences, which – if they had been critically examined – could have challenged the accepted female domestic role. For the first time, many women regularly went out of the house without their children to meetings and demonstrations, they also made prison visits to husbands, boy friends and relatives. For those women with small children, there were considerable difficulties in arranging such visits. The uncomfortable and tedious journey to Long Kesh or Magilligan usually took the whole day. A survey of internees' families records:

> In a number of families the children may miss one day's schooling a week in order to visit Long Kesh with their mother. Yet again, they may be kept off school to look after the young ones whilst their mothers visits. Very often the mother had to take all her children with her to Long Kesh, as there was no one to look after them. As they never knew how long they would be away, most mothers felt they couldn't ask their neighbours to look after their whole family. (Ragg, Doherty, O'Hara and Buckley, 1972, p. 7)

The difficulties were obvious. The lack of community facilities for mothers with young children became strikingly apparent, but these were problems confronted and dealt with – partially on a collective basis, but largely by individual women themselves. The sheer organisational effort of arranging one or two days out per week, with or without children, undoubtedly contributed to a situation where women felt a new sense of self-confidence. This feeling of self-reliance also applied to those women who for the first time had to collect social security benefits as well as dealing with the family budget. In normal circumstances, the social security office refused to pay out money to a woman whose husband was available. As one wife explained, 'I had never claimed benefit in my life, I had thought that those who did were scroungers, but when I got to that office I felt entitled to the money and not one bit ashamed. I also felt sorry for those people who had been going there longer than me.' Despite the fact that the wives of internees were soon supplied with regular weekly payment books, the women rapidly realised how to survive not only as single parent families, but also as claimants.

Another change for these wives of internees was the break from frequent pregnancy. Given the tradition for Irish Catholic women to have a number of children in the early years of marriage, this 'break' allowed them a degree of freedom they might not otherwise have had. It is worth noting, however, that two out of the four women interviewed had babies within twelve months of their husbands' release from prison; it is thus difficult to generalise about how welcome the respite from pregnancies was to the women themselves. This is particularly so because the attitudes among the younger generation to the use of contraceptives are definitely changing despite the influence of the churches.

Finally, women who had initially been somewhat reluctantly caught up in the civil rights struggle were suddenly the focus of world publicity. Perhaps for the first time in their lives, many women found themselves to be figures of importance to others outside the sphere of their immediate family and community. They were responsible for direct action as traffic stoppages. Their demonstrations and protests, showing their new collective power, appeared on television and in the press. Bernadette Devlin summed up the response in her autobiography:

> We had an influx of foreign revolutionary journalists searching for illumination on the Theory of Petrol Bomb Fighting. The people of the Bogside thought it was fantastic; they didn't know how to spell revolution, never mind work it out, but they were really delighted with themselves that people should come from the Sorbonne to ask the unemployed of the Bogside where they learned to fight so well. (1969, p. 205)

Similarly in the working-class Nationalist areas of Belfast, such as the Markets or Turf Lodge, local public meetings were held with wives of internees or other female relatives on the platform. They would address the audience and should a British Army patrol venture into the vicinity, a few remarks would be thrown in their general direction. Inevitably, these women developed a new sense of self-awareness and, indeed, virtually a new social identity. Their struggle, however, was fought entirely in the cause of their menfolk and did not include feminist demands even though they returned to face the problems of surviving as temporary single parent families.

Community and family support for these women was forthcoming as long as they followed the strict moral code demanded of the wives of prisoners. If they did not conform, or indeed if any women from such areas flouted community rules, then retribution was swift and vicious. In the city of Derry, for example, at least one Catholic women was tarred and feathered because she courted a British soldier. In another instance, a woman's head was shaved because she had a male friend while her husband was in prison. In the Loyalist community, there was the notorious 'romper room murder' of July 1974, when two women beat Ann Ogilby to death with her young daughter in the adjoining room. The motive of the ten women involved in the case came out in reports of the trial: a detective stated that the murdered woman was 'associated' with the husband of one of the women.

Women leading campaigns

Women did not confine their activities to the issues deemed important by the Civil Rights Association. In 1971 a number of mothers in the Ormeau Road area of Belfast decided to mount a 'Milk Campaign'. This began when the then Minister for Education, Margaret Thatcher, stopped the supply of school milk for children over the age of seven. Protest letters were sent to the newspapers and mothers began gathering to discuss the matter. A picket was arranged for the City Hall and some 200 women and children turned up with banners and placards.

The atmosphere of sectarianism in Belfast prevented the untroubled development of this campaign. Although women from both sides of the religious divide were affected by the Government decision, it was claimed by some that the 'Milk Campaign' was a Catholic conspiracy, that since Catholics had more children they would therefore be more adversely affected by the stoppage. The local press gave headlines to this argument; consequently sectarian fears escalated and Protestant support for the campaign was less forthcoming. Even this apparently straightforward issue of social concern was to be damned by the age-old tensions of Orange and Green politics.

In May 1971, the mothers staged a march from the City hall to Stormont, a distance of some six miles. They lobbied local MPs and put their case to Captain Long, the Stormont Minister for Education. The support of several MPs, including the Reverend Ian Paisley, was pledged but not publicised. In this particular campaign at least one Protestant woman from East Belfast, who spoke on behalf of the group on television, was intimidated at work for agitating alongside Catholics. This woman was a school meals attendant and was told not to go back near the school again. She wrote to the campaign organisers wishing them well but explaining why she and her friends could not participate in any further protests.

Nevertheless, the campaign continued. With the aid of Transport House, 'The Mothers of Belfast', as they now called themselves, produced a petition against withdrawal of school milk and distributed this to over one hundred schools, mostly primary. All the heads (except from two schools, Botanic Primary and Ballygomartin) signed the petition against the withdrawal of the school milk. Support also came from many trade unions, the Irish National Teachers' Organisation, the Child Poverty Action Group and a number of political parties. The women lobbied the Belfast City Council to ignore the 'no school milk' order as the Merthyr Tydfil Council had done in Wales. A protest march was held at the City Hall, complete with two cows provided for the day by the Farmers' Union. Although the Council did not adopt the proposed action, they did pass a resolution requesting the Belfast Education Committee to ask the Stormont Government to reconsider the decision to stop school milk. This was passed unanimously on 1 June 1971, probably one of the few uncontested decisions ever made by the Belfast City Council.

Despite the considerable success achieved by the mothers' campaign, the decision to stop the supply of school milk was not rescinded. The campaign itself was dropped in August 1971 when internment without trial was introduced. In the face of mass arrests, brutal interrogations and extensive civil unrest, the movement for limited social issues lost its momentum. This problem was to re-emerge over the following decade as community and single issue campaigns struggled to reassert themselves over the bitter political divisions in the Province. Women were to be at the forefront of many of these campaigns, not least in the many area committees against the plans to redevelop Belfast which entailed the destruction of many well-established working-class communities. Some success was achieved by the combined community pressure.

In terms of organisational involvement, the most noted development to draw on large numbers of women was the formation of the 'Peace People' in August 1976. This was set up after the death of three young children in Andersonstown. The incident occurred when soldiers shot dead an armed Provisional IRA man in a car which then went out of control and killed the children. The children's aunt, Mairead Corrigan, and another Andersonstown woman, Betty Williams, spoke out in the media at their distress over the children's deaths and their opposition to the IRA. The media immediately identified the group that resulted as 'Peace Women', and it is important to note that at first the movement was formed entirely of women. Again the theme of family concern was noticeable; women feared that their children would be caught up in the apparently unending round of sectarian and political conflict.

The 'Peace People', renamed as men took part, seemed to offer solutions that were both peaceful and non-sectarian. For the first time in many years there was an air of optimism. When it became clear that there were few simple solutions to the problems of Northern Ireland and the direction of the movement became increasingly controlled by middle-class and church elements, working-class support in both Loyalist and Republican areas fell away. Moreover, many individuals and organisations, including the Civil Rights Association and the Irish Congress of Trade Unions, took the view that substantial political and economic changes would have to be made to ensure lasting peace in Northern Ireland.

Republican and Loyalist women

Women have a long tradition of active participation in the Republican organisations, although largely through separate units and in ways dictated by the male-dominated movement. Throughout this century, however, women active in the Nationalist and Republican movement *have* raised issues of feminism and equal rights. Margaret Ward describes how in the late sixties younger women in the Republican movement 'began to express their disillusionment and disaffection with their subsidiary role and urged strongly for their integration into the IRA' (1983, p. 258). In recent years, moreover, feminist demands have received at least a gesture of recognition, specifically since the value of English feminist support for the traditional Republican struggle has been appreciated. Some individual women have gained prominence in the Republican movement and have suffered as a result. In 1976, Maire Drumm, the vice-president of Provisional Sinn Fein, was shot dead; and in 1980, Miriam Daly, who was influential in the Irish Republican Socialist Party, shared the same fate.

The methods used to discriminate against women in such organisations are, not surprisingly, mirror-images of the society they live in. One women from the official Republican movement pointed out to me:

> The myth that women were not to be involved in politics was maintained through a number of ways. The fact that politics often revolved around the pub and pub discussions; no woman would go into a pub on her own. Also the men found it beneficial to keep the wife in the dark about certain activities. The relationships between man and wife was very strained, the wife couldn't ask where he was going or what he was doing. This is one of the reasons why open public activity was welcomed by women, especially the anti-internment struggle, where for the most part it was our women who were involved, our men being in danger of being lifted.

On at least one occasion, women picketed a Republican drinking club in West Belfast because of its restrictive rules against women. The men, however, dismissed such actions as petty and as diverting attention from the 'real' struggle. Other feminist demands were scorned in this manner. An attempt in the late 1970s by the 'Women against Imperialism' to re-adjust the balance within the Republican movement had some measure of success when the group began to link the demands of Republican women prisoners in Armagh prison to feminist ideas. This was mainly achieved by using International Women's Day, 8 March, as a day of protest. Public demonstrations on that day began in 1976 when the Northern Ireland Women's Rights Movement organised a rally in the centre of Belfast and have continued each year since. In 1979 protests at Armagh women's prison were started to express solidarity with the women in jail. These demonstrations took place outside the prison itself and a number of English feminists responded to the invitation of Sinn Fein and 'Women against Imperialism' to take part.

The women's department of Sinn Fein was established in 1981 and at the 1983 Ard Fhies, the annual conference of Sinn Fein, the policy of positive discrimination for women was adopted throughout the movement. This policy agreed to reserve seats for women either by co-option or votes for at least one quarter of the Ard Comhairle (National Executive Committee), to ensure that women were selected as candidates in elections and employed equally in Sinn Fein advice centres and offices and, in general, to avoid stereotyped roles for women. On more controversial issues, however, change was less forthcoming. The attempt to delete the sentence, 'We are totally opposed to abortion', from their policy documents was unsuccessful, although the word 'totally' was removed. Nor did Sinn Fein support the Anti-Amendment campaign in the Republic, a campaign against the inclusion of a clause in the Irish Constitution enshrining the illegality of abortion. (Only one political party in Ireland has publically supported a woman's 'Right to Choose' – the Communist Party). The 1984 Ard Fhies came out for the acceptance of contraception and for divorce rights. These changes showed a marked contrast with previous years, as Margaret Ward states:

> In 1979, a full ten years after the start of the latest round in the nationalist campaign, Sinn Fein was forced to admit that 'apart from a few articles in the Draft Charter of Rights and a short declaration made at a press conference in 1972, nothing has ever been said or written on the subject (of women)'. (1983, p. 255)

Within the Loyalist organisations, the involvement of women has been at a more limited level. This may well reflect, however, the lack of local community support for extreme Loyalist groups relative to their Republican counterparts. Nevertheless, the wives of Loyalist internees have demonstrated on a number of occasions and have taken part in prisoner status protests; indeed, from time to time, the wives of Loyalist and Republican internees joined forces to make their protests heard. In terms of the Orange Order and

Unionist Parties, the traditional function of the women's sections would appear to be the organisation of jumble sales and refreshments, while throughout the annual 12th of July celebrations the women's role is confined to that of cheer leaders. Despite this, in recent years an increased number of female candidates have been put forward at elections by the different Unionist parties. Such women, however, are never noted for their feminism, and tend to be more vehemently conservative than their male colleagues.

In something approaching desperation at the lack of feminist awareness and concern, the Northern Ireland Women's Rights Movement was set up in 1975. The intention was to establish it as an 'umbrella' for all interested organisations and thus to create a united women's movement bringing together women from Protestant and Catholic areas around common demands. This gained wide support from the labour movement; a number of trade unions, women's groups, political parties and individuals were affiliated. The Women's Rights Movement highlighted issues such as the lack of nursery schools, inequality of pay, the delayed implementation of the Sex Discrimination Order, 1976, and parity of rights with women in Britain on divorce, abortion and other legal rights. In 1975 the NIWRM formulated a Charter for Northern Ireland with seven feminist demands: (1) equal opportunities in education, training and work; (2) equal pay for work of equal value; (3) equality of legal and social rights; (4) the right to maternity and child care facilities; (5) parity of rights for women in Northern Ireland with women in England; (6) improved family planning services; (7) recognition for non-working wives and mothers. This organisation also initiated discussion and debate about issues such as rape and abortion, which were later taken up as campaigns by a range of women's groups. By establishing the first women's centre in Belfast and through activity and research, the Northern Ireland Women's Rights Movement has succeeded in highlighting feminist issues.

Living in an 'armed patriarchy'

During the last 15 years the 'troubles' in Northern Ireland have been subject to debate, mainly at times of increased tension. The media tend to direct attention only when 'newsworthy' incidents occur, like bombings or events during the hunger strikes of 1980 and 1981. Yet for many Northern Irish families, especially those working-class areas, violence has become part of daily living. Under these circumstances, it is often the woman, in her role as wife or mother, who has the heavy responsibility of trying to bring up a family in a situation similar to a war environment. At the same time, Northern Ireland appears under the veneer of a 'normal' state in a liberal-democratic country.

Husbands and children are the main victims: killed, maimed or imprisoned. Teenagers in particular are vulnerable to violence; many young people become involved in joy-riding in stolen cars, housebreaking and armed robberies. Over the last few years, such criminal activities ('hooding'), and the resulting deaths, have dramatically increased. 'Hooding' is a spin-off from paramilitary activity; the young people use knowledge gained on the fringes of illegal groups in order to benefit themselves. Joy-riding and 'hooding' are subject to another analysis, of course. These activities provide some escape from boredom for unemployed youth confined to particular geographical areas because of poverty and sectarianism.

The Irish Republican Army and the Irish National Liberation Army have their own way of dealing with a 'hood', in a manner that can only be described as rough justice – i.e. 'knee-capping', shooting the victim in the knees. In Derry a young person bled to death after being knee-capped. In a society with a high level of violence, this form of punishment is becoming more and more accepted. In 1982 the IRA executed a young boy because of his continual involvement in 'anti-social' activities, and in 1984 the INLA executed a 24-year-old man (married with two children), because he used its name while participating in robberies. A number of youths, while joy-riding, have also been shot or killed by the British Army or RUC.

Another area of violence is that caused by the British Army using rubber bullets or shooting people outright, as in the case of 'Bloody Sunday' in Derry 1972, when the British Army killed 13 people. Between 1971 and 1981, 13 other people, 6 of them children, were killed by plastic or rubber bullets (Curtis, 1982, p. 6).

Violence is, of course, created by the paramilitary organisations on both sides: the Irish Republican Army and the Irish National Liberation Army; and the Ulster Freedom Fighters and the Ulster

Volunteer Force. Many young people join these paramilitary organisations and, as a result, finish up behind bars or in coffins. Both Maread Farrell and Bobby Sands were eighteen years old when they were convicted for their activities in the IRA. Similarly, on the other side of the conflict, as Sarah Nelson points out:

> Loyalist prisoners, who provide a captive sample, show that like the IRA, most Loyalist militants at this time (1973) were broadly representative of their age group and community. They were mainly young working-class men between 17 and 22 who differed little from others in their area in terms of education, employment and police records. (1984, p. 118)

Some acts of violence are indiscriminate, such as bombings; others not so indiscriminate. This is the most publicised form of violence and one that at times has spilled over into the streets of Britain.

It is difficult to estimate the effect that the deaths of over 2000 people in 15 years, and many more injuries, has had upon the lives of families in this country. In a society that is already divided, it may be that further polarisation takes place. In 'normal' times, a family suffering bereavement receives sympathy from the community. It is quite straightforward to sympathise with a family whose son or daughter is killed in a bomb incident, an innocent bystander who happens to be in the wrong place at the wrong time. But the political conflict in Northern Ireland has produced problems and injuries much deeper than this. The death of a 'hood' or member of a paramilitary organisation receives different reactions from different sections of the populace.

If women as mothers have received little sympathy, then women as wives have received even less. Those who endured sexual or domestic violence were practically unknown until the formation of the Northern Ireland Women's Aid Federation in the mid-seventies and the Rape Crisis Association in 1981. Domestic violence has its own special dimension. Being a member of a paramilitary organisation or of the Ulster Defence Regiment, for example, may give a man a certain amount of protection from being prosecuted for domestic crimes. In the first study of domestic violence in Northern Ireland, Eileen Evason comments that in Northern Ireland a battered woman may face unique difficulties in seeking help.

> Firstly, husbands may use the power they have as members of paramilitary organisations to control their wives by, for example, threatening relatives who try to assist. It must be said that, through membership of such organisations and indeed the UDR many more men have access to weapons here, and women in Northern Ireland live in what can only be described in an armed patriarchy. Secondly, many battered women live in areas where the police are not welcome and the community bias is against calling for police assistance. The argument here obviously is not about the rightness or wrongness of membership of this or that organisation. Nor is it suggested that any of the organisations endorse or support violence against women in the home. The point is simply that the power gained outside the home may be deployed within it, adding an extra dimension to all of the means men normally have for oppressing women and engendering fear. (1982, p. 73)[1]

Evason makes the point: 'Women married to men in non-manual occupations are not much less at risk than those married to manual workers' (1982, p. 17). The interviews conducted by Eileen Fairweather, Roisin McDonough and Melanie McFadyean (1984, pp. 128–133) also attest to wife-beating and other forms of male violence in all sections of society, not just the working-class as is commonly supposed.

It is to the credit of Women's Aid that in difficult political circumstances they have been able to provide refuges in 'neutral' areas, where both Protestant and Catholic women can find protection. In cases of rape, some members of the police and army have been cited; rape at gun-point has also been recorded. At least one woman reported being under threat from a paramilitary organisation, thus suggesting the protection of one of its members. Evason's point about power raises questions: if sections of the population resort to violence to achieve various political or personal ends, how will this affect the power relationship within the marriage, and will the future generation experience more violence within the home?

Awaiting reciprocal action

Women have clearly been active in a wide range of political organisations, social movements and specific movements and specific campaigns; they have been motivated in most cases by their perceived family responsibilities. Yet the collective power and social identity that women acquired through their public activity have not been reflected in an altered position within the home. Few have effectively challenged the idea that women, whether employed outside the home or not, are virtually solely responsible for household chores and child-rearing. If a woman continuously queries her husband's perception of her role, she places her marriage in jeopardy. To demand that her husband should also look after the children and the house, to insist that she has a right to an individual life, leads to three possible consequences. The husband may concede to some of these demands; he may disagree with his wife and the relationship may be tested, to the point of breaking up; or he may attempt 'to put her in her place' through violence.

An interest in women's issues has grown, slowly but continuously, since 1975, yet for the most part this awareness has not permeated the mass housing estates in Belfast, Derry and other cities, and has had even less emphasis in rural areas. Melanie McFadyean writes, 'The war has politicized people; these years have inspired the debate between feminism and nationalism, have made women question the institutions that generations before them had taken for granted – marriage, the church, birth control, the law' (1984, p. viii). A somewhat overstated view, but some of the younger women involved in the women's groups in Belfast have begun to challenge ideas and promote changes in policies of the various political parties. Since 1980, several women's centres have opened; women's education projects and organisations helping rape victims have come into existence. The Women's Information Group and Northern Ireland Women's Rights Movement work actively to create a non-sectarian women's movement. Added to this is the network of Women's Aid and the growth of women's participation in the trade union movement. These are signs that more women are becoming aware of the need for collective action.

Debates and activities regarding feminism and nationalism, however, have concentrated mainly on the issue of feminist support for the 'armed struggle' and whether or not women's groups should give support to women Republican prisoners in Armagh jail,[2] and less on women's rights to contraception and abortion and men's responsibilities within the home. Interviews with local women from a working-class estate in Belfast confirm this situation. Those women conscious of the need for greater independence tended to barter for it quietly. As one wife commented, 'If he could force his opinion on me, I would be just like a wee snail in here waiting for him to come in. Just build your whole life around him and that's what he would like. Every woman should have a bit of independence and I think getting out to work gives you that.' She pointed out that with her part-time job as a home help, she had to do extra housework in her own home in the evenings. When asked how her husband felt about her working, she replied, 'So long as it doesn't interfere with him, he doesn't mind. He would say, if you can't cope then don't do the job, stay in the house. He's a bit of a male chauvinist pig is Jimmy.'

Where women are less successful in negotiating an element of freedom, frustration can build up over the years. Another wife (30 years old with four children) illustrated some of the feelings that many working-class women have about their role in the home:

> He just sits there, he doesn't lift a finger to help me. There are times when I could scream. He doesn't seem to see the frustration I am in at all. But what can I do? If I stop cooking, who will feed the children? He won't. He can walk out of the house at any time without any explanation. I sometimes wish I could do the same. But I can't. To all extents and purposes, the kids are my responsibility, I can't just walk off and leave them. There's nothing really I can do but put up with it. I've often felt like picking up the dirty dishes and hurling them out of the window, but that would not be a solution, would it?

She reveals yet again how the feeling of responsibility the woman has for her family limits her self-expression and perceived options. The fact that in many working-class communities the extended family network has not only remained, but been reinforced by the 'troubles', provides a further barrier to the development of female independence. Widescale intimidation gave rise to extensive squatting, which resulted in families and relatives being housed in the same neighbourhood. The men in the family along with their male friends form a close-knit group which serves to reinforce each other's ideas, prejudices and stereotypes. The women, on the other hand, are not guaranteed support from female relatives if they are viewed as flouting the community norms and conventions influenced by the local churches.

It is not for sectarian reasons that most of the women featured in this chapter come from Catholic Nationalist backgrounds. Although reference is made to other activities, the Civil Rights Movement received most attention because of the enormous amount of political activity generated within this organization and because so many women participated. The nature of the Civil Rights Movement tended to dictate who would be involved, just as the Civil Rights Movement in America did, regarding black people. This is not to deny that there are many aspects to the political conflict in Northern Ireland, affecting different people in different ways. The women portrayed in these pages are those who have expressed fear, anger and protest because of the internment and mistreatment of their husbands, brothers and sons. The feelings of these women allowed them to react on behalf of their relatives or neighbours, but rarely on their own behalf. In the very best sense of humanity, of course, this activity is in reality an action on behalf of themselves. A final quote from a woman whose husband was interned indicates that women are still awaiting reciprocal action from their husbands regarding the elimination of injustices which women experience in the home. This woman, active in the Civil Rights Movement in the early seventies, describes her social life in marriage:

> On our night out, he goes off to the club, I put the children to bed. I arrange for the babysitter to come and then I get ready to go out. I go to the club, sit down and Peter, when he sees me, comes and buys me a drink. Then he goes off to talk to his friends. I sit all night on my own, and mostly buy my own drink. Then I go home. Peter has to stay – so he says – to help clear up the club. I then pay the babysitter and that's our night out.

Since her husband works 'voluntarily' for this drinking club, he is out most nights. She comments, 'he sits up there in the club, talking about when he was in Long Kesh, he doesn't give a damn about me. This bloody house is like Long Kesh to me, at least he had friends to talk to inside. I'm in here on my own staring at these four walls.'

Notes

1. Evason credits Cathy Harkin from Derry for the phrase 'armed patriarchy'. Now deceased, Cathy was renowned for her activities in the labour community and women's movement.
2. Many political parties, trade unions and women's organisations have supported the campaign to stop 'strip searches' of female prisoners in Armagh jail, carried out on remand prisoners as they leave and enter the prison to attend court. Since the prisoners are always escorted and never come into contact with any member of the public, such humiliating searches are considered by many to be unnecessary. In addition, prisoners who receive visits from friends and relatives have an element of physical contact, yet are not strip searched; the contention that such practices are necessary for security reasons does not stand as a valid statement.

References

Brody, Hugh (1973) *Inishkillane* (Harmondsworth: Penguin).

Central Citizens Defence Committee (1970) *Law and Orders. The Story of the Belfast Curfew, 3–5 July 1970* (Dundalk: Dundalgan Press).

Connolly, James (1981) *Breaking the Chains. Selected Writings of James Connolly on Women* (Belfast: Unity Press).

Curtis, Liz (1982) *They Shoot Children* (London: Information on Ireland).

Devlin, Bernadette (1969) *Price of My Soul* (London: Pan).

Edgerton, Lynda and Brown, Pat (1983) *Must We Be Divided for Life?* (Belfast: Northern Ireland Women's Right Movement).

Evason, Eileen (1976) *Poverty. The Facts in Northern Ireland* (London: Child Poverty Action Group, Poverty Pamphlet 27).

Evason, Eileen (1982) *Hidden Violence* (Belfast: Farset Co-op Press).

Fairweather, Eileen, McDonough, Roisin, and McFadyean, Melanie (1984) *Only the Rivers Run Free. Northern Ireland: The Women's War* (London and Sydney: Pluto Press).

Hamilton, Roberta (1978) *The Liberation of Women. A Study of Patriarchy and Capitalism* (London: George Allen & Unwin).

Marx, Karl, Engels, Frederick, Lenin, Vladimir, and Stalin, Josef (1950) *Women and Communism. A Selection of Writings* (London: Lawrence and Wishart).

McFadyean, Melanie (1984) Introduction to Fairweather, McDonough and McFadyean.

Nelson, Sarah (1984) *Ulster's Uncertain Defenders: Loyalists and the Northern Ireland Conflict* (Belfast: Appletree Press).

Ragg, Doherty, O'Hara, and Buckley (1972) *Survey of Internees' Families* (Belfast: Northern Ireland Civil Rights Association).

Ulster Defence Association News, May 1972.

Ward, Margaret (1983) *Unmanageable Revolutionaries. Women and Irish Nationalism* (London: Pluto Press and Dingle, County Kerry, Ireland: Brandon Book Publishers).

5 The Coal War: Women's Struggle during the Miners' Strike

MOIRAM ALI

Britain has no female mineworkers, yet women became the driving force behind the miners' strike of 1984–85. The media portrayed these women as the supportive wives and daughters of miners, dutifully performing a domestic role that enabled their men to maintain the strike. Women were shown mainly carrying out activities associated with the soup kitchen and, at times, standing 'behind their men' on the picket line. In this chapter, I challenge this view of women acting only in a supportive capacity to their men. It is true that some women limited their participation to the practical and domestic sphere, but others became more actively involved in the political scene than some of the men. Furthermore, as the strike progressed, women developed new insights: they came to regard the strike as their own struggle, rather than one they backed solely out of loyalty to their menfolk. I examine here this awakening of women's awareness to wider issues and its implications for the future.

Not all women backed the strike, it is important to recognise, and a small group initiated a Miners' Wives Back-to-Work Movement. Of much greater significance, however, in terms of numbers and extent of commitment, were those involved in local women's support groups and the nationally-based Women Against Pit Closures. My observations are based on women belonging to this organisation in Sherburn-in-Elmet, a small town of 4167 people (1981 census) in North Yorkshire. Without its own pit, Sherburn is not a pit town in the orthodox sense. Many of its inhabitants have arrived in recent years in the relocation of overspill populations from nine separate coalfields in Selby district and parts of West and

North Yorkshire. Some miners have lived in the town for about fifteen years, but this is a short time in the annals of mining communities. Although specific to the women of this location, my analysis also draws on evidence from other mining areas, particularly South Wales.

Why women took up the strike

The miners' strike began in March 1984, prompted by the National Coal Board announcement that a programme of pit closures would lead to the loss of 20 000 jobs in just one year. Men at Cortonwood Colliery in Yorkshire, a pit under direct threat, walked out. In Scotland, too, miners came out over the projected closures. Within days the strike spread through Yorkshire, Scotland, South Wales and Kent.[1] This was not the first miners' strike, of course; previous ones had taken place in 1972 and 1974, as well as in the earlier period of 1921 and 1926. What made the 1984–85 strike unique, however, was the active involvement of women on a scale and in a form never before witnessed in any British industrial dispute.

Although women were active in the strikes of the 1920s, it is difficult to assess their involvement because labour historians (mainly male) have seldom been interested in recording their activities. Carole Harwood has recently traced the militant action of women in Wales during this period as part of a long and continuing tradition of women's struggles in the Welsh mining villages:

> They were out on picket lines and also gave scabs rough music when they returned home, beating a barrage of smashing kettles, cans and frying pans. Such women had reason to be angry as they entered that period known as the Depression. By the 1930s, Welsh doctors were reporting cases of babies contracting rickets in the womb. In 1934 alone, 1007 babes under the age of 4 weeks died. The government's response was to cut benefits, and by early 1935, women were out on the streets in protest. (1985, p. 28)

Women have also fought for women's jobs and for better pay and working conditions for women; Grunwick in 1976–77, for example, shattered the stereotype of the passive Asian woman. But 1984–85 was the first time so many women throughout Scotland, England

and Wales became engaged in a nationwide industrial protest.

This was in contrast to women's role in the relatively brief coal strikes of the seventies. In both 1972 and 1974 (lasting six and four weeks), miners' wives encouraged their men to return to work, often regardless of whether a settlement had been reached. Women found it hard to live on strike pay and disliked the strain of having their husbands around the house all day. Quite simply, they could not relate their own interests to the demands of the strikers for more pay. Even in Wales, as Barbara Bloomfield relates:

> It is fair to say, however, that some of the Maerdy wives were not particularly sympathetic to the NUM in the early seventies and that those strikes were seen as 'men's strikes' over pay rather than as disputes which affected the whole community. (1985, p. 16)

In 1984, the strike was not over pay, but over pit closures, the resulting unemployment, and the widespread effect this would have on people's lives. This explains why women became so active in their support. Pit closures would mean mass unemployment extending into the future. Clearly, this would affect not only men, but the family and the whole community. Losing a dispute over pay would not have terrible consequences for women, but losing this battle to save pits would result in profound changes in the character of affected villages. Even in Sherburn-in-Elmet, where mining takes third place after agriculture and manufacture, local pit closures would mean mass and permanent unemployment for the town. One Sherburn woman remarked:

> I've a lad, nineteen, and he must have his name down at thirty different places locally, but it's useless. He doesn't think he'll ever get a job at this rate, and he's a bright lad. If the pits went, so would all the chances of a job. It would be a ghost town – frightening thought, isn't it?

Pit closures would directly affect the present and future lives of everyone in the community. This was not a question of shunning mining jobs in other areas or other types of work because unemployment was rising steadily in most parts of Britain. Glynnis Evans from the women's support group in Maerdy was asked during a phone-in programme on Radio Oxford why they were fighting to keep such a dirty and dangerous job open for their children instead of moving to find work elsewhere. She told how she loved her community, the Rhondda, and asked why she should dig up her roots to roam the country searching for work that didn't exist. She concluded, 'If we took up Tebbit's suggestion and got on our bikes we'd end up over the white cliffs of Dover' (Sweeney, 1985, p. 69).

Women found themselves caught up in the conflict: on the one hand, negotiations between the NUM (National Union of Mineworkers) activists and the NCB (National Coal Board); and, on the other, direct and often physical conflict within their towns and villages between strikers and strike-breakers (known as 'scabs'). War-like conditions ensued, with a heavy police presence, sometimes accompanied by military-style protective riot gear and curfew-style road blocks. Pitched battles between police and pickets, and between strikers and 'scabs', created a tense atmosphere in those villages with divided loyalties to the union. Many of the women I spoke to compared the strike to a war. A woman from Sherburn-in-Elmet told me:

> We've had media against us, we've had government against us, we've had DHSS (Department of Health and Social Security) against us. We haven't just been on strike, we've had all the forces against us as well. It's been like a state of war.

Women's support groups

Of necessity, women organised themselves to feed and clothe their families. The DHSS assumed that all miners were receiving £15 at first and later £16 per week in strike pay (which they did not receive because the NUM could not afford it) and consequently deducted this amount from the Supplementary Benefit that the strikers' families were entitled to. Since single miners failed to qualify for any assistance, they had no income. With savings of miners' families dwindling and debts mounting, women's support groups began to emerge all over Britain. At first, women responded to the needs of their communities, rather than becoming actively involved. The struggle was between the NUM and the NCB. Women's support groups provided the organisation to survive during this conflict. Such organisation was not only new, but in contrast to the traditional lifestyle of women from mining communities, described as 'a life of exclusion and isolation, welded to a *culture* of solidarity and support, though that support has no clear organised form for women' (Campbell, 1984, p. 8).

The sudden and rapid emergence of these support groups was followed by a link-up of groups and the formation of a national network, the Women Against Pit Closures. The primary function of support groups was to help ease hardship and suffering in the community, but these groups served another, perhaps equally important, function for women; they built solidarity among women and lessened the feelings of despair and isolation that had been so great during the strikes of the seventies. As Tina Worboy from Sherwood Colliery in Nottingham put it:

> The women's support group was started by me, because I was in the '72 and '74 strikes . . . I felt isolated when my husband used to come back and say everything that had happened while he was out . . . I thought, I would get all the women together, so that there was somewhere they could go with one another, like the men in the '72 strike, it would help the women. (Kendall and Norden, 1985)

Generally, women's support groups were set up by one or two women, with others then becoming involved. Sheila Capstick started the Sherburn-in-Elmet group by booking a room in a local public house, the Oddfellows Arms (the only pub in the town allowing women to meet), and then publicising the meeting. Initial response was good and the group grew from strength to strength, meeting weekly throughout the strike and afterwards. Sheila was no stranger to political activity. Having participated in local Labour Party and trade union affairs, she had a clear idea of how to attract new members and how to organise them. But most groups were established by women who had never been remotely involved in political action; this was their first experience.

So great was the success of such women that in mining communities throughout Britain these groups grew to rival the union as the principal vehicle of organisation. The women's support groups became the focus of attention, the hub of the community. Women in these groups were more in touch with what was happening locally and they knew exactly who would be sympathetic towards particular causes. Their greater intimacy with local people and local issues meant that they were much more effective than the union in gathering support for events and activities at a community level. The union's skills lay in organising men nationally, but their procedure was too bureaucratic and impersonal to be as successful at a local level. In the early days of the strike, however, these women's groups were not always so strong. Members lacked confidence and involved themselves in the kinds of support most familiar to them; they were concerned with what amounted to an extension of their domestic duties as wives and mothers. Women felt it was their responsibility to provide their families with, at the very least, the basic requirements of a 'normal' life – a balanced, healthy diet and decent, clean clothes. The first vital requirement was provided by the organisation of food parcels and soup kitchens.

Ensuring that no one in the community goes hungry may appear to be a simple enough task requiring little more than mass-catering skills. But where did all the food come from? There was no money to buy it. Where was it cooked? How was it distributed? This apparently simple task of running a soup kitchen engaged women in all of the unseen activities of feeding a penniless community. The first of these hidden activities – getting the food – was carried out in a variety of imaginative ways. Food was obtained either directly from street collections and donations or by raising money to buy it. Fund raising for food involved women in activities ranging from conventional jumble sales to more outrageous stunts like sponsored strip-teases and bed-pushes. One such sponsored bed-push took the women of Sherburn-in-Elmet over the North York Moors: 'It were so hilly that the person in't bed had to get out and help push.' Fund raising was not a series of one-off events; in order to maintain enthusiasm, it had to be continuous and involve entertainment aspects.

Once the food was obtained, it then had to be cooked, or parcelled and distributed to needy families or single miners. Packaging and distribution was easily carried out, though it was necessary to make sure that no parcel exceeded a value of £4 (which would then be counted by the DHSS as income and deducted from a family's benefit). At Maerdy Lodge in Wales, for example, the support group sent out 700 food parcels a week to miners' families all down the valley as far as Porth. Volunteers describe their work:

> We can only afford to put in the basics: eight pounds of potatoes, a tin of corned beef, a tin of veg, rice pudding, fruit, sometimes sugar, tea bags, tins of beans or spaghetti and so on. We have to raise money ourselves through raffles and socials and going away to speak at meetings. We did well last week – from meetings in Birmingham and Oxford we brought back £1000. If someone's in real need, they can ask for more food – single men are the worst off. They're never turned away if they come and ask. (WCCPL and NUM, 1985, p. 34)

Despite the problems posed in cooking and serving food, women often found this more rewarding than distributing food parcels. Soup-kitchens and canteens brought people together, not just physically, but emotionally, too, and created a sense of common cause. Soup kitchens demanded a local venue suitably equipped for large-scale catering. Such was rarely to be found in pit villages, whether in the local church hall, miners' welfare or village hall. Women had to make use of whatever was available; this could be a single four-ring cooker to prepare over 200 meals a day. Improvisation solved most problems. In one Pontefract soup kitchen, large plastic baby baths were used for washing up. Despite the difficulties, women coped with determination, resourcefulness and humour. The story of the Serbian bean soup provides an example. A woman's support in Woolley received a consignment of Serbian bean soup from a French trade union, but this delicacy was not to the taste of the traditional pie and peas palate of Yorkshire miners. Indeed, even the very hungry miners were reluctant to eat it. Betty from Woolley remarked, 'I kept six tins back to throw at the police if they got too heavy but that still left twenty or more.' In an attempt to disguise the Serbian soup, the women added carrots and potatoes and passed it off as 'beef barbecue'. Such was the popularity of this dish that for weeks afterwards the miners were asking when there would be more of it. Stories of this type have emerged by the score, with each pit village having its own variation on the standard themes. The oral tradition of mining communities will ensure the survival and elaboration of these anecdotes for a long time to come.

The women not only set up soup kitchens and distributed food parcels, but arranged stores of shoes, clothing and household items for the needy. They became recognised for setting up, in effect, 'an alternative welfare system', as Hywel Francis writes:

> This new kind of alternative welfare system has created in many places a very resilient and tough resistance movement. Everyone should now acknowledge that the network of women and mixed support groups has given rise to an alternative, community-based system of food, clothing, financial *and* morale distribution which has sustained about half a million for nearly a year. (1985, p. 14)

Hidden hardships

Lack of money caused suffering for everybody, but real hardship was felt most by women, who made the most sacrifices. Hilary Rose reports the effects of the strike in the words of women from Upton in West Yorkshire:

> The little things they couldn't buy constantly niggled – a chafing reminder of poverty: 'Shampoo, soap, sanitary towels, tights – that's a luxury. Everything has to go for food.' (1984, p. 328)

Other women could appreciate the effects of these deprivations. Oxford University Women's Group, for example, launched an appeal through the colleges to raise funds for sanitary protection, an expensive but essential item for the women in mining communities. Great quantities of sanitary towels and tampons were soon collected for distribution (Sweeney, 1985, p. 80).

Rarely did miners' wives have any money to spare. What there was went on the children or the husband; women would do without. They frequently skipped a meal because there was not enough food to go round, but they did not look for recognition for their sacrifices. Indeed, they often concealed the fact that they were going without by claiming that they were not hungry or that they had already eaten. Money paid by the Union directly to miners for local picketing (£1 per day) rarely reached the women and children. This income the men regarded as their private income, to be spent as they wished – usually on cigarettes or on beer in the local pub. Rose observed, 'These differences in access to food and small treats, as between men and women, marked most households' (*ibid.*). This was echoed by the women of Sherburn, where one said to me (referring to her husband), 'I'd rather go without m'self so that he'd get a good meal inside him.'

Most women would not acknowledge even to themselves that they were depriving themselves for their families. Instead, they consoled themselves with the view that others in the village were worse off and they should be thankful. Pat, the treasurer of the Sherburn-in-Elmet Women's Support Group, told me, 'I'd never had a struggle or any problem until the strike, but I can't complain. There were lots in this village that knew real hardship.' I was told of a widow who lived with her son, a single miner receiving no state benefits. The small income the woman had was spent trying to keep the two of them fed and clothed. Life was hard, particularly during the bitter winter, one of the coldest on record this century. Her son's free coal allowance had been stopped because he was on strike. With no heating in the house, she could bear it no longer. Shivering with cold, she took an axe to her wardrobe and chopped it for firewood.

Women on the picket lines

As the strike progressed, women started to question their part in the dispute. No longer content with traditional women's roles, many became actively involved on the picket lines. In South Wales this happened within a few months after the strike started and by July they had organised themselves on an area basis with regular meetings where groups could plan and share experiences. One woman tells of her progression:

> I'm a nurse. I have to be gentle in work. I never thought I'd be like I am today on a picket line. I never thought I'd be on a picket line. We've fought for our pay rises, but it was a different kind of fight. There wasn't the same angriness. We are fighting for our community. We're fighting for survival. (WCCPL & NUM, 1985, p. 32)

Another from Neath and Dulais Valley talks of women's emerging understanding of how anger flares up in a tense situation:

> We hadn't been on the picket line before. Our men had come back with all these stories of police violence and provocation, and we thought maybe it was an exaggeration. But we found out that

> it wasn't. You see a convoy coming out and your're seething with rage. I did a V sign at one of the drivers and a policeman told me I could be taken away for that. So I turned my fingers round the other way. But the drivers made signs like that at us – and no-one threatens to arrest them. (*Ibid.*, p. 37)

She tells of their commitment:

> Now the women in our valley would go on any picket line anywhere they were needed. Not at the beginning of the strike – we wouldn't. Now it's all changed. (*Ibid.*)

Women developed their own tactics in dealing with the police, as one woman describes their experience at Port Talbot:

> The police were surprised because we were women. They didn't know where to put their hands, because when they touched us we gave them abuse. They didn't know how to react. They tried to joke with us and get information out of us – asking how far we'd travelled – but we stayed quiet. We did an inspection of them – they didn't have proper uniforms on and we told them, and they didn't know how to react. There were about 150 women. Some were nervous, as you can understand. But once the lorries came . . . the frustration inside you. (*Ibid.*, p. 31)

When Mary Coombes from Maerdy threw an egg at a coke lorry at Port Talbot, she was arrested and charged with breach of the peace. She tells her story:

> I said (to the police) I didn't see why I should be treated differently to a farmer's wife who a month previously had thrown an egg at Mrs Thatcher, and that day nobody was charged, but when a miner's wife throws an egg at a lorry you're charged with a breach of the peace and locked in a cell. (*Ibid.*, p. 38)

Observing that women's demonstrations in Wales were more 'peaceful' than in the past, Bloomfield suggests that the forces of the state have become much more organised and menacing than before. She cites the innovation of Maerdy women marching up and down police lines, 'inspecting' the constables, as an illustration of their use of wit and ridicule rather than muscle (1985, p. 16). Women also planned certain tactical operations, for example in responding to the sequestration of funds in South Wales:

> The women were furious at the loss of hard fought for, desperately needed, funds in South Wales. It was a woman from Maerdy and her husband who initiated the brilliant occupation of the Price Waterhouse offices in Birmingham, foxing the security guards, jamming the lifts, phoning out press releases and organising for fish and chips to be hoisted through the window. (Sweeney, 1985, p. 75)

Women move ahead

As the strike went on, women became active at three levels. First, at a practical domestic level, women worked to ensure that family life was kept as normal as possible. This enabled the men to get on with the business of the strike with few domestic troubles to concern them. In other words, women were *behind* their men providing support. At this level, women were not much interested in the politics of the strike, something they felt should be left to the men. Their concern was to maintain their material standards of living as best they could. They confined themselves to their traditional role and supported men in their traditional role; gender roles were reinforced.

The second level of involvement came when women placed themselves *alongside* men. Women and men worked together in the same activities, on the picket line or at rallies and demonstrations. These women believed they had an equal part to play in the strike and that they could best use their time and effort by carrying out the same action as men, if at times using different tactics. Some women did not move to this level. In South Wales, for example, a number of women's support groups did not go on the picket lines for various reasons.

> This often seems to be because the men put their foot down, saying it's too dangerous – and several of the women said they wouldn't want to after what they'd seen of Orgreave on television. Some were deterred by the worry that if they were

> arrested they wouldn't get the NUM's legal backing if their local lodge hadn't approved them picketing. Others were too worried about their children. (WCCPL & NUM, 1985, p. 37)

The third level brought women up front, *ahead* of men. At this level, women committed themselves to activities generally open only to men who were senior members of the Union. Obviously, this level of engagement prompted the most resentment from men. They were content to have the support of women and sometimes let women take an equal role, but they were seldom willing to allow women to take the lead. Women began to receive invitations to go abroad, making contact with members of the labour movement in Europe, North America and the Soviet Union. Their husbands generally received no such invitations. This reversal in the expected gender roles is difficult to explain. The novelty of women's keen involvement in an industrial dispute could account partly for these invitations, but a more likely explanation can be found by looking at the current trends within 'the Left'. The European Left prides itself in its recognition of the worth of women, although some women argue that it is just paying lip-service to an ideal of equality of the sexes which is not a reality within the Left itself. Women's involvement in the miners' strike gave the Left an opportunity to prove it meant what it was saying, by giving a voice to women. Here was a chance, and mining women found themselves in demand for speaking tours abroad.

At first, because of their domestic ties, women had difficulty taking on these activities, even those who had gained the necessary confidence. Childcare was seen as women's responsibility, as was housework. Men considered they had legitimate reasons for refusing to take on these duties on while their wives were off on more exciting missions. Although this lack of cooperation seriously limited the participation of women in the early stages, as the strike wore on, women's position changed. Traditionally, mining communities clearly differentiate gender roles. The ethos of masculinity requires a 'real' man to assert himself and keep the 'missus' firmly in her place in the home. Moreover, to help with domestic duties would almost certainly lead to accusations from other men of 'sissiness' and being 'hen-pecked' or, worse still, a 'woofter' (homosexual), the ultimate wound to masculinity. This tradition of defining manhood and womanhood in Victorian terms of separate spheres helps to explain men's reluctance to contribute to household chores. Such domestic activity would threaten their credibility as 'real' men. Without exception, the women in Sherburn told me that their husbands and sons would do as little housework as possible. Even women with full-time jobs were still expected to do all the housework. In effect, women acted as servants, waiting on men.

Many women suggested to me that men's reluctance to help with housework to release their wives for speaking engagements had arisen, at least in part, from jealousy. Men who helped with some domestic chores to make it possible for their wives to participate in the first and second levels of strike activity would do nothing to enable their wives to go abroad or to take on national speaking tours. These assignments were regarded as male reserves. One woman's comment on her husband echoes others: 'He didn't mind me getting involved in the strike, but he still expected to find his dinner on the table when he got in.'

The expansion of women's role to include picket duty and trips abroad forced many men to become more active in the home. Only in the woman's absence and of necessity would a man do any domestic chores. As women achieved a higher profile in the strike, men gained their first experience of housework. Previously, everything had been done for them, first by their mothers and then by their wives. One man commented that because of the strike, he now knows where the switch is on the vacuum cleaner. Evening meetings of women's support groups meant that men had to stay in and babysit. Early morning picket duty for women meant that men had to prepare breakfast and see the children off to school. Indeed, the more involved women became in the strike, the more involved men became in the home. Men realised that the strike needed the support of women if it were to survive. It was men's self-interest that allowed women to play a part. This is important to recognise: for the visibility of women could easily be interpreted as a desire by men to give women a more equal role. This was not so.

The level and type of activities women undertook closely coincided with the stage they had reached in the life cycle. Single and childless women found it easier to take on third level activities than married ones or those with young children. Most women in their twenties and thirties had babies and young children, whereas older women had older and less dependent offspring. This freed older women for a more active part in the strike; they were more able to take part in third level activities requiring them to go away from home. This does not mean that their husbands were more willing to let them go, simply that they had fewer ties to hold them back.

Younger women could travel away from home to 'strike business' as well, by taking advantage of offers made by older sisters, mothers and grandmothers to help with childcare, but feelings of guilt prevented many from accepting such generosity from older female relatives. They felt it was their own responsibility to look after their children, even if this meant more limited strike participation. They did accept offers of help (usually babysitting) from their mothers and mothers-in-law, but this was common before the strike, rather than a product of it. As a direct result of strike hardship, however, mothers and mothers-in-law extended many more invitations for meals to their married offspring, thus strengthening relationships between women of the two generations. Since family meals could be considered a social occasion rather than a charity handout, they were more readily accepted by members of the mining community who prided themselves on their self-sufficiency. This feature of mining culture explains why members of the community organised themselves to protect their own lifestyle; they did not sit back and wait for the Union to do it for them.

Defending a way of life

What is so important about the way of life in mining communities that women so passionately defended? Partly they were protecting their material security, but their reasons went beyond this. They were fighting to save communities, not just jobs. Coal communities are of a special type: close-knit, heavily male-dominated and traditional. Why should women wish to retain such communities? The view that sees the mining culture as oppressive to women comes from outsiders, especially middle-class feminists. Women within these communities do not perceive themselves as oppressed. They take comfort in the closeness of the community, for they know that such unity derives from coal-mining life. The dangerous nature of mining acts to bring people closer together. Fatal accidents in the pit are felt by everyone, not only the families of the deceased, and strengthen family and neighbourly ties. Again, intermarriage within and among mining communities has meant the development of numerous kinship ties. Losing the pits would lead to the fading and disappearance of these relationships, as witnessed in places where pits have been closed and villages partially deserted.

In defending their communities, women gained new capacities. Fran Appleyard, a woman of eighteen from Sharlston, a pit village near Wakefield, talked to me about what she had done during the strike. For about twelve months she had been involved in CND (Campaign for Nuclear Disarmament) and, four months after the strike began, she had taken part in a twenty-mile Youth CND march. The meeting afterwards was to have been opened by a miner's wife, but she failed to appear. Fran was asked if she would address the meeting because her father is a miner, as was her grandfather, and she and her mother had been active in a women's support group. She told me:

> I didn't want to do it because I'd never done anything like it before and I was dead nervous. In fact, I was in agony but I knew that I had to do it. I just sat there and said things what I was thinking and it went down really well. I got a standing ovation.

Fran felt she gained confidence from this first public meeting and she wanted to become more involved in the strike. Following her speech at the Youth CND rally, she was invited to tour Belgium on an official NUM fund-raising trip with two others. The day before she was due to leave for Belgium, she discovered not only that she was the only female, but that the other two were considerably older than she was. By this stage, however, she decided she could not change her mind because she had agreed to go, and go she must. When she met the two men, one from South Wales and the other from Fife in Scotland, she found that she could not understand their accents and they could not understand her broad Yorkshire accent either. Fran related, 'The funniest bit was when we met the interpreter. He couldn't understand any of us. To make matters worse, he spoke a Flemish dialect, so he couldn't even understand most of the Belgians.' Despite this handicap, the tour was a great success and raised over £4000 for the NUM. Fran had moving stories of kindness and solidarity to tell of her trip to Belgium:

> We stopped off at this shop to buy some chocolate. The woman behind the counter asked us (in broken English) if we were English. We explained what we were doing in Belgium. She told us that there was a lot of support in Belgium for the English miners. Then she opened the till, took all the money out and gave it to us. I was so moved by her kindness, I just cried.

This was Fran's first trip abroad. With the exception of occasional visits to London for CND rallies, she had rarely been much further than Wakefield. This strong international support Fran experienced in Belgium encouraged her to become even more active. She began travelling the length of the country addressing meetings and rallies, rarely showing the slightest signs of nervousness. Then her own village invited her to talk at the Sharlston Miners' Welfare. She was very nervous, as she describes:

> It's different talking with people you know. I kept imagining them miners were all thinking, 'What the hell does she know? She can't know owt, a lass of 'er age'. Anyway, it seemed to go down okay 'cause everyone clapped and cheered.

Indeed, it had gone down so well that Fran was now seen as a leading figure. The classic scare tactic, a brick through the window, was delivered to her house during the night. She was alone in the house, both her parents having travelled to the Soviet Union on a trip organised by one of the Soviet miners' unions. She tells of her reaction:

> I don't know who did it or why. I must admit, I were a bit shaken up by it, but I wasn't put off. If anything, I were even more determined than before to see the strike through.

The strike marked the awakening of Fran's political awareness. Although she had been involved in CND, she had never connected the issue of feminism, racism and the nuclear threat; they were a series of unrelated phenomena that she pieced together only as a result of her involvement in the miners' strike. This pattern was repeated with many of the women I came to know, although most (unlike Fran) started with no political involvement. Increasing participation in the strike was followed by membership of the Labour Party. Every woman I spoke to had joined this party by the end of the strike. The vague and naive political notions they expressed at the start of the strike had developed into advanced and sophisticated ideas they were able to articulate with confidence and commitment.

This transformation in women as a result of strike involvement was so great that I would be sceptical had I not witnessed it for myself. The women themselves could hardly believe they had changed so much. After the strike came to an end, one woman in Sherburn-in-Elmet wrote of her experience:

> I'd been involved almost from day one, my days of 'just a housewife' were over, and I'd actually enjoyed the awfulness of it all, because, through my involvement, I became a totally different woman. I became my own self, an entirely different person. A person in my own right, belonging not only to my husband and family, but to myself, discovering I'd a brain of my own, an independent soul, and a right to drop everything and go anywhere, because, for once, I was needed and depended on by others.

These women were all doing things that they could never have envisaged themselves doing before the strike. Sue, for example, had gone to the Soviet Union with her two young children at the request of a trade union in the USSR. Before then, she had never gone as far as London. During the summer of 1984, Sherburn-in-Elmet staged a miners' gala. Anne, one of the women from the support group, wrote a version of 'Cinderella' in rhyme. She had no idea that she could write while Pat, who took the leading role, had had no previous experience in acting. Earlier Pat could only find fault with herself; now her confidence grew and she began to value herself. When I last saw Pat in May 1985, she told me she was writing a book:

> I don't suppose it'll get published. I may not get round to finishing it, but I feel that it has to be told. Women held the strike together and we've all got our stories to tell. I don't want anyone to forget that.

The strike built this sort of strength and confidence among women while it lasted, but now it is over, what is the future for these women? Have the hopes and dreams forged during the strike materialised or are they forgotten? Have they become part of a strong and growing working-class women's movement or have they gone back to the kitchen sink? Returning to Sherburn-in-Elmet in May 1985, I found that the women's organisation was still very much in existence. The women's support group continues to meet, although with less frequency, fortnightly rather than weekly. During the strike months, women had been concerned with issues directly related to the struggle. With the strike over, women had the chance to stand back and assess their activity. Most of the miners are now back in paid employment and the collection of food and money no longer needs to be continued on a large scale. But sacked miners require practical help and they are looking to the women's support groups for this. Again, debts mounted during the strike, many running into thousands of pounds, and these have still to be paid. In Sherburn-in-Elmet, there are no families without debts to settle. All this means that women's support groups still are needed to help the families most ravaged by the strike. Although fewer people depend on support groups, their task has become much harder. With the strike officially over, many supporters have withdrawn their help, unaware that it is still required. Despite these difficulties, support groups carry on.

Although easing hardship is still a priority, the focus of interest has changed within women's support groups towards issues directly affecting women. In Sherburn-in-Elmet, for example, the women are raising money for sacked miners *and* campaigning against the closure of a hospital. Sheila explained:

> There's a hospital in Fulford, near York, that they're going to be closing and this is one of those things that when they start, we've got to get our teeth into, because there's no hospital around here.

The women told me they could see a parallel between cuts in the government health service and forced cuts in coal production. Furthermore, they feel that hospital closures affect women more since they usually have to take their children to hospital. 'We'll have to struggle that much further on the bus with kids while the men are at work with the car,' said one. The women of Sherburn-in-Elmet have begun to discover that no one issue can be looked at in isolation; their interest in fighting health cuts has drawn them into the battle to save public transport in their area from privatisation. The process of politicisation they have undergone during the dispute has provided them with an awareness enabling them to see the interconnections between seemingly separate issues. Making links is part of a process towards understanding how the world around us works. Mining women are beginning to see how they fit into that order.

A feminist struggle?

The fairer, though far from egalitarian, division of domestic labour between men and women in coal communities has been seen as evidence of a developing feminist awareness. Indeed, many British feminists were excited by events during the miners' strike, believing it might herald the start of a working-class feminist movement. I would argue that women's participation in the miners' strike had little to do with feminist awareness, except in a few isolated cases. True, women are beginning to question their position in a traditionally male-dominated community, and men are becoming more involved in domestic life. Usually, however, this amounts to women incorporating features of masculine culture ('mates', the pub) into a predominantly feminine lifestyle. Men may help more in the home, but they retain their masculine ethos wholesale. Consequently, accommodation occurs rather than a radical overhaul; the basic structures and relationships that maintain inequality are left unchallenged and unchanged.

Rather than deriving from feminist issues, the women's support groups arose spontaneously in response to the needs of the community for food, an issue coming as a direct extension of their domestic concerns. Contrary to what some middle-class feminists wish to believe, women's participation in the strike was not part of some wider feminist struggle. Furthermore, the working-class women involved in the strike had more in common with their working-class 'oppressors' than with their middle-class 'sisters'. Of the strike, Sheila remarked, 'It were a working-class struggle, that's what it were. I don't think it had owt to do with feminism or equal rights – it was just a class thing.'

Did the women's peace camp at Greenham Common in Berkshire influence pit women? Sheila told me, 'I think our women feel strongly and passionately for these women and what they're doing. I've the utmost admiration for them. I just wish I could go down there and be with them.' Yet the women of the mining communities felt their rise to prominence during the strike would have occurred in any case, without the existence of a women's peace camp at the USAF base at Greenham Common. Miners' wives did make connections between their battle and what the Greenham women are struggling for. Greenham women are opposed to nuclear power and nuclear weapons; pit women were aware that the phasing out of coal was likely to result in the introduction of more nuclear power. At miners' rallies everywhere, pit women and Greenham women spoke on the same platform, making the links between running down coal and stepping up nuclear fuel. Greenham women talked of the police violence they experienced while blockading the air base. Miners' wives spoke of police violence on the picket line. Greenham women expressed their fears for a nuclear future, of the destruction of the world as we know it, and saw no hope for today's young people. Miners' wives talked of nuclear power, with the destruction of pit communities and eternal unemployment for their children.

The miners' strike may not have transformed miners' wives into feminists, but it has certainly challenged some middle-class feminists. Debbie Withal says, 'For many feminists, the miners' strike has meant reassessing our attitudes to working with men, and has shown the real links between feminism and the struggles of working class women' (Kendall and Norden, 1985). The miners' strike has helped some feminists to see how gender division serves to prevent individuals from achieving class unity.

At the same time, the miners' wives have gained a much higher evaluation of themselves from the strengthening of female associations through their work in the soup kitchens, actions on the picket lines and their sharing of experience with women from other communities. Anne-Marie Sweeney tells about the Maerdy women being warned before they came to Oxford that it was full of feminists and not to pick up any of those 'strange ideas', but it was not a case of 'liberated' women enlightening the 'oppressed' so much as making friendships and talking about things of immediate mutual interest. She writes:

> Involvement in struggle has changed us all. We talked about many things – women's health, the knowledge and control of our

> own bodies, the waiting lists for operations like hysterectomies. A number of the women are in other jobs in the Rhondda – part time shop workers or in the caring, servicing jobs such as home-helps or hospital work. We talked about attacks on these jobs and services . . . and we discussed our personal lives – the pressures of being a single parent, of jealousy, the need for independence in our lives, of experiencing male violence in the home. (1985, pp. 70–71)

When the visitors left after three days, they felt they had known them as friends of a lifetime. These were the experiences that heightened women's awareness of common concerns.

Many of the women in Wales believe that their part in the strike is helping to change attitudes in the Union. One woman from Treherbert puts it this way:

> We're overcoming the problem slowly, but it is slow because the NUM is a male dominated industry. But attitudes are changing. The younger miners are better than the older ones. But there are a lot of older miners in the group and we do get a bit of hassle, but in the end they give in. (WCCPL & NUM, 1985, p. 33)

These women have taken an active part in a long political struggle, some of them moving into the public arena in a way they had never done before. Many have become more aware of the political links between their community and the nation, between the issues of coal mining and nuclear power, between the cuts in government spending and the loss of local services. They have also experienced new powers as women organising and acting collectively. But they have not become feminists in the sense of envisaging any radical change in gender roles. Rather, they are continuing their women's support groups to fight for a wide range of community causes and class interests. During the strike, a woman in Wales said:

> When the strike is over the women's support group will stay together. We're preparing things now. There's a conference being arranged which will be held every year for groups throughout the country, and we're going to have monthly meetings. We will keep in contact, and stay together as women's action support

group, and whatever we can fight, we'll fight; whoever's difficulty, we'll help them. There's no way we'll ever go behind the kitchen sink again. No way. (*Ibid.*, p. 32)

Note

1. Detailed accounts of the strike are provided, among others, by Freeman (1985), and Reed and Adamson (1985). The authors in Beynon, ed. (1985) analyse the main issues.

References

Beynon, Huw (ed.) (1985) *Digging Deeper: Issues in the Miners' Strike* (London: Verso).

Bloomfield, Barbara (1985) 'Maerdy Women's Support Group', unpublished thesis, Ruskin College, Oxford.

Campbell, Beatrix (1984) 'The Other Miners' Strike' *New Statesman* 27 July, pp. 8–10.

Evans, D. (1984) 'King Coal's Other Face' *The Guardian*, 4 April, p. 10.

Francis, Hywel (1985) 'Mining, the Popular Front', *Marxism Today*, vol. 29, no. 2, pp. 12–15.

Freeman, M. (1985) *Our Day Will Come: The Miners' Fight for Jobs* (London: Junius Publications).

Harwood, Carole (1985) 'A Woman's Place . . .' in WCCPL & NUM, pp. 25–30.

Heath, Tony (1985) 'The Miner's Wife Who Found Her Voice and Spread the Word' *The Guardian*, 5 June, p. 14.

Kendall, T. and Norden, B. (1985) 'What Did You Do during the Strike, Mum?' *Spare Rib* no. 151.

North Yorkshire Women Against Pit Closures (1985) *Strike 84–85* (Leeds: North Yorkshire Women Against Pit Closures).

Reed, David and Adamson, Olivia (1985) *Miners' Strike 1984–1985: People versus State* (London: Larkin Publications).

Rose, Hilary (1984) 'The Miners' Wives of Upton' *New Society*, vol. 70, no. 1145, pp. 326–29.

Sweeney, Anne-Marie (1985) 'The Oxford Women's Support Group' in Oxford Miners Support Group, *The Miners' Strike in Oxford* (Oxford: Oxford and District Trade Unions Council), pp. 67–91.

Vallely, Paul (1985) 'The Strike that Turned Wives into Warriors' *The Times* 4 March, p. 10.

WCCPL NUM (Welsh Campaign for Civil and Political Liberties and National Union of Mineworkers, South Wales Area) (1985) *Striking Back* (Cardiff: Cymric Federation Press).

6 Between Two Fires: Palestinian Women in Lebanon

ROSEMARY SAYIGH and JULIE PETEET[1]

Intractible, insoluble, punctuated by spasms of genocidal violence, the conflict over Palestine has brought dispersion, statelessness and chronic insecurity upon the indigenous Arab population. Such conditions inevitably have implications for women, as members of a threatened group, and as tied in specific ways to its physical and cultural reproduction. Even if not shared equally by all classes, or all parts of the diaspora, insecurity is a primary fact of existence for Palestinians, especially the 87 per cent of them, on average the poorest, who live under Israeli, Jordanian, Syrian and Lebanese rule. Being Palestinian weakens their right to be educated, work, build a home, travel, and makes them vulnerable to arbitrary arrest and deportation. Dispersion of the population is replicated at the level of the household, through high rates of forced migration. Few Palestinian mothers have all the members of their household under one roof; many cannot visit their kin; many have had their homes destroyed, not once but many times. Insecurity of existence, of the home itself, has meant that women's work of reproducing the family has become harder, at the same time as becoming charged with political meaning. Violence has invaded the Palestinian home, erasing the distinction between front line and home front, politicising women's most ordinary tasks.

As a result of the difficult conditions in which the Palestinian national struggle has developed, women's issues have been even more subordinated to national ones than in other Third World struggles, despite the early and active sharing in it by women. The dilemma is well put by a leading militant, Mai Sayegh:

> Compared with what is happening, compared with Sabra and Chatila, the dispersion of our revolutionaries, the dispersion of

> our people, and the questions they face: 'How to survive? Where to go? How to find food for our children?' – compared with all this, women's problems seem of little weight. (1983, p. 152, authors' translation)

Each of the host countries, Jordan, Syria and Lebanon, offered those who fled from Palestine during the 1948 war a slightly different legal, political and social framework. Lebanon accorded them an ambivalent status, neither nationals nor foreigners, and restricted their work rights. Assimilation was made easy for Christian Palestinians and for those with professional skills or capital. Private educational and training opportunities abounded. Indeed, from the beginning, Lebanon has been an environment of special opportunity and special danger. Insecurity has been chronic, reaching peaks in the seige of Tell al-Za'ter by the Lebanese Forces in 1976, and in 1982 with the Israeli invasion and subsequent massacre. At the same time Lebanon is the only Arab country where the resistance movement was enabled through popular backing to establish a stronghold. Though under constant attack from Israelis and their Lebanese allies, the resistance movement controlled the camps for 13 years, and was free to recruit, campaign and establish a gamut of social services. Women were involved in this transformation as cadres, workers, mothers, supporters, clients. Few were not 'with' the resistance; none were unaffected by it. Women found themselves stretched between domestic and national responsibilities and 'between two fires' quite literally as targets of both Israeli and Lebanese attack.

Some landmarks in Lebanese/Palestinian relations are: the arrival in 1948 of more than 100 000 refugees, predominantly Muslim and of rural origin; the successful uprising of the camps against the Lebanese Army in 1969, supported by a broad spectrum of Lebanese oppositional groupings; the Cairo Accords, also in 1969, which gave official sanction to the *feda'iyyeen* bases in South Lebanon; the Civil War of 1975/6, during which Palestinians and Lebanese Muslims were thrown out of East Beirut; the formation in 1976 of the Lebanese Forces, headed by Bashir Gemayel; and the Israeli invasion of 1982, the siege of Beirut and the withdrawal of the Resistance Movement.[2] The war of 1982 began a new epoch for the Palestinians who remained in Lebanon.

Situated just south of Beirut's municipal boundary, Chatila camp is a relatively small one, with an estimated 5500 inhabitants in 1983, but the area of which it is part holds perhaps 25 000 people. In the north, Chatila melts into Sabra, a mainly Lebanese Sunni quarter famous for its fruit and vegetable market, while in the east it borders on thc mainly Shi'ite suburb of Shiah. The high population density here is the result of a heavy influx of rural migrants and refugees from the war zones, who have squatted 'illegally' on waste land around the camp. Whereas the camp population is almost entirely Palestinian, the outer quarters are much more heterogenous, containing Lebanese (most of whom are Shi'ite), Palestinians, Syrians, Egyptians, and people whose status is 'under study'. What distinguished Chatila from other camps, and made it a special target for attack in 1982, was its closeness to the headquarters of the resistance movement in Sabra and Fakhany.

No visible difference marks out the camp from the low-income Lebanese housing around it. Its outer face is a tight cluster of cheap one- and two-storey breeze-block houses, damp in winter, hot in summer, their tin roofs hung with washing. The main streets are unpaved and pot-holed, dusty or water-logged depending on the season, foul-smelling from leaking sewage, but lined with a colourful confusion of small shops and street vendors. Behind lies a maze of narrow, winding alleys, the playground of small children. Glimpsed through open doors, homes are impeccably clean, swabbed down with water that often has to be fetched from distant street taps. Many homes have small courtyards lined with plants, where women do much of their work; and as in Palestinian villages, outer doors are usually left open during the day, and women inside call out to passers-by to stop in for a chat and a coffee. With so many comings and goings, homes are not at all cut off from the world outside. Women's domain teams with both political and personal news, pungent comments on people's behaviour, rumours. Increasingly since 1982, there are anxious questions about the future.

Exile and resistance in Lebanon: 1948 to 1982

The uprooting

The first years after the uprooting (*iotila'*) were ones of physical hardship, material deprivation, and psychological trauma over the loss of kin, homes and country. Conditions at the beginning were very bad, as one survivor describes: 'Seven families to a tent, some families lived in caves. There was overcrowding and sickness. Many old people and children died.' Another recalls: 'We often went to bed hungry, and suffered badly from the cold since we were too poor to buy winter clothing or shoes.' The loss of Palestine was likened to 'mourning over a dead loved one'. Belief in an imminent return, based on UN resolutions, continued for a long time after 1948, eventually to be replaced by belief in the necessity for Palestinians themselves to take action.

In 1950, UNRWA began registering the refugees and setting up camps. Whereas urban Palestinians with professional qualifications readily found work, and were able to rent accommodation in Beirut and the other coastal cities, the impoverished mass of rural Palestinians had no choice but to settle in the camps, where UNRWA distributed rations, and provided basic sanitary and medical services as well as free schooling from six to 16 years. Conditions in the camps changed little over the years. Tents were replaced by shacks made of petrol cans, and these by more solid housing; but camp sites and UNRWA services did not expand with population increase, and the state of streets, sewage, water and electricity supplies remains one of perpetual inadequacy.

On its side, the host government set up a Directorate of Refugee Affairs to deal with a group whose presence in Lebanon was accepted only temporarily, pending repatriation. With time, however, real control of Palestinians passed into the hands of the Army's Intelligence Bureau. Palestinians were seen as a problem for a number of reasons: as Muslim in majority, they posed a threat to the hegemony of Maronite Christians over the state and over the other sects making up the Lebanese body politic; as Arab nationalists, they jeopardised Lebanon's ties with the West; and from the beginning of *feda'iyyeen* operations from South Lebanon in the mid-1960s, there was fear of Israeli retaliation. Hence the authorities imposed strict surveillance over the camps to prevent any political organisation. At the same time, to discourage permanent settlement, they imposed vexatious restrictions on work, change of residence, travel, and the repair or extension of houses. Such measures were not applied with equal severity throughout the period, nor in every camp; but by the late 1960s they amounted to an oppression that stoked the fires of the uprising of 1969.

To protect its own labour force, the government enacted laws preventing non-nationals from employment in government, banks, foreign companies, and transport. Barred from obtaining Lebanese nationality, camp Palestinians were thus constrained to work in less skilled, less well paid jobs, for example in agriculture and construction. Income levels only began to rise as jobs were opened up in oil-producing countries, but as late as 1980, after three decades of free schooling, more than half the Palestinian labour force was estimated to be in 'blue-collar' jobs. Remittances from working migrants in other countries made it possible for families in Lebanon to improve their homes, spend more on food and clothing, and invest in further education for their children. These changes reduced the gap between camp populations and their Lebanese neighbours, encouraging exchange of various kinds – including intermarriage.

The uprooting began a series of changes in women's work and situation that included, though this was slow to appear, a weakening of the power of the family. The most obvious change was in the conditions of their domestic labour, which underwent sharp deterioration. Rural women's former agricultural work in communal kin- and village-based groupings was replaced by domestic work in individual households, yet, at the same time, a great number of women were forced by husbands' unemployment or sickness to seek work outside the home. The only work that illiterate women could find at that time was in seasonal agriculture, construction, or domestic service; this last had never been undertaken by rural women in Palestine and was considered dishonouring. Factory work only became available later, in the Beirut area. Palestinian women were paid less in all types of work than Palestinian men, who were paid less than Lebanese.

It was only as free schooling gave rise to a generation of literate young women that a few began to work in respected 'white-collar' jobs; until late into the 1970s, however, most camp families remained hostile to the employment of women outside the home and preferred their daughters to marry as soon as possible after leaving school. Once married, women were seen as being obliged to give priority to child-rearing and running the household. Certain aspects of traditional modes of marriage arrangement changed, for instance forced marriage (*ijbari*) was gradually abandoned, and the female marriage age rose; but families continued to play a predominant role in the negotiations leading up to marriage, and until long after the uprooting property and status in Palestine continued to be taken into account when making matches. Thus while the economic basis of family control was eroded by loss of land, its ideological expression was less affected and continued to be exercised over women long after young men, as independent wage earners, had begun to challenge it.

From the beginning, settlement in camps had mixed and contradictory implications for women: ending their village insularity, but arousing conservative reactions from men because of the forced proximity of 'strangers'; eroding the power of the *hamuleh* (clan) through loss of land and dispersion, yet reconstituting in the camps a larger, more diffuse, more censorious locus of control; schooling women and offering them employment, but also forcing them to represent a cultural patrimony in danger of attrition. Palestinians in exile found themselves faced with a dilemma that threads through their history from 1948 to the present, and in which women are peculiarly involved. On the one hand, they refused cultural changes imposed on them through expulsion from Palestine, clinging to an idealised vision of the past, and striving to preserve all forms of authenticity. On the other, as they became increasingly active in the struggle for the return to their homeland, they realised that this demanded radical social change.

Homes violated

Fatmeh recounts:

> One day my father didn't come home from work. We were waiting at home with our mother, when the Lebanese police came and kicked the door in. They tore up the mattresses and pulled down all the food, spilling the rice, lentils and chickpeas. They said they were looking for weapons. They saw a large bin of flour and asked my mother what was in it. She said, 'It's only flour.' As one of the policemen bent over to look in the bin, his hat fell into the flour. He became so enraged that he slapped my mother across the face. Then they attacked my brother, kicking, punching and slapping him. My father was in prison for a month. After that, he was often taken away for a day or two of interrogation.

Such harassment was a regular feature of life in the camps before 1969. Homes of suspected activists were targets of repression by the Army Intelligence Bureau. With activist men under arrest or in hiding, women were left at home to confront the authorities and to carry all the responsibilities arising from their husbands' absence.

Experiences like these prevented Palestinian women in camps from ever feeling 'at home' in Lebanon. They also drew women into political activity, for instance standing outside meeting places to warn of the approach of Army agents, or organising small, but vocal, demonstrations outside jails, demanding the release of detainees. Girls like Fatmeh became aware of the repression suffered by their people as a consequence of being Palestinian. The following account given by Haifa, another young woman, shows the kind of experiences that brought ordinary women into the political arena:

> We used to live in Nabatiyeh camp in South Lebanon until it became unbearable because of constant Israeli attacks [the camp was destroyed in an air raid in May 1974]. Then we moved to Tell al-Za'ter camp in Beirut to be more secure and to find jobs. But in Tell al-Za'ter the police would come and take our possessions, and put them on trucks and order us to return to the South. People would plead with them: 'In the South there is no work. We need to work to feed and clothe our children.' They beat up several people, but we managed to stay.
>
> My mother worked as a servant in rich Lebanese homes. She also gathered herbs to sell in the market. When I was 16, I started to work in the factories near the camp. We didn't earn as much as Lebanese workers and there was a difference in wages between men and women for the same work.
>
> In the camps, we weren't allowed to make any repairs to our huts. Once my mother attempted to repair our leaking roof. The police came and fined her.
>
> During the 1976 siege of the camp by the Fascists, women had to run under heavy fire to get water for their children. Once from the underground shelter I watched as a woman carrying a water container on her head was hit by a sniper's bullet. She slowly sat down, holding the water container with one hand, the other hand on her chest. There was no choice: either children died of thirst or

their mothers died trying to bring them water. My father was also killed by a sniper's bullet.

During the battle for the camp I worked in the clinic and the bakery along with many other young women. Before that, most girls weren't allowed by their families to work in the Resistance clinics, or to go out with boys, or go out in general. But after the battle of Tell al-Za'ter, no mother would prevent her daughter from going out. On the contrary, she would tell her to go out and work to help her people.

Supporting the resistance

For women, although membership in a Resistance group was rare before 1977, most felt proud of, and committed to, a national movement that gave them hope of eventual return to Palestine. Their support was important to the resistance movement because of its broad strategy of rousing the whole Palestinian people to understand its situation and mobilising them to struggle to change it. Rather than waiting passively for the Arab governments to produce a solution women must be willing to give their sons as fighters, and to join the resistance movement as workers, supporters, and members.

All the groups competed to increase their membership and support in the camps through programmes for women. Before local cadres were recruited and trained, this work was undertaken by women cadres of long standing, mainly middle class, educated women from outside the camps. Initially their work in the camps was difficult and tedious; as outsiders they had to build a visiting network and acquire community trust without a kin or neighbourhood foundation. The fact of their being members in a mixed organisation at first created a cultural barrier between them and women in the camps. But even if camp women hesitated to take the final step of joining organisations, they were prepared to be active in other ways and the cadres found many ways to approach them. Everyday social activities like visiting, women's gatherings, work, and anniversaries became channels of politicisation. Whereas middle class women were most often recruited at university, camp women were usually first involved through kin and neighbourhood networks.

Visiting networks, crucial for initiating contact with camp

women, were established by the cadres in a number of ways. For the outsider this process required precision and delicacy. Samira, a full-time Fateh member recruited as a secondary school student, worked in a Beirut camp for ten years, and by 1982 she was well established and respected in the camp. At the beginning, she faced difficulties since, as a single girl, her behaviour was subject to suspicion and scrutiny. Immodest clothing or casual friendliness with men would have aroused doubts about her. Samira describes her method:

> As a girl, it's easy for me to enter homes in the camp. Building a relationship with families makes it easier to mobilise their girls. I focus on women who have a brother, father or husband in the Resistance. I tell their fathers or brothers to encourage these girls to come to demonstrations and celebrations. Another way of approaching such a girl is by weekly visiting. For example, if I find a girl who would make a good cadre, I visit often, though I don't discuss politics until we are better friends. I go for informal visits and discuss everyday things.

The cadres' decision to focus recruiting campaigns on unmarried rather than married women made sense given their greater freedom for scheduled activity, their generally higher levels of education, and their malleability. Yet it had consequences that became apparent later, in particular a high rate of loss of local cadres as they got married. Housewives who were not linked to the Resistance through their menfolk, or who did not spontaneously join demonstrations, also tended to be neglected by the cadres.

Not all visits were successful. Sometimes a cadre would inquire about the problems of a woman she was visiting, as a way of building ties by helping with concrete needs, only to be met with embarrassed silence. Many housewives were welcoming but did not want to become involved; either they feared 'complications' with their husbands or their housework left them no time for activities outside the home. Widows generally welcomed the cadres' visits as a chance to share their troubles, and find out about possible aid. Younger women, often eager to find a way into salaried work or political action, needed the cadres' support in arguments with their families.

Unless she was supported by an activist brother, a camp girl might be prevented by her family from certain kinds of political activity, for example attending meetings after dark. Outright defiance or disobedience was unlikely because of the severity of sanctions. Even middle class girls had difficulties with their families, and in the early period of the resistance movement a small number of them, determined to devote themselves to full-time political work, broke completely with their families. Leila tells of her experiences:

> Initially my parents agreed to my political work because I was writing articles and giving speeches, but when I started going to mixed meetings they began to react negatively. The more I was involved, the more they worried. I tried not to have an outright confrontation with them: no love affairs, no outings to the cinema or parties, nothing they would disapprove of. I wanted them to know that I was only doing political work when I was away from home and that I wouldn't do anything to harm the family honour. It was when I left to live in the camps that they told me never to come home. They threatened to burn my books, throw out my bed and my favourite jasmine plant. Later they sent me very emotional letters asking me to come home. I wrote back that I was working for our people. Later when I moved back to Beirut, we were reconciled and I started visiting them again.

It would be inconceivable for such a break between a girl and her family to occur in the camps. There, crowded housing and neighbours' intrusions makes any absence immediately noticeable. The closely knit clan and camp neighbourhood has a more effective authority than middle class families, which are residentially scattered and more permissive with daughters. Middle class girls are also more able to support themselves should the need arise.

If all other arguments failed, a girl whose family continued to prevent her from undertaking national work might accuse them of 'treachery'. But such escalation was generally avoided, and the cadres advised against it, believing that traditional sectors of the population should not be alienated, but rather 'talked into' accepting the need for women to take part in the national struggle. The counselled patient persuasion, never directly challenging the principle of family authority, nor encouraging young women to rebel. In fact, girls' struggles with their families were seen as a vital stage in their development ('If she cannot face her family she will not be of much use to the movement'). Not only this, girls were seen as a medium for politicising the family.

Dropping out of the revolution

However strong their emotional support for the resistance movement, however ready to welcome the cadres into their homes, the majority of camp women still perceived their primary social roles to be those of wives and mothers. As a cadre working in the camps, Leila remarked on the low number of women formally members of the organisations:

> The problem is not housework or even the overall division of labour, but the socialisation of women to be wives and mothers, the feeling that childbearing fulfils their social duties.

Political activism corresponds closely to specific stages in women's reproductive cycle. It is in the so-called 'dangerous years', from puberty to marriage, that women are most likely to have strong political feelings, to want to be politically active or to join the workforce. Longer schooling and later marriage expanded the 'dangerous years', while the resistance movement made it legitimate for women in this stage to work in offices, hospitals, or political parties. Neither the resistance movement as a whole, however, nor the women's sector within it, ever challenged marriage and childbearing as woman's primary goal. Once married, many women dropped out of active membership, or diluted their activism.[3] Seasoned cadres bitterly remarked of such a woman, 'She has graduated'.

Women's involvement is cyclical in another way, tending to peak at times of crisis and subside between them. During the Lebanese Civil War of 1975–76, women staffed clinics, baked bread, prepared food and carried it to the fighters, brought water under gunfire, and even fought to defend the camps. Some would join Resistance groups during such crises, only to leave once the military threat subsided. The cyclical character of women's activism was more of a prblem for the women cadres than for the movement as a whole, by making it difficult to build up a corps of skilled and experienced organisers. For most resistance leaders, it fitted a strategy of mobilising women within traditional structures and relations.

'Land before honour'

'My mother is illiterate and worked as a servant in Lebanese homes. I finished intermediate school and work in an office. My younger sister is a medical student.' These words of a 27-year-old woman reflect the very different opportunities arising for women depending on their generation.

When the resistance movement moved to Beirut in 1970, it set up medical services, social assistance and educational programmes.[4] Productive enterprises were also created to give work to the widows of 'martyrs';[5] the Movement's numerous departments and offices generated jobs mainly filled by women. Women's earning power was increased by setting up training centres, and through generous subsidies enabling them to obtain advanced professional qualifications or go to university.

Salaried work outside the home was often considered by women cadres as a necessary first step towards further involvement. Huda states:

> I try to mobilise women to work first. Mobilisation is not just political: it is to get women to participate in society; it is to get rid of social obstacles through being involved in production. In this way women build up their self-confidence. Then I try to tie in work with politics.

Women's entry into the world of work was legitimised under the Resistance by its relation to the national struggle and by the informality of work settings. Resistance workshops were situated in or near camps; women's work in them was to a large extent an extension of their traditional domestic labour, for instance embroidery, machine sewing, teaching, cooking, cleaning, social work. The absence of time clocks and stringent production schedules allowed women to respond to family crisis, such as a sick child. Motherhood was honoured as a national duty and a natural event; maternity leave with full pay lasted from 40 days to two months. Women could also work at home on a piece rate basis.

Some men continued to oppose women's employment outside

the home, but such opposition was weakened by the need for additional income and by the feeling that such ideas were old-fashioned and an obstacle to national struggle. Intent on mobilising women, the Resistance campaigned against traditional notions of honour and fostered new symbols of a culture of resistance. The slogan *'al-ard qabl al-'ird* (land before honour)[6] became part of everyday speech and had a strong effect by putting two sacred values in opposition, thus forcing people to choose between them. Other factors that weakened opposition to women assuming roles in public life were the loss of young men and the ever-deepening crisis.

In the Resistance workshops and offices, women also picked up the language of political analysis, which enabled them to argue with their families and defend their positions with confidence and vigour. Women's new educational levels often outstripped those of their fathers; this, together with their new political consciousness, raised women's self-esteem more than the money they earned through employment. Women working with the resistance often saw themselves as politicisers of their families. Arriving home from work, they initiated lively discussions, bringing news and analyses of the latest military and political events, as well as information about new services and projects in the camps, thus linking the family with the larger world outside the home and neighbourhood.

Um Khalid,[7] an active housewife

Mother of eight children, born in a village in Galilee, but brought up in a camp in South Lebanon, 33-year-old Um Khalid has lived in Chatila since the early 1970s, though neither she nor her husband, a full-time civilian member of the resistance, has any relatives there. Unlike many camp women of her age, Um Khalid finished intermediate school. She was a good student, and an older school-teacher brother encouraged her to study, but in 1966 there was no question of girls in camps continuing their education.

When newly married, she went to live with her husband's family in a camp in north Lebanon. Although they are also her aunt and uncle, her parents-in-law treated her badly: 'I couldn't go out or visit freely, and if I did go out my mother-in-law would come with me.' The move to Chatila gave her freedom to come and go as she pleased, a freedom she uses to the full.

In 1981, a diploma from a teachers' training course equipped her to conduct the first adult literacy class in Chatila. The pay is small but the short work hours, from 3 to 5 p.m. daily, suit her heavy domestic work load, and the fact that two of the children are not yet in school. One of the reasons she works is so that her eldest daughter, Muna, can go to private secondary school.

Um Khalid's day begins around 6 a.m. After rousing the children and helping the youngest to dress, she prepares them a quick breakfast. Abu Khalid leaves the house only to return for lunch and supper, leaving Um Khalid to cope with all the housework and childcare. She is lucky to have five daughters to help her, especially the eldest, 14-year-old Muna. Um Khalid often expresses guilt at putting too much housework on Muna, leaving her too little time for study. This is the main cost of her own out-of-the-home activities. But she does all the heaviest work (washing clothes, bread-making, buying food, cooking) herself. Breast feeding the youngest child is fitted in between other tasks.

A job too important to be delegated is the daily trip to the market, ten minutes' walk away, to buy fresh vegetables, fruit and meat. Lunch, the main meal of the day has to be ready by the time Abu Khalid and the children come home, usually at different times because of variation in school and work shifts. She spends on average three hours a day, on alternate days, washing clothes or baking bread.

All through the day friends and neighbours drop in to chat and drink tea or coffee. After lunch, if there is time, Um Khalid visits friends before her mid-afternoon class. Her visiting network is voluminous, extending all over the camp into surrounding Lebanese neighbourhoods. Many visits are to women she meets through her husband's political work or women members of the resistance. She frequently assumes the role of 'broker' for her friends, relaying messages and requests to her husband. Since she is literate, she is sometimes asked to read newspapers to groups of women. They are interested in general news, but are most intensely concerned with news of wounded or dead fighters. Um Khalid also tries during her visits to mobilise young men into the resistance, offering her husband's help if their situation requires it.

After her class she often visits her students' families, or they may gather at her house. Especially if the students are young, visiting their families helps to build strong relations, and prevent drop-out. When there are lectures, demonstrations, or funerals, she may take the class as a group; or if there is a *nedweh* in the neighbourhood,[8] she takes them to attend it. Held in the homes of ordinary camp women, and led by women members of the resistance, the *nedwaat* are weekly seminars covering a wide range of topics, from child health-care to the current political situation.

Um Khalid rarely loses her calm, although when shelling occurs she must make quick and difficult decisions: whether to continue the class or rush home to her children, whether to go to class or take her children to the shelter. Sometimes, if shelling is light, her class gathers at her house to talk and wait out the hours until it is safe to go outdoors. Even when talking with visitors, Um Khalid keeps busy knitting, sewing, or breast-feeding her baby son. On holidays and feast days, she bakes quantities of cakes for the fighters or for friends and relatives.

Um Khalid still believes that it is better for girls to marry young, but asserts, 'My daughters will be free to marry whomever they wish.' On this subject she argued vigorously with a neighbour who advocated 'the old way of getting married', a position that Um Khalid calls 'backward'.

Though not a member of the resistance, Um Khalid considers herself a 'struggler' by virtue of her community activities and her teaching job. She is very proud of the way Palestinian women are taking part in the national struggle and sees them as 'the most advanced women in the Arab world'.

The case of Um Khalid illustrates several critical aspects of the lives of Palestinian women caught up in protracted, violent conflict. First, it shows how primordial domestic labour remains, compounded by large families, low incomes, poor facilities, and the absence of change in the division of household labour. Domestic work is shared between mother and daughters, particularly the eldest, which often means that she gets less schooling than her younger sisters. New tensions arise as girls acquire aspirations towards university and professional training. Um Khalid's dependence on her daughters for help with housework points to the break-up and dispersion of the extended family. This is a change that has both positive and negative consequences for women, relaxing control, but depriving them of the support of adult female kinfolk.

It is as an 'active housewife' (*mara' nasheeta*) that Um Khalid most forcefully illustrates how women in camp settings stretch their traditional domestic and social role to include new activities.

Sustaining such role expansion requires unusual strength, and for this reason Um Khalid exemplifies an ideal to which many women aspire rather than a large category. Yet other politicised housewives can be found in Chatila, combining management of a large household with political work and sometimes a salaried job as well. Although the resistance movement encouraged the *mara' nasheeta* in ways that included employment, free training, programmes for children and the *nedwaat*, two points must be noted. First, the women cadres focused their mobilisation efforts on unmarried women (*binat*) rather than on housewives. Second, the *mara' nasheeta* type was not created by the Resistance but has existed since the beginning of the Palestinian struggle,[9] and should be seen as an indigenous and specifically women's response to British occupation and Zionist colonialism.

Um Khalid does not openly criticise the rules that place all the responsibility for house management on her shoulders; and like most other women of her generation, she is proud to have many children. But younger women frequently grumble at the heaviness of housework, and most of them intend to have fewer children: 'Four and that's it!' Further, Um Khalid never criticises her husband for leaving her to cope with everything, including sick children and parent/teacher relations. On the contrary, she serves him and defers to his wishes as much as, if not more than, other wives. But she also stands up to him in arguments, whether on domestic or political issues, and resists his pressures to spend more time at home. Such self-confidence is not new to Palestinian women but it has new implications, arising from their recent experience of taking part in the national struggle. As they cross into public space, they become aware of their potential equality with men and conversely, of the reality of their subordination. Involvement in politics has developed women's confidence in their own abilities, while their consciousness of their oppression as women has grown sharper as they encounter opposition, discrimination within the Movement and the triple burden of domestic, political and salaried work.

Mothers of martyrs

While the resistance movement opened up new roles and identities for women, it also consecrated their reproductive role and charged it with new political meaning. Recurrent crisis and physical hardship have changed camp women's view of their lives, making them describe their daily chores as 'struggle' and themselves as 'strugglers' (*munadilat*). Their daily routine of shopping, cooking, cleaning and child-raising is fraught with difficulty and anxiety. The whereabouts of children must constantly be monitored in case of shelling. Homes must be continually repaired, or new ones found. The frequency of widowhood is a constant reminder that this may be their fate.

As conflict enters the home, motherhood is increasingly expressed as a national act and duty. This view is particularly strong among older, uneducated women who lose no chance to express their nationalist feelings and believe that women should contribute to the struggle as mothers, without challenging tradition. Um Muhammad, a survivor of Tell al-Za'ter and mother of several martyrs, expressed this viewpoint when she said proudly at a meeting, 'We Palestinian women have a *buten 'askeri'* (literally 'military womb', meaning 'we give birth to fighters'). Another elderly peasant woman who lost her husband and four sons in Tell al-Za'ter, said, 'We Palestinian women, we give birth to them, we bring them up and we bury them for the revolution.' At a meeting in Chatila, a middle aged woman stood up and declared defiantly, 'I'm giving the Israelis a hit too – my four sons and my husband are all with the *feda-'iyyeen'*.

Though the 'martyr's mother' may never have been politically active, her maternal sacrifice is extolled as a supreme political act. Women, givers and sustainers of life, whose status in the community traditionally rested on the number of sons they bore, are not expected willingly to sacrifice their children and it was out of respect for this symbolic giving that mothers of martyrs were always visited on religious and national commemoration days. In addition, they were invited to attend Resistance celebrations with the leaders and received visits from them. It was said of them, 'They have the ear of the Resistance' and because of this many played an active political role in camp life as intermediaries.

The status and respect awarded by the community to mothers of martyrs epitomises the politicisation of women's reproductive role. That this process began early in the Palestinian struggle is suggested by the important place given by the national tradition to Jamjoom's mother, a woman celebrated for her refusal to mourn when her son was executed by the British in 1929. Later during the Great Rebellion (1936–38), women's capacity to suppress mourning for killed fighters became a practical necessity, to avoid retaliation against their villages. Like the active housewife, the martyr's mother is an indigenous Palestinian Arab form of woman's struggle.

Martyr's widows are also respected and supported but they have less time than older women for missions outside the home. The historic form taken by widows' struggle is to refuse re-marriage and work if necessary to bring up their children.

At a deeper level, maternal sacrifice has become a symbol of the extent of Palestinian loss and suffering. Over time, several rituals and practices have evolved to console grieving mothers, including this chorus often sung at funerals:

> O mother of the martyr, rejoice,
> For all youths are your children.

Aftermath: from 1982

By mid-August of 1982 the war seemed over. Though the Israeli Army was still on the outskirts of Beirut, the Habib Accords had been signed, the resistance movement was about to withdraw, and a multi-national force was arriving to supervise the transition to peace. The people of the camps who had taken refuge in less exposed parts of the city returned to clear away the rubble and repair their homes. Reassured by Lebanese and American guarantees of protection for non-combatant Palestinians contained in the Accords (Cobban, 1984, p. 124), they were nonetheless worried that Bashir Gemayel, elected President on 23 August, would, once in office, sweep Palestinians out of West Beirut.[10] If their homes were rebuilt, it would be a little harder to carry out such a plan. But on 14 September, Bashir Gemayel was assassinated; on the 15th, the Israeli Army advanced into West Beirut, surrounding Sabra and Chatila.

The home of Um Fady, whose account follows, lies in the quarter outside the camp through which the Special Unit of the Lebanese Forces assigned to 'clean' Chatila entered the area.

> On Thursday afternoon we were sitting in this room when the shelling started. That's when the water-tank on the roof was hit,

and the verandah. You see the verandah, how it's all torn away? With every explosion dust was coming down on us.

I said to Abu Fady, 'For God's sake, get us out of here.' He said, 'If I could have got you out, wouldn't I have done it?' At first he couldn't get the car out because our neighbour's house had been hit, and rubble was blocking the road. But finally, somehow, he got it down the alley. He asked me, 'Do you want to go to your aunt's?' I said. 'What are we still waiting for?' So he got us out, and all the while he was making the children laugh, to take their minds off the shelling. When we left, none of these houses were destroyed; that happened later. They hadn't started the killing. We knew nothing about the massacre then, we fled because of the shelling.

Once we reached my aunt's home in Sabra, I said to him, 'For God's sake, Abu Fady, don't go back to the house. Stay with us.' But he said, 'No, I must go back to get the children's clothes and their milk.' So I sat and waited for him, and I waited and I waited. Two days I waited, but he didn't return.

My aunt said, 'He must be hiding somewhere.' I said, 'Out of the question! If Abu Fady were separated from us for a single day, he would do the impossible to see his children.' I wanted to go back home, but they wouldn't let me. On Sunday I managed to get away. No one would come with me, neither my aunt nor my husband's brother.

At first I felt lost. I couldn't recognise anything. I couldn't find the house, not even the road. The whole quarter had changed, what with the bulldozing and the bodies. The first person I saw was a foreign journalist. He asked me in English, 'Where are the dead children?' I shouted at him, 'I don't know. Leave me alone. I'm looking for my husband.' I looked around: here a dead woman, there a man, there a pile of youths. I reached our house. The outer wall was all broken down. I looked through the debris. There was no smell of a corpse. I looked for the car and didn't find it. That gave me hope. I took the milk and a few clothes for the children and went back to my aunt's.

He still didn't come, so the following day I went back again. I searched and searched, and couldn't find him. I was sitting weeping – my son was just six weeks old – when a woman passed and asked me what was the matter. I told her the story. She said 'Sister, there's one over there, go and look.' I went and looked. It was my husband. They had scooped debris over his body after killing him; his head and neck were under the rubble, and his clothes were all torn, nothing left except his underpants. I went to the Civil Defence workers who hadn't seen him yet, and they moved him away for burial. He had been lying five or six days in the sun.

The full death toll from the massacre was not registered at the time. The Civil Defence and Red Cross workers on the spot were overwhelmed, and could not make a complete count. Some bodies had been removed for burial by relatives before they arrived on the scene; others already lay covered in mass graves. Given the massacre's duration, around 38 hours, and the population density in the quarters attacked, an estimate of 3000 is more realistic than those given by the Kahane Commission (700 to 800) and the Lebanese government (326).[11]

The new repression

Chatila after the massacre looked as if a giant had trampled over it, smashing its matchbox housing. Rubble was strewn everywhere, blocking streets and alleys. In the southern quarters, where the massacre had been concentrated, bulldozers had attacked every structure they could reach. Among the ruins women in black wailed, screamed curses, searched, quarrelled over remnants, or wandered about in a daze. It was not merely the scale of loss and destruction that made the situation so catastrophic, it was the lack of a single authority to take charge. After previous battles, the Resistance Movement had undertaken repairs and compensated people for losses. Now the Resistance was gone: Palestinians and others in Beirut's 'poverty belt' were at the mercy of the political forces whose programme was signalled by the massacre. The Israeli invasion had cleared the scene for the reassertion of the authority of the Lebanese state.

Chatila's Popular Committee dissolved itself,[12] and once again authority was represented by the UNRWA director's office and Lebanese Army checkpoints. What had been public, political space under the Resistance now reverted to domestic or commercial use: homeless families took over Resistance offices and clinics; the Lion Cubs' training ground became a parking lot.[13] People said, 'We are back to '48, back to zero.' Just as after the uprooting, there was a persuasive sense of disaster, of mourning for better days. Every family had suffered losses; everyone had kinsfolk or friends among the departed fighters.

As soon as the Israelis left Beirut, mass arrests by the Lebanese Army began in and around the camps. The arrests were intended to intimidate the Palestinians, and prevent them from re-organising; also to screen out anyone with false papers, or not entitled to reside in Lebanon, or believed to be a member of a resistance group. The arrests continued sporadically through 1983, together with kidnappings carried out by the Lebanese Forces who were now able to circulate freely in West Beirut, until February 1984, when militias opposed to the government forced the Army out of West Beirut. Italian units from the Multi-National force posted around Chatila intervened on several occasions to stop brutality, but they had no mandate to prevent the authorities from making arrests. Most adult male members of the community were taken for interrogation during this period; women were occasionally included if they were reported as having belonged to the resistance, or as having gone to the Beka', where Palestinian fighters were still stationed.

The problem of unemployment was as serious now as were war damage and insecurity. Many arrests took place on the streets, or in workplaces, so that men hardly dared to go out to look for work. New labour laws further restricted jobs that non-Lebanese could take, and the Ministry of Social Affairs stopped issuing work permits to Palestinians. Stagnation of the Lebanese economy caused by continuing political crisis brought unemployment to Lebanese and Palestinian workers alike, and threatened income levels already undermined by three months of war. A small field study carried out in February 1983 estimated that only 12 per cent of Chatila men were employed.[14] People summarised these various pressures as *khanq* (strangulation), and saw them as a covert continuation of the massacre.

Coping with chaos

The war and the massacre created a category of women who had lost their main provider, whether husband or son, as well as home and possessions. In the past, the resistance had compensated all victims of war damage without discrimination but in the aftermath, national and residential criteria were strictly applied. UNRWA helped Palestinians inside the camp to rebuild their homes, but many of the new widows were squatters on 'illegal' land and so were disqualified by most of the aid institutions from receiving indemnities. The PLO's Social Affairs Institute, set up to support the families of war victims and prisoners, was too harrassed by the authorities to register the new widows until the end of 1983. Most of the new widows were illiterate and had never worked outside the home. They had little or no savings and most had three or more children to care for.

In the aftermath, a bewildering assortment of local and foreign donor institutions arose, to assist in reconstruction. Their offices were widely scattered over Greater Beirut. Aimed at different clienteles, each had different offerings as well as different rules and procedures. New widows had no one to guide them through this maze of institutions. The women cadres had not been trained for this kind of work and had problems of their own to cope with.

For the bereaved women, loss was compounded by confusion, misinformation, exclusions, delays and shortages. Reconstruction indemnities ran out long before all damaged homes had been repaired. Scarcity of help engendered bitter competition and strained norms of neighbourly solidarity. Even kinship, the usual bedrock of support, frequently failed. Widows complained that relatives had turned them out or stopped visiting them. One accused her husband's brother, the person most obliged to help her, of appropriating an indemnity she had succeeded in obtaining.

Yet a certain substructure of solidarity remained as well as the practice of weaving social relations, reasserting themselves as the worst of the shock wore off. Women began to form new relations and friendships that partly compensated for the breakdown of old ones, and for paralysis of national and community structures. One of the older widows, with sons abroad, took under her wing a younger woman whose problems were more complicated than most. Nadia's husband was among the 950 'missing' men who had been rounded up during the massacre but whose bodies had never been found. Without a death certificate, their wives were not considered eligible for a SAI pension or UNRWA special assistance. For Nadia and the other wives of 'missing' men, their ambivalent status seemed to be more disturbing than widowhood, for which there exists a strong pattern of community respect and support. In addition, her husband had not been registered with UNRWA, which meant that her four young children had no claim to residence in Lebanon or UNRWA services. When Nadia eventually left Beirut for the Beka', she stayed there with a married daughter of the older woman who had befriended her in Chatila.

Breakdowns were few but many symptoms of strain short of breakdown were visible, and they did not only affect widows. Women generally complained of insomnia, pain in the back, head and knees, and difficulty in breathing. Doctors spoke of an increase in cases of diabetes, thyroid problems, intra-menstrual bleeding, tension and high blood pressure. Such symptoms increased as turmoil in Lebanon dragged on. Older women bore up better under stress than young ones who had only known the good days of the Resistance.

'Faith', a political as well as a religious quality for Palestinians, also played a part in Chatila women's capacity to cope with hardship. Men turned to religion through stricter observance of prayer and attendance at the mosque; among women, religiosity took a different form as they discarded the secular 'look' associated with the Resistance period (T-shirts and jeans) for long-sleeved dresses and head scarves. Women's conversation became heavily loaded with invocations of God's compassion and power. In the aftermath, the name of God was used as if it has power to heal, with people in pain or mourning or fear admonished to 'Say "Allah!"'. Besides their profound psychological effects, such ritual utterances serve to bridge the gap between the more and less unfortunate, and remind people of their common bonds as Muslims.

Um Fady, a new widow

One of the widows who coped most energetically with her losses was Um Fady, whose description of escaping the massacre was quoted earlier. Her situation typifies that of other widows, even though her response is in some ways idiosyncratic. Though on 'illegal' land, Um Fady's former home had been relatively spacious, with two storeys, and a courtyard. After the massacre, nothing was left of the upper floor but a dangerously hanging fragment of wall, and all the groundfloor walls had been breached. By February 1983, five months after the end of the war, Um Fady had managed to procure building materials from the only donor agency in Chatila that helped everyone. She worked on the house herself, along with a hired labourer, bringing her baby son and two little girls from the abandoned school in Sabra where she had taken refuge, along with other homeless families.

At this time her only possessions, beside the ruined house, were the baby's push-chair, a suitcase full of childrens' clothes, some blankets, and a two-ring gas burner, Her furniture, equipment, and most of her clothes had been looted. A pre-war photo showed her in glamorous décolleté; now she always wore the same black dress, and left her greying hair dishevelled in mourning. In contrast to neglect of herself, she kept the children neat and well clothed.

Apart from her aunt, she had no close relatives nearby. Her own family were in the South, and she had quarrelled with her husband's brother. A Palestinian in a predominantly Lebanese neighbourhood, without the protection of male kinsfolk, Um Fady needed to establish warm relations with her neighbours. This required constant effort and skill. Anti-Palestinian feeling was rife in the aftermath, and could take the form of verbal hostility, theft, encroachment, or complaints to the nearby Army checkpoint. Another reason why Um Fady needed her neighbours' goodwill was that she had been more successful than others in securing aid. She had received a building indemnity from an agency that had refused to help others in this quarter. Alone among the Palestinians there, she had received help from an Iranian-sponsored committee directed to Lebanese Shi'ites. In addition, she had been helped by the Lebanese Red Cross, the Italian contingent's medical team, and the Austrian and Norwegian social aid centres. This she managed alone, mostly on foot, pushing or carrying the baby.

A few other widows placed some of their children in orphanages, as a way to have them temporarily looked after without losing parental rights. Um Fady despised those who took this step. She dotes on her children. Hugging them and planning their future seems to help her. She intends to look for work when the baby is old enough to go to kindergarden. She worked before marriage as a child-minder and knows how to use a sewing machine. She will try to rent part of her home to respectable tenants. People pitied Um Fady as one of the hardest hit of the massacre victims and admired her resourcefulness in finding aid: 'She's *awiyya* (strong, bold) but she deserves every penny she gets.' Yet in her own quarter, there was envy and gossip. Her success was not easy to hide in a milieu where homes are open to neighbours. Though Um Fady did her best to please them, it was impossible completely to avert their ill-will: two of them made trouble for her with one of the donor agencies. Sympathy for her was restored when police broke down her newly repaired walls as part of a protection racket.

Um Fady shunned the other Palestinians in her quarter and they in turn complained bitterly that she never helped them with information about the donor agencies. Dissociating herself from them was doubtless one way of strengthening her ties with her Lebanese neighbours. Such dissociation was made easier by the distance of her quarter from the camp and its relative isolation. Chatila people disliked visiting there because of the proximity of a Lebanese Army checkpost. After the battle of February 1984,[15] the Army withdrew from Chatila and Um Fady gradually re-established ties with former friends in the camp.

One important element in Um Fady's ability to steer between the rocks and whirlpools of her situation was the speed with which she grasped the main features of the post-war scene, with the Lebanese authorities back in control and foreign agencies as the main source of help. She had a higher level of education than most of the other widows, knew a little English and had worked before marrying. This made her enterprising. Others waited for help to reach them or for neighbours to tell them where to go. Um Fady went out and searched. Some of the other women exaggerated their losses, whereas Um Fady stuck close to the truth. This gave her credibility with the mainly middle class employees of the donor agencies. In spite of disappointments, most other widows relied on kin and neighbours for moral and practical support. Um Fady sought out foreigners and dissociated herself from Palestinians. The weakness of her Palestinian links differentiates her from Um Khalid, whose loyalties remained unaffected by the massacre.

In other ways Um Fady typifies Chatila women faced with disaster and loss. In the tradition of Palestinian widows, she clung to her children, rebuilding her life and home around their future. With a 'little from here, a little from there', she succeeded in patching things up. If not equally enterprising, others managed to do the same. One opened a small shop. One began taking an adult literacy class so as to be able to find a job. Others rented out a room. A few left Chatila, if they had kin in other areas who could put them up; but most stayed. One who had miscarried after searching among the corpses for her husband, re-married. Only one case of complete breakdown was reported. Discussing the rarity of collapse, women would say, 'Who would look after my children?' The identification of women's role with motherhood, which resistance cadres had criticised, showed up in the aftermath as a source of will to carry on.

Return to protest

The Women's Union was one of the few PLO institutions that did not close down after the war; its Chatila centre was repaired in time to celebrate International Women's Day, 8 March 1983, with Palestinian songs and *debkeh* (a national dance). Few women cadres remained to keep up the former activities. It was dangerous for well-known figures to be seen in the camps and many local cadres had left with the resistance, whether because they were married to fighters, or because they wanted to carry on political work. There was no longer scope in Lebanon for the mobilising and recruiting campaigns that they had worked at before.

The repressive measures being taken now were all too familiar to older people who could remember how things were before 1969. But their scale and the political conjuncture made them far more alarming. As intended, the massacre engendered fear of repetition; several panic flights occurred in the year that followed. Fear gave rise to a mood described as *hayt al-hayt* ('keep to the wall', keep out of trouble). A protective veil was drawn over the past: photographs of children in Lion Cub uniform were hidden, pictures of fighter sons taken down from the wall; books on Lenin and the Resistance Movement were removed from bookshelves, leaving encyclopaedias and school text-books. Since there is no family in the inner camp, people say, that did not have one or more members in the Resistance, all had to search for the narrow ground where honour and dignity is preserved but safety not rashly jeopardised. This posed especially delicate problems for wives of men who had had political responsibilities, who might still be visited by people in need, such as widows. Too many visitors might indicate political activity, but to turn visitors away transgresses the sacred law of hospitality, and exposes offenders to contempt. Everyone with a political history had to assume that he or she was being observed.

Given the arrests and the informers, it was remarkable that there continued to be any manifestations of national feeling. Here, women took the lead, because there was less danger of their being arrested or physically assaulted. The first of these political events took place on the fortieth day after the massacre, when women from the Chatila branch of the Union organised a commemorative march to the mass graves;[16] three of the leaders were detained by the Lebanese Army on charges of incitement to riot, but were released the same day. Other national commemorations such as Fateh's anniversary on 1 January, and the Day of the Land on 30 March, continued to draw mainly women participants. Though Lebanon is pledged to the same support of the PLO as other Arab League states, there was real danger in taking part in such marches at that time.

Individual confrontations also took place daily in the camp, between women in their homes or on the streets, and units of the Lebanese Army patrolling it. Women recounted these incidents in their visits, savouring how so-and-so's daughter had answered back to a patrol that had insulted her, and how so-and-so's wife had called down God's anger on soldiers breaking down a newly repaired wall. For though there was fear, there was also defiance. People recalled other such confrontations they had heard about or witnessed as children, before the Revolution, for instance how women had hurled stones at police who came to evict squatters. The Army recognised how formidable these women could be: 'You Palestinian women ride your men' was the insult hurled at one of them, a double insult because of the sexual allusion and the implication that Palestinian men are weaklings.

Women were also activated by the arrests. Many who had never demonstrated before joined marches and sit-ins now because they had a husband, son, or brother in prison. A woman whose son or husband had been arrested would not only demonstrate, she would confront the local Army Commander, and, if this failed, she would demand an audience with any prominent Lebanese Muslim politician, including the Prime Minister. Women from Chatila even crossed over into the dangerous Eastern sector where the prisoners were kept, to try and visit their menfolk, or get them released. A young woman whose husband was missing after the fighting in Tripoli in November 1983, made two journeys to look for him across the most notorious of the Lebanese Forces' roadblocks, where many kidnappings of Palestinian women had occurred.

Such action by women in defence of male kinsfolk has ancient

Semitic roots, and is accepted as a legitimate extension of their 'natural' role; it is precisely *as women* that they have right of access to the powerful, and the task of moving them to compassion. As an extension of women's domestic role that carries them effectively into the sphere of power, it warns us once more to question the common dichotomy between public and domestic spheres. When circumstances demand it, women perceive themselves as interchangeable with men, capable of carrying out all their functions, even though temporarily and by default. Such interchangeability of gender roles is illustrated by a placard carried by a woman during the farewell demonstrations for the resistance fighters in September 1982: 'We will take your place!' It could be taken as a message from the whole female population to the male fighters.

The ability of ordinary, unorganised Palestinian women to sustain political action is demonstrated in a story told by one of the few top-level women cadres to remain in Lebanon after the war. She had gone to one of the camps to tell women there about a sit-in to be held next day in protest against the kidnappings and arrests.[17] Since it was dangerous for her to circulate in the camp, she asked an older woman, whose son was in prison, to spread the news, though without instructing her what to say. Um Ali went round telling other women, 'Today it's my son who is in prison, tomorrow it may be yours. Who will march with you tomorrow if you don't march with us today? Isn't every young man in this camp the son of all of us?' The cadre commented, 'It's because we have such women that our revolution will never die.'

Some questions

Chatila women appear here under two radically different sets of conditions: between 1969 and 1982 the resistance movement was firmly established in Lebanon and women were involved in it at several levels and various ways. In the period after 1982, the resistance has left and women are coping with destruction and threat as the Palestinian community enters a new phase of uncertainty. Such sharp transitions have occurred before in Palestinian history and prompt the question whether women in such conditions develop or get conscripted into gender-specific tasks of minimising the trauma of change, of normalising the new situation? Our data suggests this may be so, but the question bears closer investigation, especially because such a 'normalising' role for women is likely to obstruct changes that many community members call for as 'progressive'.

Particularly after 1976, work among women of the camps ('mass work') was adopted as a priority by the women cadres and we see them developing effective methods of mobilisation and recruitment. Yet the auxiliary functions and slight means allocated to the Women's Union by the resistance leadership suggests that the cadres' work was not seen as a priority. This impression is strengthened by the reluctance of all except the leftist groups to press for change in gender relations and the division of domestic labour (Abu Ali, 1975). This raises questions as to the purpose of the mobilisation of women by the Resistance: what were the real roles allocated to both cadres and ordinary women by the different groups?

For women, an important effect of resistance movement mobilisation was the opening up and legitimisation of new roles and identities: as militant, martyr, worker, cadre, prisoner. Can these roles and identities be sustained after the political framework that gave birth to them is removed? How lasting are changes that take place at the level of consiousness in a minority of women, without being institutionalised?

A universal feature of Muslim societies is the urban middle class ideal of the *sitt fil-beit* (lady in the home), but when the resistance cadres entered the camps, they brought a new model of the middle class woman as active (*nasheeta*) and committed (*multezema*). What is the strength of this new model among women of other classes? Will it be sustained after resistance withdrawal, or does it require an economic basis, employment in the movement, to be effectively realised? Will the pressures of consumerist society press women back into the home?

In the aftermath of the war, Palestinian women are seen to be coping with unusual difficulties with little institutional help. They also carry on political protest with few or no directives from above, taking risks at a time when men hardly dare show themselves on the street. Such capacity for spontaneous action calls up a number of questions: how much of this is due to emergency dimensions of women's conventional domestic/social role: how much to the effect of resistance campaigns? How much is the result of a pre-resistance gender- and culture-specific tradition of struggle? Does it guarantee that women will exercise more power in a future Palestinian society than Algerian women have so far in theirs? Or are legal and institutional changes essential *during* national struggle in order to prevent women's liberation from being consigned to the bottom of the national agenda?

Finally, our data emphasises the 'stretched' roles that have evolved for ordinary Palestinian women during more than 70 years of conflict, such as the 'martyr's mother' who gives her sons to the struggle and bears their loss stoically, the widow who refuses remarriage and works so as to bring up her children, and the 'active house-wife', who undertakes political actions without challenging the community's expectations of what married women do. Western researchers often assume that Third World women's political functions can be measured by formal membership in parties or election to office. Hence, they have neglected forms of struggle that women themselves evolve within their own cultural framework. It would be valuable to know more about the processes through which Palestinian women have developed these 'stretched' roles and how they have handed them on. How will these roles be modified as women attain higher educational levels and higher rates of employment?

Notes

1. The first part of this study, 'Exile and resistance in Lebanon: 1948 to 1982', was written mainly by Julie Peteet and is based on the fieldwork for her PhD dissertation, which was carried out from September 1980 to May 1982. Rosemary Sayigh began work in Chatila in December 1983, and is responsible for the second part: 'Aftermath: from 1982'. The authors wish to thank the Diana Tamari Sabbagh Foundation and the Institute for Arab Studies (Boston), for helping to fund their research.
2. Lebanese/Palestinian relations are complicated by the way the presence of the Palestinians has interacted with Lebanon's internal conflicts, generated by its sect and class structure. For good accounts, see Khalidi (1979) and Cobban (1984).
3. By the end of the 1970s, younger women were beginning to insist on continuing their political activities after marriage. This was particularly the case with members of radical Resistance groups, and was a likely outcome when spouses were members of the same group.
4. The PLO set up the embryo of a state in Beirut, including departments dealing with Foreign Relations, Health, Education, Economy and

Industry. There were also the mass unions: Workers, Women, Students, Teachers, etc. In addition, the larger Resistance groups ran social institutions. Altogether, the movement employed a large part of the Palestinian civilian labour force as well as many Lebanese and other nationalities.

5. In Islam, the term 'martyr' (*shaheed*) is used for one who sacrifices his life for the faith and for the *'umma* (Muslim community), an act that is both religious and political, hence different from the English usage. Palestinians also use *feda'i* (one who sacrifices, pl. *feda'iyyeen*) to refer to the Resistance fighters.
6. *'Ird* is specifically women's honour, or honour derived from control over women's sexuality. It is distinct from *sharaf*, honour pertaining to individuals or groups, without sexual connotations.
7. *Um* (mother) and *abu* (father) are used in conjunction with the name of the first-born son to designate the parents. This custom is still followed in rural Arab communities.
8. The *nedwaat* were one of the most effective forms of mass mobilisation practised by the women cadres. They gave women not accustomed to speaking in public a chance to 'find their voices' and women used them freely to ask questions, raise demands and air grievances.
9. Women from villages were killed demonstrating against the British occupation in Jerusalem in 1929. Other women are reported to have hurled missiles at British soldiers from their balconies.
10. This was in fact Bashir Gemayel's intention. See Schiff and Ya'ari (1985, p. 246).
11. Kapeliouk (1984) gives an estimate of 3000. This may be a little high. For interviews with survivors, see Barada (1983).
12. From 1969 to 1982 all camps had Popular Committees representing the local population and Resistance groups.
13. The Lion Cubs (*ashbal*) were children aged from five to 15 years enrolled in a PLO-directed programme that combined physical, educational, political and paramilitary elements. Girls were included.
14. Mahmoud al-'Ali, '*Terbiyat al-Tifl beyn al-Mu'essessat al-'Usra wa al-Mu'essessat al-Ta'limiya*' (Arabic), mimeo, 1983.
15. Opposition to the Amin Gemayel regime mounted throughout 1983, with fierce gun battles being fought out in West Beirut and the Southern suburbs between the Lebanese Army and the various Muslim militias, mainly Amal (Shi'ite) and Jumblat's PSP (Druze). In February 1984, the Army was forced to leave West Beirut; only units friendly to the Opposition were allowed to remain.
16. The fortieth day after a death is an occasion for renewed mourning. When deaths have political connotations, as in the case of the Sabra and Chatila massacre, the *'arba'in* (40th) gives rise to political demonstrations.
17. During this period, Lebanese Sunnis, Shi'ites and Druzes were also being kidnapped. Lebanese women formed an ad hoc committee to organise protest. Lebanese Christians have also been kidnapped, though not on the same scale.

References and further reading

Abu Ali, Khadija (1975) *Introduction to Woman's Reality and her Experience in the Palestinian Revolution* (in Arabic) (Beirut: GUPW).

Antonius, Soraya (1979) 'Fighting on Two Fronts: Conversations with Palestinian Women', *Journal of Palestine Studies*, vol. 8, no. 3.

Antonius, Soraya (1980) 'Prisoners for Palestine: A List of Women Political Prisoners' *Journal of Palestine Studies*, vol. 9, no. 3.

Barada, Layla S. (1983) in 'Invasion of Lebanon', special issue *Race and Class*, vol. 29, no. 4.

Beck, Lois and Keddie, Nikki (eds.) (1978) *Women of the Muslim World* (Cambridge, Massachusetts: Harvard University Press).

Bendt, Ingela and Downing, Jim (1982) *We Shall Return: Women of Palestine* (London: Zed Press).

Canaan, Tewfiq (1931) 'Unwritten Laws Affecting the Arab Woman of Palestine', *Journal of the Palestine Oriental Society*, no. 11.

Cobban, Helena (1984) *The Palestine Liberation Organization: People, Power, Politics* (Cambridge: Cambridge University Press).

Graham-Brown, Sarah (1980) *Palestinians and their Society 1880–1946* (London: Quartet).

Graham-Brown, Sarah (1984) *Education, Repression and Liberation: Palestinians* (London: World University Service).

Haddad, Yvonne (1980) 'Palestinian Women: Patterns of Legitimation and Domination', in Khalil Nakhleh and Elia Zureik, eds. *The Sociology of the Palestinians* (London: Croom Helm).

Kapeliouk, Amnon (1984) *Sabra and Shatila: Inquiry into a Massacre* (Belmont: Association of Arab-American Graduates).

Khalidi, Walid (1979) *Conflict in Lebanon* (Cambridge, Massachusetts: Harvard University Press).

Mogannam, Matiel (1937) *The Arab Woman and the Palestine Problem* (London: Joseph).

Pitt-Rivers, Julian (1977) *The Fate of Shechem, or The Politics of Sex* (Cambridge: Cambridge University Press).

Sayegh, Mai (1983) 'Choisir la Révolution' in Monique Gadant (ed.) 'Femmes de la Méditerranée', special issue of *Peuples Méditerranéens*, nos. 22–23.

Sayigh, Rosemary (1981) 'Encounters with Palestinian Women under Occupation' *Journal of Palestine Studies*, vol. 10, no. 4.

Schiff, Zeev and Ya'ari, Ehud (1985) *Israel's Lebanon War* (London: Allen and Unwin).

Schneider, Jane (1971) 'Of Vigilance and Virgins: Honor, Shame and Access to Resources in Mediterranean Society' *Ethnology*, no. 10.

Seger, Karen (ed.) (1981) *Portrait of Palestinian Village* (London: Third World Research and Publishing Centre).

Shaikh, Zakaria al (1984) 'Sabra and Shatila 1982: Resisting the Massacre' *Journal of Palestine Studies*, vol. 14, no. 1.

Tawil, Raymonda (1980) *My Home, My Prison* (New York: Rhinehart Winston).

7 Kibbutz Women: Conflict in Utopia

ALISON M. BOWES

Since their foundation, the Israeli kibbutzim have been involved in a series of wars, obvious and direct manifestations of political conflict. Unless their communities were in border areas, and therefore vulnerable to direct attack, kibbutz women have for the most part experienced these wars second-hand, either seeing their male relatives and friends going off to fight, or, if they were doing army service themselves, working behind the front line, supporting the troops. Yet their lives have been directly conditioned by conflict, not only that in the Middle Eastern context, but also within Israeli society itself. At the same time, they have been involved in their own struggle for emancipation within the kibbutz movement, a struggle which, many argue, they have lost.

This chapter explores conflicts within the kibbutz movement which have involved women, and some of those conflicts in the wider Israeli society which relate ultimately to 'the war', as the perpetual tension with the Arab world is known in Israel. I examine how kibbutz, national and international conflicts are interconnected. I use Kibbutz Goshen, where I did fieldwork between 1974 and 1976 as the basis of the discussion.

Goshen is a fictitious name for a real kibbutz of the Kibbutz Artzi Hashomer Hatzair, politically the most left wing of the kibbutz federations and affiliated to the Labour Party coalition government at the time of fieldwork. Goshen was founded in 1949 near the town of Petach Tiqwa and the pre-1967 Jordanian border. In 1975, it had 139 formally elected members and candidates for membership, and a total population of about 300. The non-member population consisted mainly of members' children, and also of volunteer workers, a few visiting soldiers and the retired, aged parents of some members. To become a member required the vote of those already elected.

Economically, Goshen was a communally worked mixed farm, producing cotton, chickens (for meat), citrus fruit, avocados, pears, and roses (as cut flowers), all for sale rather than subsistence. In 1975, a small factory producing metal goods was being set up. The community also had services typical of all kibbutzim, including a kitchen, dining-room and laundry, and children's houses, in which children were collectively reared in age-groups, spending only the late afternoons, early evenings and Sabbaths with their parents. Members ran the kibbutz through the General Assembly, a weekly plenary meeting, and by means of a series of committees with delegated powers. All were obliged to work in Goshen's economy, and all were entitled to housing, food, clothing and the care and education of their children.

The early days

The vast majority of kibbutz pioneers belonged to the Socialist Zionist arm of the wider Zionist movement. From 1910 when Degania, the first kibbutz, was founded (Baratz, 1954), until the 1920s women comprised a tiny minority of kibbutz pioneers. Although at that time changes in the position of women were seen as necessary and desirable, there is very little evidence of conscious attempts to effect them. In the 1920s women themselves began to fight much more deliberately for a place in the pioneering effort, forming their own work teams, training centres, farms and so on (Maimon, 1962; Katzenelson-Rubashow, 1976; Rein, 1980). They campaigned to work alongside the men in the movement and, importantly, to do the same jobs, especially agricultural labour and roadbuilding, both ideologically highly valued in the pioneering movements. At this time, the traditional women's work that they had done in the *shtetl* (the Jewish community of Eastern Europe whence many of them had come), such as housekeeping and childcare, was simply unnecessary: living quarters were humble and there were very few children about to be cared for.

The attitudes of male pioneers to the women's efforts seem to have ranged from outright hostility to amused tolerance (Rein

1980). Certainly, there is no evidence of the kind of radical re-examination of the roles of men and women that many feminists today argue is necessary for change to occur (e.g. Oakley 1981). The pioneer women seem to have thought that if they built a society in which they were economically independent of men, they would be liberated: the form of this liberation would be the freedom to 'take on the occupations, attributes and goals of men' (Mednick 1975, p. 3).

This was an asymmetrical egalitarianism (Bowes, 1978), for the men were not pressed to take on the corresponding 'occupations, attributes and goals' of the women. As children were born and as living standards improved, kibbutz women took on the new work involved. This was seen as a 'natural' development within the kibbutz: no man could do such work. Paradoxically, the women pioneers had colluded in their own subordination: by striving to become involved in manual labour in the fields and on the roads, they had helped to devalue women's traditional work, and by the time they took on jobs in collective childcare and housekeeping, these were classified as 'unproductive work', a necessary burden on the community, and a distraction from 'productive work' in agriculture. The terms 'productive' and 'unproductive' work are internal categories, used both in official movement statistics and in common kibbutz parlance.

The contemporary kibbutz

As many as 90 per cent of women kibbutz members today work in the 'service branches' (Rayman, 1981)[1], and the situation on Goshen reflected this general picture. In fact, very few jobs in the productive branches were considered suitable for women, and most of these were occupied by younger women, not yet mothers. Members of Goshen said that the work in productive branches was 'too hard for women', referring to a generally accepted assumption that most women were, by nature, physically weaker than most men. Sometimes, further comments were added: for example, I was often told that women who drove tractors 'damaged their insides', thus reducing their ability to bear children. The only woman who drove a tractor (once) during my fieldwork was in her late thirties and unmarried. At this age, she was thought unlikely to have children, and her insides did not therefore require protection. It should be noted that there was no sense in which she was thought to be 'more like a man', stronger than other women and therefore more suited to tractor driving. In fact, she was very small in stature, and physically quite delicate. Women were thought to have qualities especially suited to certain jobs, notably childcare: this was justified by reference to their assumed nature. When a man asked for work with the children, he was laughed at, both by men and women, and when a man recovering from illness was allocated the so-called 'light work' of ironing, not only was he completely unable to do it, but his appearance at the ironing board gave rise to great hilarity.

There were exceptions to the general picture: for example a middle-aged woman who worked with the hothouse roses was widely admired for working in a productive branch. The women in the hothouses did not do exactly the same work as the men: some tasks, such as cutting the flowers and pruning were shared by both sexes, whereas grading was done by women and packing by men. In distinctions like this, it is difficult to see the prevailing notions about strength and weakness operating: indeed, the women often said that their work was harder, because it was continuous while the men 'just lazed about' between packing sessions, waiting until there were enough graded flowers to fill a box before starting. But the notions did operate, in that women did not work with the flowers in the summer (the off-season), the justification for this being that they would not be able to bear the intense heat in the hothouses.

There were some men who had service jobs and escaped criticism: sometimes, this was because the job was considered a man's job, such as being a mechanic, but other men who had widespread respect in the community could carry off service work without damaging their reputations (a pioneer, who had made a considerable productive contribution to Goshen in the past, could be put in charge of allocating shoes). But in general, unproductive work was associated with women, and productive work with men: the exceptions merely reinforced accepted views of female and male capabilities.

The ideologically low value accorded unproductive work, and its association with women are clearly and closely related, in the kibbutz movement generally, to (particularly male) evaluations of women themselves, which refer to their failure to participate actively in kibbutz life, their lack of interest in kibbutz politics, and their general dissatisfaction with their lives. Often, when couples were unhappy on Goshen, or left the community, this was blamed on the woman's failure to adapt to kibbutz life or to act as a kibbutz member should. Such reasons were considered so commonplace on Goshen that they were used instead of explaining their real reasons for wanting to leave. In reality, the structure of women's lives makes it difficult for them to be good kibbutzniks in the generally accepted sense, that is, to get permanent jobs and to take an active interest in local politics.

Many women in Goshen, working in the services, did unskilled work, and thus failed to conform to the now accepted norm that kibbutz members should be skilled workers (cf. Shepher, 1972). Being unskilled handicapped them in the search for permanent jobs: a main avenue to job tenure was to make oneself indispensible by acquiring, through training, skills which others did not have. Having a permanent job is today a mark of establishment as a kibbutz member: without one, a person may be derided as a *pkak* (a cork, a person who floats about between jobs) (*ibid.*). There were very few opportunities for women on Goshen to acquire skills, become indispensable, and thus obtain permanent jobs. This was in part because they were concentrated in the services in which there was necessarily much unskilled work, and also because Goshen, a rather poor kibbutz, had invested few resources in modernising the services and training service workers. Due to the profit-making orientation which Goshen shared with other kibbutzim (Cohen, 1966), 'productive' branches were consistently given priority when opportunities for investment arose.

It is true that there are opportunities for women kibbutz members to acquire skills, for instance as *melaplot* (children's nurses). Such opportunities are greater on the richer kibbutzim where there has been more investment on the service sector. Even so, the culturally defined, conventional rhythms of women's lives hamper their ability easily to obtain permanent jobs. As women usually start to have children in their early twenties, they may change their jobs several times in the course of their lives.

On Goshen, a typical woman continued with her normal work during the first six months of pregnancy. Then, after a few weeks of doing lighter work, for example in the kitchen, she went on to sew in the *communa* (clothing store). After the baby's birth she was given six weeks off work so that she could attend to the infant all day. Thereafter, with the child in the communal nursery, the mother built up her working hours again, starting with light work and perhaps eventually returning to her original job, if it had not been taken by someone else.[2]

This routine on Goshen has been practised since its foundation in the late 1940s. Before that time kibbutz women worked harder and longer hours when they were pregnant. Members of Goshen believed that their system was introduced because it was more humane and better for mother and baby; it was in fact possible to introduce the system because of better living standards for which earlier kibbutzim had striven (cf. Cohen 1966).

Constant changes of unskilled jobs meant that women on Goshen acquired knowledge about the workings of the kibbutz economy with difficulty, if at all. While a man with a permanent, skilled job had in-depth knowledge of a particular branch, and was involved in planning that branch's role in the economy as a whole, most women were effectively excluded from such decision-making processes, and therefore from a large area of kibbutz affairs. This lies at the root of the complaint that women do not participate actively in kibbutz politics: much of the very technical know-how and experience needed to do so is simply not available to them, and the areas in which they do not participate are considered to be among the most important of community concerns.

Many women on Goshen were dissatisfied with their lives, and particularly their work. They complained either that they could not find a job, or that their existing work was monotonous. Of five young women who left Goshen during my fieldwork, three had been unable to find work which suited them (the fourth married out, and the fifth left after an unhappy love affair). An older women, who had been removed from her job as kibbutz nurse because she gossiped too much, had spent years looking for alternative work: finally, in desperation, an ancient knitting machine was resurrected from a store room, and she tried to make it work. This kept her busy for some weeks, but the general opinion was that she would not stick to the knitting, and would never find a 'proper job'.

Among the younger men of Goshen, particularly those who had come as adult immigrants, there operated an informal ideology about women (not officially sanctioned), which many people in the

West would consider sexist. They frequently, publicly and unashamedly, discussed the attractiveness (or otherwise) and sexual availability of young women on Goshen, especially those who came as volunteer workers. When a television programme on 'Women's Liberation' in America was screened, it was greeted by these young men with derision and ribaldry, and references to the sexual frustrations of 'women's libbers' (a derogatory term which expresses their attitudes fully). A suitable wife for these men had not 'slept around': although all couples lived together before they got married, such arrangements were normally seen as preludes to marriage, not casual affairs. Whereas a young man who had had a number of affairs was to a degree admired, a female equivalent was considered a tramp. But, once married, men were fiercely protective of their wives. During my fieldwork, one of them had to be physically restrained from assaulting another who, he thought, had been looking with too much interest at his wife. It was clear that wives were seen as property, to be treated as the man wished: I observed cases in which wives were publicly humiliated by their husbands, and there were cases of wife beating (which also occurs on other kibbutzim). Wife beating can be seen as 'coercive control' (Dobash and Dobash, 1980, p. 15), expressing the fundamentally patriarchal nature of a society in which women are the inferiors and possessions of men.

Older male members of Goshen, together with some of the kibbutz-educated younger ones, professed disgust at the ideas and behaviour just described. Their attitudes towards women were much more liberal, and they treated women more like equals. Older men felt that women kibbutz members had already been emancipated by the kibbutz, especially by comparison with their former *shtetl* sisters; women were no longer confined to the nuclear family home, housekeeping and looking after children. In the kibbutz, they had education and the opportunity to take part in politics, and no woman was financially dependent on her husband. Among this liberal group, there was evidence of the failure to examine all the causes and consequences of and remedies for the subordination of women referred to in the discussion of the early kibbutz pioneers.

For example, when Simone de Beauvoir, the distinguished writer, came to Israel to receive an award in 1975, a party from Goshen (two thirds women, one third mainly older men) went to a meeting arranged by the kibbutz movement, chaired by a male pioneer of Goshen, at which she was interviewed. The chairman made a speech to open the meeting: he said that while he admired her, and the work she had done for women's emancipation, he must set the record straight by stating that the main purpose of the kibbutz movement was the struggle for socialism. With the achievement of a truly socialist society (outside the kibbutz as well as within it, he implied), women would be emancipated automatically. Modern feminists were diverting attention from the real struggle, and were bourgeois. De Beauvoir replied to the effect that women's struggle had to be independent because women had to fight both capitalism and patriarchy: if they failed to do so, male oppression would continue. This brought no reaction from the audience, which otherwise applauded frequently, especially when she gave support to Israel and the kibbutz movement. Later in the meeting, some women in the audience stood up and argued for a modern type of feminism. They were jeered at and shouted down by other members of the audience, though not by the party from Goshen: this party comprised people who were better educated and more concerned about political issues generally and feminism in particular than most members of Goshen. They enjoyed the meeting, and were interested to hear what de Beauvoir had to say; one pioneer woman, asked her opinion of the chairman's views, replied 'Oh, take no notice of him: he's always had verbal diarrhoea.'

Her dismissive attitude is indicative of the fact that whatever the ideology and behaviour of male kibbutz members, many kibbutz women do not passively accept the attitudes and actions which most men try to impose upon them, nor do they meekly adopt the roles and status which kibbutz structure seems to indicate. First, women of Goshen and other kibbutzim have developed alternative ways of influencing kibbutz affairs; secondly, they have recently been seeking new sources of satisfaction in their lives; thirdly, there are examples of efforts to develop a more radical analysis of the position of women in the kibbutz movement.

Though kibbutz women are effectively barred from participation in public kibbutz politics, they are very active in the informal decision-making arena. This involves the discussion of matters which may eventually be considered more formally – sometimes a formal gathering such as the General Assembly, the weekly meeting of all the members of a kibbutz and its highest authority, may 'rubber stamp' decisions already arrived at through informal discussion. There are also certain matters which are decided upon purely informally, generally those which are considered, for one reason or another, inappropriate for formal, public discussion. On Goshen for example, the reputations of individual kibbutz members with their fellows were important for the success or failure of their various enterprises in the community, such as finding suitable jobs, getting permission for study leave, driving lessons, sundry other luxuries and the like. Building on a good reputation, it was possible to collect support for a vote in one's favour at the General Assembly. The development of people's reputations and the mobilisation of support took place in the informal political arena. Judgements on moral and personal issues were also reached informally: for example, those who misbehaved could be ostracised through the spread of rumour and gossip, prospective candidates for membership could be assessed, then welcomed or otherwise, and messages of criticism could be passed through the communication network.

Women's high level of activity in the informal political process can be partly explained by two facts. First, they tended to work together in rather quieter work places than men. Secondly, because all community members used the services and therefore came into contact with the service workers, women tended to have wide networks of regular contacts throughout the community. But it is also true that Goshen's women actively sought participation in informal politics, knowing that this was the main way they could influence at least some community affairs: many of them were very skilled at passing on just the right kind of information to just the right people, and were conscious of the influence they could exercise.

Return to familism?

Latterly, women in the kibbutz movement have demanded greater involvement in their children's upbringing. This so-called 'return to familism' has taken two main forms. The first is that women now spend more time with their children and the regime in the children's houses has become less rigid than it once was. In the 1950s on Goshen, mothers were allowed to see their children only at specified times during the day, whereas by the 1970s, they were in the habit of making more frequent, casual visits. In some kibbutzim (not Goshen), extra rooms where children may spend the night have been built onto family homes (at considerable expense). Secondly, work in the children's houses has become the most desirable kind of work for women themselves. This contrasts with the situation in the early days of Degania, the first kibbutz, described by Baratz (1954), when one woman caring for all the children was seen as a convenient way of keeping as many mothers as possible at work in the fields and the other services. On Goshen, competition among women for work in the children's houses was fierce and such work was considered infinitely more pleasant and desirable than the alternatives. Training for the work was available, and it therefore offered the advantageous opportunity to become an indispensable permanent worker, a 'good kibbutznik' (though pregnancies could still disrupt women's careers).

Rosner (1967), Tiger and Shepher (1975) and Spiro (1979) have seen the return to familism in its various forms as a resurgence of women's biological predisposition to care for children. I disagree fundamentally with such an interpretation, particularly in view of the many social, cultural and historical factors, quite independent of biology, which have given rise to the trend (Bowes, 1978). Classic anthropological evidence of the very wide variation in male and female roles which are possible in society, whatever the biological constraints (e.g. Mead, 1977), strengthens my disagreement. The 'return to familism' can be more usefully interpreted as an attempt by kibbutz women to win themselves a more valued role in their communities. While cooking, cleaning and laundry are derided as 'unproductive work', childcare, expressing faith in children as the future of the kibbutz (cf. Spiro, 1972) and offering possibilities for women to become 'good kibbutzniks', is respected.

Compared with other Israeli women and many Israeli men, kibbutz women are actually in a position of some privilege. At least they can choose to 'return to familism'. The presence of non-member workers on the kibbutz in the form of volunteers from abroad aids members' careers, helping them become established in permanent skilled jobs, as volunteers do less skilled or seasonal work (cf. Bowes, 1980). Although permanent skilled jobs are available more readily for men, this mechanism still operates for women, freeing them from the very lowest status jobs such as washing up, serving at table and ironing, which might be 'women's work'. Because volunteers do such jobs, women are freed to do what they see as rather more interesting and valued work, particularly in child care. A similar argument holds with respect to hired workers, who can amount to up to 50 per cent of the labour force in kibbutzim with industrial branches (Leviatan, 1973), and almost invariably do unskilled, monotonous work.

Although one rationale for setting up industrial branches is often said to have been the provision of fine work for women's nimble fingers (e.g. Don, 1977), it is clear that women have rejected the opportunity offered to them. The work is done by hired workers (some of whom are women), the kibbutz prospers, and the women members pursue the 'return to familism'.

Younger women on Goshen were divided in their aspirations. Most hoped to get married and have families, but they foresaw different ways of doing so. At least three women in their twenties, sabras of Goshen,[3] stated that their ambition was to 'be a housewife', that is, to give up kibbutz life for a husband and a house to care for. Others were horrified by such a suggestion: they believed themselves equal to men in every way, and entitled to participate fully in communal life. Some questioned the current roles of women and men's attitudes towards them in the kibbutz movement generally, and began tentatively to work towards change, for example through writing articles for the kibbutz news-sheet. These women were influenced by the contemporary European and North American women's movements, but were hesitant about starting their own groups. When a group was initiated on another kibbutz, the response was mixed. On the one hand they were shocked to realise that such a thing was necessary in a kibbutz where women were after all, already independent (here, their views accorded with those of the pioneers). On the other hand, they were beginning to realise that groups might be useful. They were sure of their opinion of the sexist ideology I described, considering it despicable, calling those who subscribed to it 'disgusting', and vigorously fighting any suggestions that women were, or should be, inferior or subsevient to men. They tried to argue with those who wanted to be housewives, though gave up when they made little headway.

'The problem of the woman'

In the kibbutz movement generally, there has long been concern with what is termed 'the problem of the woman'. Leon (1964) sees the root of the problem, which has made many women dissatisfied with kibbutz life, lying in the area of women's work, their concentration in the low valued services and the lack of skill and training opportunities. In 1958, the General Council of the Kibbutz Artzi (a meeting of delegates and officials of the constituent kibbutz) called for more discussion of women's roles and status, constructive attempts to improve their job satisfaction (by more training), an end to the view of women as inherently suited for service work, and recognition of the fact that many kibbutz women were restless because of the status to which they had been relegated (Viteles 1967, pp. 331ff). The issue was brought to the Council by a group of women involved in movement administration who had sent questionnaires to Kibbutz Artzi kibbutzim and collected responses indicating widespread dissatisfaction among women. The General Council, it should be noted, had no power to direct kibbutzim to specific courses of action. It could only make recommendations which the communities might or might not implement. It is clear that in many kibbutzim of the 1970s, not least Goshen, there had been few improvements in the position of women in the 20 years since the General Council's recommendations. Furthermore, it should be noted that the delegates to the General Council and other such bodies tended, and still tend to be drawn from the minority of, predominantly male, kibbutz members, interested in wider political issues and prepared to do long hours of committee work. Much of the information presented to meetings today still comes from surveys, now carried out by movement institutes, which are much removed from the everyday life and everyday concerns of the average kibbutz member. Cynical kibbutz veterans say that social surveys are the new ideology of the kibbutz movement.

The seeming isolation of movement-level discussions from the kibbutzim, and the apparent lack of effect of movement-level recommendations on the position of women suggest that change within the kibbutz movement in the position of women is unlikely to come from its formal policy making bodies. It may be that the recent discussions such as those I observed on Goshen, and the famous 'return to familism', which has come from kibbutz women themselves, are more likely to be decisive in the long run if change, in whatever direction, is to occur.

The Israeli context

Thus examination of movement history shows how kibbutz women have attained their present roles and status, and how the kibbutz itself has become, ideologically and structurally, increasingly patriarchal since its early days. In a longer historical perspective, instead of one woman being dependent on one man, as was the case in the *shtetl*, all the women members of the kibbutz are now dependent on all the male members. There is constant evidence that the women have been unhappy with developments, and that many have actively resisted them. Their dissatisfaction and resistance appear to have had relatively little impact however, except regarding childrearing, for which women are in any case thought to be especially suited. In order to begin to evolve a full explanation for these developments, and particularly for the fact that the kibbutz women seem to have lost out despite their efforts on the contrary, it is necessary to look at several things: first at aspects of the role of the kibbutz movement in Israeli society as a whole, secondly, at the interaction between the kibbutz movement and the wider society, and finally at the way in which political conflicts are expressed at different levels, ultimately conditioning the role and status of women kibbutz members.

The investigation of these issues is complicated by more general problems of social scientific research in Israel, which has tended, consciously or unconsciously, to be ideologically biased (Cohen, 1965; Asad, 1975; Teeffelen, 1977). Studies of the kibbutzim have tended to conform to movement ideology, for example, by defining the kibbutz rigidly as a community of members when in reality, as Shepher (1980) points out, its boundaries are more ambiguous; by minimising conflict within the community (even Evens (1975 and 1980) heavily disguises the case of embarrassing conflict he analyses); and by isolating the kibbutz analytically from the wider society (cf. Rayman, 1981). Movement-allied research (e.g. Rosner, 1967) places disproportionate faith in questionnaire surveys. One of its main purposes is to argue that kibbutzim offer lessons for other societies (e.g. Blasi, 1980; Bartolke *et al.*, 1980) and it adopts unquestioned, ideologically-based assumptions about the nature and history of the kibbutz movement (cf. Bowes, 1978). By paying more attention to the conflict dimensions of the kibbutz and Israeli society, the present discussion intends to avoid the problems of earlier material, and to offer fresh insights into the position of women in the kibbutz movement.

The early kibbutz pioneers were certainly idealistic and committed to building a socialist way of life, but they were also caught up in the wider Zionist movement upon which they depended for land and financial support. Early in the history of the Yishuv (the pre-State Jewish settlement in Palestine), the Zionist establishment tended to be suspicious of the kibbutz 'communists', but once it had realised the economic and military strengths of kibbutz settlement, it gave the kibbutz movement increasing material and ideological support (Kanovsky, 1966). The kibbutz movement was furthermore not an inward-looking utopia, but aimed to act as a series of revolutionary cells, both as examples for other elements of the Yishuv to follow, and as active workers for the achievement of socialism throughout the Yishuv and the creation of a socialist state. Kibbutzim therefore welcomed opportunities to develop close relationships with the Zionist establishment, and by the latter part of the British Mandate over Palestine they had themselves joined the pillars of that establishment. Not only did they come to represent the public face of the Jewish pioneer, fighting against all odds to 'make the desert bloom', but representatives of the kibbutz movement became directly involved in the highest echelons of the political and military hierarchy.[4] The roots of the alliance between the capitalist elite and the socialist elite, which Hanegbi *et al.* (1971) see as crucial to the structure of Israeli society today, are therefore to be found in the Yishuv.

By the 1930s, many elements in the Yishuv were working towards the establishment of a Jewish State. The overwhelming importance of the campaign for all sectors of the Yishuv, even those which did not support it (Elon, 1983), cannot be denied. Since the kibbutz movement was firmly tied to the rest of the Zionist movement, it was to be expected that its internal character would correspond, at least to a degree, with the character of that link as a whole, and that it would be coloured by the nature of the struggle for the State. The kibbutz movement supported the moves for statehood.

Rein argues that the constitution of the fighting force in pre-State Zionist activity was crucial in conditioning the legal, ideological and practical position of women in the State. She writes:

> At this critical time for the Jews of Palestine, the establishment of a viable fighting force created a basis for the nation-state. While the British Mandate ruled politically, and political decisions were being taken elsewhere, the growth of a serious fighting force became a symbol of potency for the aspiring nation. At last, Jews were showing their strength and power. The men who had come from generations of emasculated manhood were at last fulfilling their deepest needs to assert themselves and gain recognition. Any success achieved by women in this field would have threatened this image. The men were fighting a private fight from which women were excluded. (1980, p. 47)

In fact, women did fight alongside men, especially in the Palmach.[5] Rein shows that their contribution was systematically undervalued, and that from early on, they were placed in separate units, away from front-line action, and given jobs as wireless operators, nurses and the like. She sees the army as a symbol of manhood, and argues that it was therefore inevitable that women should be excluded or at least relegated to a service role. Certainly, their contribution was given little ideological value, and as the armed struggle 'made specific the tone of the country and allowed the elitism of the fighting male Jew to take hold of the culture and mould the lives of the people' (Rein, 1980, p. 48). Women's secondary position in Israeli society became entrenched.

Hazleton (1977, p. 137) makes the parallels between women's position in the army, the kibbutz and Israeli society as a whole explicit:

> The Israel Defence Forces (IDF) and the kibbutz are probably the two most famous images of Israel. They symbolize the duality and simultaneity of life and death – sword and plowshare. And they are the stars in the firmament of the myth of Israeli women's liberation . . . But . . . though their afterglow lingers on, both the army and the kibbutz are prime examples not of the liberation of Israeli women, but of their imposed and accepted regression into the feminine stereotype.

By the 1930s, kibbutz women were struggling to take on the roles of men, and had achieved some success within the kibbutz movement. But they were already moving into service work as more children were born and as living standards improved. Women's involvement in the physical struggle for the State paralleled their experience in the kibbutzim, and, it seems, added even greater ideological kudos to 'men's work' and, importantly, to manhood. Despite their struggle on other fronts and the fact that women's roles in the kibbutz had changed from those of tradition, the kibbutz women were unable to penetrate this male preserve. In addition, because the army became an overridingly important symbol of the state, that state itself became another male preserve, and women's roles in the kibbutz, the army and the state were similar. If there were forces within the kibbutz movement itself militating against the success of women's struggles, outside it such forces were infinitely greater, inexorable and unopposable.

The character of the Israeli state today, like all states, is determined by historical experience. The ideology of manhood identified by Rein (1980), Hazleton (1977) and others, persists, and has a powerful influence on the position of women in the country as a whole, as well as within the kibbutz movement. It enjoys considerable institutional support which ensures its efficacy.

One example of this institutional support lies in the operation of the Women's Equal Rights Law (WERL) of 1951. This is a general and somewhat unspecific measure which outlaws discrimination against women, gives married women equal rights to handle property, and to custody of their children. It prohibits unilateral divorce by men without court authorisation, and allows consenting adult litigants to have cases judged according to religious courts if they so wish. Lahav (1977) shows that these measures were passed in a deliberate attempt by the ruling Labour Party to eradicate inequalities between men and women, and were supported both by radical and moderate wings of the party. The Labour Party remained in power, however, only by maintaining a coalition with the religious parties, and in the case of WERL had to make concessions to the traditions of religion in order to get at least some measures through. One concession was the inclusion of the option of religious jurisdiction for those who wanted it. The law also left marriage and divorce within the jurisdiction of religious courts, although it did include a clause stating that civil laws protecting 'women as women' would take precedence over WERL.

Lahav (1977) gives three reasons why WERL failed to give women equal rights: first, it was too general and vague, difficult to apply in specific cases – more a declaration of principles than a piece of workable legislation. Secondly, the legislature and courts were not really committed to it, Lahav says, being rather conservative and traditionally minded, and unwilling to tighten up its clauses so that they could be used properly. For example, she notes that the law allowed for the imprisonment of a man who refused consent to divorce, but that this measure was very rarely used. It involved not only greater concessions to women's rights, but also a contravention of religious tradition. Thus, both legislature and courts seem to have deferred to tradition in the form of religious law, even where they were not obliged to do so. Thirdly, and according to Lahav, most importantly, WERL failed because it perpetuated religious jurisdiction over nearly all matters pertaining to marriage and divorce, and protected 'women as women'. Religious law, she argues, is one of the major forces in Israel preserving traditional gender roles, doing so in a way which discriminates against women. Under religious law, for example, a woman who does not wish to divorce cannot prevent a divorce taking place, whilst a man can veto a divorce, and 'keep his wife in marital bond forever' (Lahav, 1977, p. 199). With regard to the laws protecting 'women as women', she points out that these too reinforce traditional sex roles, 'women as women' meaning 'women as mothers' in practice, childcarers and weaker than men. So what the protection of 'women as women' amounts to, then, is that women may not do night work by law, and they retire from extra-domestic work at least, earlier than men. Thus traditional stereotypes, particularly religious ones, are perpetuated.[6]

The influence of religious authorities pervades the whole of Israeli society. For Jewish women. this means visits to the *mikvah* (ritual bath) before they can be married. As Tamarin (1973, p. 109) reports, the visit to the *mikvah* can be humiliating and disturbing experience for a non-religious woman. One said:

> I do not want to recall it at all. It is hard to decide whether the dominant sensation was repulsion . . ., madness . . ., or ludicrousness . . . I controlled myself for the sake of finishing as quickly as possible. Such madness in the twentieth century.

The visit is essential before marriage can take place, as only religious marriage is recognised in civil law. Should the marriage break up, a religious divorce ceremony is required. Kibbutzim of the Kibbutz Artzi federation are officially atheist (other kibbutzim are agnostic, and a tiny minority are religious), but their members must still comply with the law. They choose to go through legal marriage, saying their children must be recognised as legitimate by the state of which they are members, and for which they will be required to fight. 'They write "bastard" on the birth certificate,' one woman said, 'my children aren't bastards: I won't have them labelled like that.' Most of Goshen's marriages took place in town, deliberately set away from the kibbutz to minimise contact with religion. After the ceremony, there would be a big party on Goshen, to which the whole community was invited. In 1975, when one couple, much-wanted new members, held their marriage ceremony on Goshen itself, the development was criticised by other members. 'What is that rabbi doing here?' they asked. 'Why can't those two get married in town like the rest of us?' Their complaints were silenced by arguments about how much Goshen needed new members, and that the couple's parents had paid for all the food and lavish entertainment after the marriage.

Describing the divorce ceremony, a divorced woman from Goshen said:

> It was so stupid: there was my husband throwing an old shoe away. I suppose he was throwing me away really. But it seemed ridiculous.

Though they were uncomfortable with all the religious ritual, members of Goshen had no choice but to conform to it in matters of marriage and divorce, since they wanted legal marriage and legitimate children.

Conformity to religion, however, also appeared where it was not required by law. During my fieldwork, three non-Jewish women, who married into the community, underwent conversion to Judaism, a process strictly regulated by the religious authorities. This can be interpreted as a means of acquiring the 'cultural baggage' of an atheist Jew, necessary for full participation in kibbutz life. This was particularly important in connection with the community's ceremonial life, which involved certain Jewish festivals being celebrated without religious referent, but with an agricultural and historical emphasis. Furthermore, according to Israeli law, the child of a Jewish mother is automatically Jewish, and Zionist ideology has, not surprisingly, subscribed to the idea of Israel as a Jewish state (though some Zionists have argued for a bi-national state). There are many ambiguities which cannot be discussed here (but see Bowes, 1982) in the notion of a Jewish, atheist, citizen of Israel which operates in kibbutzim like Goshen. The general point is that, despite their atheism or agnosticism, kibbutz women cannot escape the influence of religion, and indeed this has increased since 1948.

The organisation of the modern Israeli army gives further institutional support to the ideology of manhood. Men do three years' army service between the ages of 18 and 21: thereafter, they do periodic reserve duty, for up to two months every year until they are 56 years old. Unmarried women do two years service, working as secretaries, guides, teachers and the like. They might work folding parachutes, a job described by Tiger and Shepher (1975, p. 189) as 'by far the most glamorous of all female tasks in the army.'[7] Official statements of the women's branch of the army reveal the women soldiers' role:

> A very important contribution of the woman soldier to the Army . . . [as well as her actual job] . . . is her very femininity that makes everything more delicate, softer than usual in the Army, which is always alert to fight. The woman soldier inspires the Army with a cultural atmosphere and helps to create social cohesion. (Tiger and Shepher, 1975, p. 187)

After their two years' service, women too may be called into the reserves, but this is very rare, and all married women are exempt from call-up.

Women in the kibbutz movement are faced with a multi-dimensional undervalued position. Within their communities, ideological evaluation of service work is low, kibbutz organisation and, its protestations notwithstanding, kibbutz ideology mean that women do service work, and that as people, they too are ideologically undervalued. Outside the kibbutz, even stronger structural forces devalue women themselves and the jobs women do: the legislature, the laws it passes, the judiciary, institutionalised religion and the army all place women generally in a subordinate position, and kibbutz women are directly affected by these structures. On the simplest level, the kibbutzim are subject to the laws of the land and must therefore comply with legislation protecting 'women as women'. This means that kibbutz men and women can only marry (and divorce) in Israel under religious law, as there is no civil marriage, and kibbutz men and women must do army service and reserve duty. In these fields, there is little opportunity for the kibbutz to be autonomous, and even where people agree to live together instead of getting married, the nature of kibbutz ideology and organisation mean that such an opportunity for autonomy is not taken up, so that, for example, great importance is attached to marriage (cf. Bowes, 1982).

The relationship between Israeli society and the kibbutz movement is not, however, a simple case of determinism whereby the 'outside' (Israeli society) impinges on the 'inside' (the kibbutz movement) and shapes it, because the kibbutz is not an autonomous enclave, but has a major stake in the Israeli state and society as a whole. The kibbutz movement forms part of the Israeli elite. Hanegbi *et al.* (1971) argue that the Israeli 'ruling class' consists of an alliance between a bourgeoisie (the elite of the private capitalist sector) and elite representatives of the labour movement (the public sector, including kibbutzim). The country itself is supported by outside aid, which is funnelled through the elite to other sectors of the society, and is thus the main basis for elite control. Hanegbi *et al.* (1971) argue that class conflict in Israeli society is thereby suppressed, as potentially antagonistic groups compete for a share of the largesse, rather than attempting to overthrow the system. In turn, this is reinforced by the commitment to national security, 'the war', which they argue overrides class interests, and such interests are further blurred by the existence of ethnic differences which divert people's attention. According to this formulation, the kibbutz movement is tied to Israeli society by much more than ideology, much more than legal, religious and military factors: it is directly involved in maintaining the very existence of the state *vis à vis* other states, and in reinforcing the existing state structure.

Labour and Likud

At the time of my fieldwork, the vast majority of kibbutzim were formally allied to the Labour Party under Prime Minister Rabin, or one of its coalition partners, and played a large and direct part in the formulation and implementation of government policy (cf. Aronoff, 1977). Representatives of the kibbutzim worked for the Labour Party, on secondment, and the kibbutzim formed a reliable base of Party support. Since the foundation of the state in 1948, the kibbutzim themselves have been involved, for example, in passing of the WERL, the increasing influence of institutionalised religion (due to the Labour Party's concessions to religious political parties in return for their coalition support), the organisation of the army, and various other measures. Kibbutz women's attempts to improve their position were thus further hindered by the fact that kibbutz representatives (mainly men) were, at state level, involved in developing far-reaching institutional supports for the 'ideology of manhood'.

After the victory of Begin's right-wing Likud government in 1977, the kibbutzim generally lost not only their direct involvement in government, but also much of their prestige and ideological dominance (Sherman, 1982). After the shock of defeat the Labour Party and its left wing coalition partners now had to recognise that it was no longer the guaranteed party of government, and the kibbutzim that they were no longer necessarily a dominant voice in the land. The consequences of these changes are as yet (1985) unclear, but it is doubtful whether they will alter the position of kibbutz women. The Labour government in power was subject to the will of the religious parties, which strove to maintain the traditional position of women in Judaism. In opposition, it faced a government committed to the same policy, and, in any case bound to it, for Likud, too, was dependent on religious party coalition support to stay in power. The same was true of the Peres Labour government of 1984, and, given the system of proportional representation in Israel, there is no reason to suppose that religious parties will lose their power in the near future. Furthermore, issues such as protest about the Lebanon invasion in 1982, and involvement in the peace movement preoccupied those kibbutz members concerned with wider politics. Like the push for the state in the Yishuv, such preoccupations are likely to continue to crowd out active work for change in the position of women.

Since the early days of the kibbutz movement, women kibbutz members have fought for their place as equal partners within their communities. They were successful in their fight to be allowed to do 'men's work', but their very success actually contributed to the devaluation of 'women's work', and the subsequent devaluation of women themselves. The structure of the contemporary kibbutz places women in a subordinate position to men, excluding them from 'productive' work and important areas of politics. Attitudes of kibbutz men and women to this situation vary, but generally the women still fight for improvements, either asking for more direct control over childcare or less commonly espousing modern feminism.

I have argued that the women's own activities are more likely to result in change than the discussions at movement level, which are out of touch with ordinary kibbutz members. But, as I have shown, it is essential to consider the kibbutz women's fight for change in the context of Israeli society as a whole. It is clear that legal, religious, political and military state-level structures impinge directly on the kibbutz, and, in particular, tend to reinforce traditional gender stereotypes. At the same time, it is essential to recognise that the kibbutzim themselves have been intimately involved in the development of the state, and are therefore responsible for structures which perpetuate traditional sex roles. Therefore, if it can be demonstrated that state structure is dictated by national-level conflict, as Hanegbi *et al.* (1971) suggest, then this must also be true for the position of women in the kibbutz. Then for change in the kibbutz and women's position within it, change is necessary in the state and society as a whole, which, it seems, can only come with peace.

Notes

1. Very few men have permanent service jobs. And many of those to be seen in the kitchen and dining room will be doing *toranut*, extra work for which turns are taken. It should be noted that kibbutz men treat work in the dining room and kitchen, done as part of their *toranut* duties, very lightly, as rather a joke.
2. These arrangements differ significantly from those elsewhere known as 'maternity leave'. There was no employer-employee relationship, the women's situation being dictated by the fact that they were kibbutz members, required to work for the community whenever and wherever they were available. Particular jobs were not *de jure* the prerogative of particular individuals, though *de facto* this might develop because of the process of getting skilled. So for example a trained *metapelet* (children's nurse) might return to the same work after her baby's birth,

but be allocated to a different children's house. Or an unskilled kitchen worker might be put back in the kitchen, or find herself in the *communa*.

3. *Sabra* = (lit) a prickly pear, (fig) someone born in Israel, described as tough and thorny outside, and sweet and tender underneath. 'Sabras' is an anglicised plural.
4. Davis (1977, p. 27) states 'though barely 3 per cent of the total Israeli-Jewish population, people of kibbutz origin contribute approximately 25 per cent of Israeli cabinet members, 22 per cent if not higher, of the Israeli middle and high military command and constitute the overwhelming majority of air-force pilots, the elite unit of the Israeli army'.
5. Palmach (shock troops): a kibbutz-based, elite group of Jewish fighters, founded in 1941. For opposing analyses, see Segre, 1971 (Palmach as heroic) and Weinstock, 1979 (Palmach as villainous).
6. The study of the interactions and conflicts between civil and religious law in Israel is very complex, and can only be touched upon here. Lahav's (1977) article gives greater detail on the conflicts over women's rights, and provides useful references for further research. Furthermore, there are disputes about the nature of religious law: for example, Webber (1983) indicates that protection of 'women as women' (which originates in the *halacha*, the orthodox religious law) can be seen negatively as a form of discrimination, but also more positively as a means of freeing women to fulfil their primary duties, domestic work and childcare.
7. A few women, at least from 1979, acted as instructors for men doing basic training, due, it seems to a shortage of men. This is thought by some to be more glamorous than folding parachutes (thanks to a former soldier for this information). However, it is still the case that women's position in the army is a subordinate one, and they are not involved in combat.

References

Aronoff, Myron Joel (1977) *Power and Ritual in the Israel Labour Party* (Assen, Netherlands: Van Gorcum).

Asad, Talal (1975) 'Anthropological Texts and Ideological Problems: An Analysis of Cohen on Arab Villages in Israel', *Economy and Society*, vol. 4, no. 3, pp. 251–282.

Baratz, Joseph (1954) *A Village by the Jordan, Degania* (London: Harvill Press).

Bartolke, Klaus, Bergmann, Theodor and Liegle, Ludwig (1980) *Integrated Cooperatives in the Industrial Society. The Example of the Kibbutz* (Assen, Netherlands: Van Gorcom).

Blasi, Joseph (1980) *The Communal Future: the Kibbutz and the Utopian Dilemma* (Norwood, Pennsylvania: Norwood Editions).

Bowes, Alison (1978) 'Women in the Kibbutz Movement', *Sociological Review* (NS), vol. 26, no. 2, pp. 237–262.

Bowes, Alison (1980) 'Strangers in the Kibbutz: Volunteer Workers in an Israeli Community' *Man* (NS), vol. 15, no. 4, pp. 665–681.

Bowes, Alison (1982) 'Atheism in a Religious Society: The Culture of Unbelief in an Israeli Kibbutz', in Davis, J., ed. *Religious Organisation and Religious Experience* (London: Academic Press).

Cohen, Abner (1965) *Arab Border Villages in Israel* (Manchester: Manchester University Press).

Cohen, Erik (1966) 'Progress and Communality: Value Dilemmas in the Collective Movement', *International Review of Community Development*, nos. 15–16, pp. 3–18.

Davis, Uri (1977) *Israel: Utopia Incorporated* (London: Zed Press).

Dobash, R. Emerson and Dobash, Russell P. (1980) *Violence Against Wives: A Case Against the Patriarchy* (London: Open Books).

Don, Yehuda (1977) 'Industrialization in Advanced Rural Communities: the Israeli Kibbutz', *Sociologia Ruralis* vol. 17, nos 1–2, pp. 59–74.

Elon, Amos (1983) *The Israelis: Founders and Sons* (Harmondsworth: Penguin).

Evens, Terence M. S. (1975) 'Stigma, Ostracism and Expulsion in an Israeli Kibbutz' in Moore, Sally F. and Myerhoff, G. B. (eds) *Symbol and Politics in Communal Ideology* (Ithaca and London: Cornell University Press).

Evens, Terence M. S. (1980) 'Stigma and Morality in a Kibbutz' in Marx, Emanuel (ed.) *A Composite Portrait of Israel* (London: Academic Press).

Hanegbi, Haim, Machover, Moshe and Orr, Akiva (1971) 'The Class Nature of Israeli Society' *New Left Review*, no. 65.

Hazleton, Lesley (1977) *Israeli Women* (New York: Simon and Schuster).

Kanovsky, Eliyahu (1966) *The Economy of the Israeli Kibbutz* (Cambridge MA: Harvard University Press).

Katzenelson-Rubashow, R. (1976) *The Plough Woman: Records of the Pioneer Women of Palestine* (Westport CT: Hyperion Press, first published in 1932).

Lahav, Pnina (1977) 'Raising the Status of Women through Law: the Case of Israel', *Signs*, vol. 3, no. 1, pp. 193–209.

Leon, Dan (1964) *Kibbutz – A Portrait from Within* (Tel Aviv: 'Israeli Horizons' in collaboration with World Hashomer Hatzair).

Leviatan, Uri (1973) 'The Industrial Process in Israeli Kibbutzim: Problems and Their Solutions', in Curtis, M. and Chertoff, M. S. *Israel: Social Structure and Change* (New Brunswick NJ: Transaction Books).

Maimon, Ada (1962) *Women Build a Land* (New York: Herzl Press).

Mead, Margaret (1977) *Sex and Temperament in Three Primitive Societies* (London: Routledge and Kegan Paul, first published in 1935).

Mednick, Martha S. (1975) *Social Change and Sex Role Inertia: The Case of the Kibbutz* (Givat Haviva, Israel: Publications Department).

Oakley, Ann (1981) *Subject Women* (London: Martin Robertson).

Rayman, Paula (1981) *The Kibbutz Community and Nation Building* (Princeton NJ: Princeton University Press).

Rein, Natalie (1980) *Daughters of Rachel: Women in Israel* (Harmondsworth: Penguin).

Rosner, Menachem (1967) 'Women in the Kibbutz: Changing Status and Concepts', *Asian and African Studies*, no. 3, pp. 35–68.
Segre, Vittorio Dan (1971) *Israel: a Society in Transition* (London: Oxford University Press).
Shepher, Israel (1972) *The Significance of Work Roles in the Social System of a Kibbutz* (Unpublished PhD thesis, University of Manchester).
Shepher, Israel (1980) 'Social Boundaries of a Kibbutz' in Marx, Emanuel, *A Composite Portrait of Israel* (London: Academic Press).
Sherman, Neal (1982) 'From Government to Opposition: the Rural Settlement Movements of the Israel Labor Party in the Wake of the Election of 1977', *International Journal of Middle Eastern Studies*, no. 14, pp. 53–69.
Spiro, Melford (1972) *Kibbutz – Venture in Utopia* (New York: Schocken, first published 1956).
Spiro, Melford (1979) *Gender and Culture: Kibbutz Women Revisited* (Durham NC: Duke University Press).
Tamarin, George R. (1973) 'Primitive Pollution Fears and Compulsory Premarital Ritual' in his *The Israeli Dilemma: Essays on a Welfare State* (Rotterdam: Rotterdam University Press).
Teeffelen, Toden van (1977) *Anthropologists on Israel: A Case Study in the Sociology of Knowledge* (Amsterdam, Universiteit van Amsterdam, Anthropologisch-Sociologisch Centrum).
Tiger, Lionel and Shepher, Joseph (1975) *Women in the Kibbutz* (New York: Harcourt Brace Jovanovich).
Viteles, Harry (1967) *A History of the Cooperative Movement in Israel* (Book 2: The Evolution of the Kibbutz Movement) (London: Vallentine Mitchell).
Webber, Jonathan (1983) 'Between Law and Custom: Women's Experience of Judaism', in Holden, P., ed., *Women's Religious Experience* (London: Croom Helm).
Weinstock, Nathan (1979) *Zionism: False Messiah* (London: Ink Links).

8 Brittany: Politics and Women in a Minority World

MARYON McDONALD

Ethnicity and women

This chapter deals with two topics which have, in recent years, become well-established as proper and fashionable objects of study: ethnic or minority identity, and the position of women. Brittany is the home of a much-publicised Celtic-speaking minority and, in this publicity, Breton women have often been metaphorically summoned on to a national and international stage and required to be the most authentic repositories and guardians of Breton culture. The following paragraphs might be seen as a contribution to an understanding of ethnicity and to the study of the social identity of women. However, theories of ethnicity and of the position and role of women are very much a part of the subject-matter under study. By this I mean quite simply that the people under study have their own theories of who they are and of how they should behave.

One of the implications of this is that certain ideas which we may ourselves accept and live by, and which may sometimes inform, and be the tools of, our analyses, have here to be treated as part of the subject-matter under study. For example, a determination to restore minority identity, to rescue it from majority oppression, or similarly to save women from male domination, and from frills and false consciousness, have become well-established ambitions of the educated, the committed, and the concerned. They are, by the terms of their own constitution, ambitions of self-proclaimed praiseworthiness. Oppression and false consciousness cannot be good. I do not decry the practical virtue of such ambitions but I do find them interesting, and they can be treated as part of the ethnography. Part of my research in Brittany has involved the study of well-educated people who, in various ways, pursue self-evidently virtuous ambitions of this kind. They are people who may be very much like us: very much like those who write and, one might presume, those who read these chapters.

These well-educated people are the members of the Breton movement. This movement is devoted to a defence of Breton language and culture, and, in the political arena, it is a movement of broadly 'autonomist' or separatist ambition. It is common for militants and activists who speak on behalf of minority or ethnic populations to appropriate other people's problems and to dress themselves in every available metaphor of oppression. The Breton movement, and other minority movements in France, have busily amassed images and self-images (for example, of being 'colonised' peoples) which appeal to an educated and politically radical morality. So, too, have various sections of the women's movement. Structural analogies and conflations with other conflicts or problems are common. France's ethnic minorities and the women's movement have also appropriated each other's image of oppression; this is a point to which I shall refer again, specifically for the Breton case. The modern causes of the Breton movement and women's liberation have been made one, in opposition to the majority/male 'system'. Ethnic identity and female identity have thus been drawn into mutual support, but this is true of their nineteenth-century, romantic construction as well as of the modern desire for 'liberation' from these very same constructs. In the nineteenth century, Breton identity and femininity were drawn up out of a common oppositional symbolism; then, in the twentieth century, and particularly since the late 1960s, Breton identity has been aligned with the oppositional symbolism of feminism. Before expanding on these points, I want to give a brief introduction to the political context of France, the majority context in which the minority and female identities in question exist.

The French context

France is a country with large indigenous minorities, and there has been no strong desire in the past, on the part of France's central authorities, to summon these minorities into official existence. In comparison with Great Britain, the history of France appears as one of insecurity and frequent constitutional change, and much of the political reflection which, in Britain, could be invested in conjuring internal minorities into existence, was concerned, in France, with the existence of the French nation itself. France has been occupied by foreign forces, enemies and allies, four times in the last two hundred years, and, from a combination of external interference and internal self-consciousness, has tried to define its way, over the same period, through two monarchies, one consulate, two empires, five republics, one definitive revolution, the Paris Commune, the Vichy regime, and May 1968. Faced, since 1789, with this succession of external threat and internal upheaval, Paris has never been sufficiently sure of the integrity of France to wish into existence other identities within it – that would have risked rendering even more problematic the nature of France itself. On the contrary, France and the Jacobin State have given to the world a model of directive centralisation. This French State has not, until very recent years, been a sufficiently secure definitional unit for it readily to tolerate the theoretical or actual possibility of variety within its boundaries. There was no comfortable political space that a minority could occupy.

The French language and French national identity have been inextricably linked, and it is only in relatively recent times – since the new, self-consciously international context of the post-war years – that the cause of promoting any regional language or dialect has become respectable in national, political debate rather than being cast as dangerously reactionary or seditious. And it is only since the 1960s and 1970s that the cause of a regional language such as Breton has moved from being the property of political reaction to being the property of the political left. This cause became the property of the political left under a broadly right-wing regime, giving the national left an oppositional ticket and the possibility of co-opting the vote of the 'minority' enthusiasts. Decentralisation was also on offer. The groups and societies that make up the Breton movement tend nevertheless to take a definitional distance from the national parties of the left, and try resolutely to remain un-French. Moreover, many would not see the decentralisation of France as in any way synonymous with their own vision of an autonomous, and distinctly un-French, Brittany. At least part of this vision derives from a wistful and provocative comparison with the position of other Celtic areas such as Wales and Scotland; however, the internal structure of the United Kingdom might readily permit such areas a political autonomy and nationhood in a way that the French context would not.

The ethnography which illustrates certain aspects of the Breton situation may appear singularly undramatic within a volume that deals with other situations where political struggles are vigorous and deadly. The Breton movement has the ability to be noisy, to engage in guerilla-like strategies, to throw bombs, and is not without its history of bloodshed. However, it is very much more a movement whose force and continuity resides in the elision of a Breton/French opposition with whatever political conflicts have otherwise been rife in France. I focus here on just two conflicts which seem to be particularly relevant (for further details, see McDonald 1982). The two conflicts are these: first, in the nineteenth century, the 'Breton' cause was one recension of national church/state battles in France. Second, in more modern times, it has been an important feature of post-1968 leftist opposition to the Fifth Republic. In the ranks of the Breton movement, this was a structural and political opposition in which 'Breton' gained, in contra-distinction to the 'system', an image of all that established proprieties were not. This could, according to faction or context, mean anything from a rightfully autonomous Breton nation to a 'let-it-all-hang-out' liberation. These two conflicts are particularly relevant not only because they each mark a high point in the Breton movement's own history – its beginnings in the nineteenth century and then its modern hey-day – but also because each has invoked women, or an image of them.

The political imagery of women and of regional languages such as Breton have often been closely associated at the national level. It is of some significance here that women in France gained the vote only in 1945: it had always been feared that women were too closely linked with the church and the forces of clerical reaction. I shall be outlining some of the ways in which images of Breton and of women have been associated both by those who uphold French and by those who, on the contrary, have conflated an image of women and of Breton culture in opposition to the majority, French world.

Two worlds

My research in Brittany began in 1978. I spent a year based in the regional capital of Rennes, studying, meeting, travelling, and demonstrating, with members of the modern Breton movement; and then a year living in a peasant village in Finistère, the most western, and traditionally the most solidly Breton-speaking, *département* of Brittany. In a sense, this covers two worlds: the world of the militants of the Breton movement, and the world of the peasants. Each of these worlds has a view of the other, and each has its own means of resolving any contradictions posed by the other. The militants of the movement are educated, urban outsiders, and they are usually seen as such by rural populations even if they can summon up (as much of France, and especially Brittany, still can) rural origins for themselves. Since the early or mid-1970s, a few militants have been living in and around the Finistère village of Kerguz (which had a population of thirty-two, including myself, when I first moved there in 1979). Kerguz is a village situated within the parish and administrative 'commune' (*commune*) of Plounéour-Ménez (population: 1245). It is in Kerguz that I spent my second year, and the two worlds have met here in a quite concrete way. The majority of the members of the Breton movement overall are, and always have been, well-educated, often to university level, and almost all have studiously learnt some Breton at least, having been otherwise well-schooled in French (see Beer, 1977). The peasants of Kerguz are native Breton-speakers, and have had relatively little schooling. This is an important, if not wholly surprising, difference between the militants and the 'people' on whose behalf they claim to speak.

Femininity

A political femininity

In France, femininity as an ideal image of woman, her nature and her place, became firmly established in the nineteenth century, and particularly during the reign of Louis-Philippe. Much of the structural imagery involved in the feminine/masculine duality (with all its positively or negatively evaluated correlates of irrationality/rationality, and so on) was carried on from the elite salons of the eighteenth century. The fighting women of the Revolution were placed in parentheses, and by the 1830s, under Louis-Philippe, the *citoyenne* of the 1789 Revolution had already become, once again, *Madame*. The dominant political opposition groups of the nineteenth century – the republicans on the one hand, and the Ultra-Catholic and aristocratic legitimists on the other – both sent their ideal woman back to the home, and to wifely and maternal duties, but not without a certain charm and glamour.

This was also a time of wider material and secular prosperity. The rationalism of this new technological age, under the 'bourgeois king', Louis-Philippe, was quite explicitly characterised in some educated circles as a 'masculine' force, and in contra-distinction to this, the moral and spiritual values of sentiment, intuition and prudent tradition became equated with a 'femininity' that might counteract rationalism's excess.[1] The idea of women as the guardians of morality and tradition was not an entirely new notion, but the symbolic dualities involved now took on a coherence they had never had before. The influential Breton writer, Emile Souvestre (much influenced by other writers such as Fenimore Cooper and Chateaubriand) wrote the first major work to present the Breton language and people in a romantic aspect, as a sadly disappearing world. The symbolism he used is particularly interesting. Although a French-speaker himself, Souvestre turned from Paris to invest his native Brittany with an untouched and disappearing, rural traditionality – a pure 'virginal beauty', he called it, that he loved as he 'could have loved a woman' (Souvestre (1835–7) 1971, pp. xiv–xv).

The metaphorical femininity which Brittany thus received, in a new romantic topography, gained confirmation from other sources. The traditionality that Souvestre had accorded Brittany was also attractive in the circles of clerical and aristocratic opposition, where political nostalgia for the *ancien régime* was rife. In the Breton case, political opposition of this kind found expression in the changing philological kinships of the French and Breton languages. After a flurry of Celtic France under Napoleon, when Breton had been boasted as surviving proof of France's peculiar Gaulish Celticness, French settled, under Louis-Philippe, into being a predominantly Latin language. The philological revolution, with its own German romanticism, also handed over to Breton an appealing, minority Celticness that linked it with insular Celtic in Britain. Such an idea was keenly taken up by certain members of a wistful Breton aristocracy, now severely threatened by the bourgeoisie in France, and, in a series of still common conflations, this new definition of the Breton language became an un-French origin and culture for the Bretons. A number of Breton nobles, scholars and clerics learnt Breton with a new political and moral enthusiasm, and they weeded out obviously 'French' terms, and actively imported some Welsh. In Britain, the image of the Celt was drawn up in opposition to the majority rationality of the Anglo-Saxon in the same way, and out of the same structures, that drew up an ideal femininity in opposition to masculinity (see Chapman 1978). Much of this was drawn from French sources.

Minority and majority, however, are tied together in mutual definition and self-definition, and the minority Celt in France is a construct of a political context different from that of the Celts in Britain. In France, the symbolism of femininity and the Celt could lend itself well to anti-republicanism. From the 1830s onwards, several Breton aristocrats, supported by a number of clergy, defined the entire Breton world into a peculiar spirituality and femininity, using the symbolic oppositions of femininity and masculinity, and Celtic and Latin, to describe and define a Breton culture and Breton nation in moral and political opposition to the self-consciously rational and increasingly secular French world that threatened their own status and influence. This was the beginning of a learned nationalist historiography in Brittany, organised around a Breton/French divide; such historiography still vaunts a Celticness in opposition to things 'French', and ancient Britons and all the insular Celtic worlds and Celtic women are summoned to voice nineteenth-century and more modern, political preoccupations (in, for example, Gwegen 1975; Markale 1976).

By the end of the nineteenth century then, we have a recognisable metaphoric of 'femininity' amongst the bourgeoisie in France, as well as amongst the clergy and the fading ranks of the aristocracy. We also have an educated conflation of this femininity and Celticness. From some members of the Breton aristocracy and clergy, who are now seen as founders of the Breton movement, and who saw themselves as moral and spiritual defenders of a distinctly 'Breton' world, we have Breton language and culture turning an oppositional and metaphorically feminine face to France. The sentiment that divided and opposed Breton and French, and Brittany and France, in this way, was one conceived by well-educated men in the context of French internal politics. Any French origins for Breton language and culture were nevertheless denied by it, as were nearly 2000 years of Latin and, notably, French influence.

Brittany, however, is in France. It has been officially part of France since the early sixteenth century, by which time some form of French had already been the language of power and nobility within Brittany for a few hundred years. Since at least the 1789 Revolution, when the French Republic was first established, the Breton population has, in one way or another, been living a certain Frenchness. In order to understand the Frenchness, and the evaluations of Breton, lived by women in Brittany, we have to return to the wider context and look briefly at the question of education. Here we find both women and Breton invoked in the quarrel of church and state, the clerical/republican battle that has so dominated French life.

Women and education

Where formal education for girls existed in the nineteenth century, it was overwhelmingly religious education, in church-run private schools, and especially so in Brittany. Yet women had, by all parties, been allotted the prime role of wife and mother, the great moral and educative force in the nation. Jules Ferry, the ardent republican who brought compulsory, free and lay education for both sexes and to all parts of France in the 1880s, was driven in 1870 to speak of women's 'secret and persistent support' for the old order, for 'the society that is passing and which we are going to chase out forever.' He went on:

> The Bishops know full well that he who holds sway over the women holds all, because he has influence firstly over the children and secondly over the husbands . . . That's why the Church wants to hold on to the women (but) democracy has to choose, on pain of death: either the women belong to science or they belong to the Church. (cited in Prost, 1968, pp. 268–9)

Ferry might well have added that either they learn some French, or continue with only Breton. It was of constant concern to educationists and politicians, right on into the early years of this century, that Breton women might know little or no French. More boys were schooled, and they also had military service, where the national language was learnt. Girls meanwhile usually had only poor-quality religious schools, if any, and often knew only Breton pious works. Women were under the church, and under the influence, too, of self-consciously Breton clerics who were known to fear the 'invasion' of French and sin in single focus. In the republican camp, therefore, it was feared that women in Brittany were in danger of being isolated and, moreover, of not bringing up French citizens.

The importance of French in the construction and maintenance of the French Republic, and French identity, is a point to which I have already alluded. Since the 1789 Revolution, France has made the French language the very definition of the French nation, of that 'single and indivisible republic', and, in a spirit of 'liberty, equality and fraternity', the authorities had set about securing the simultaneous spread of French, of rationality, and of citizenship. Confirming republican fears of Rome, of 'superstition', and reaction, however, the Breton movement, increasingly clerical, went on into the twentieth century to conflate the Breton language, faith and salvation into an ever purer, isolated, rural simplicity that was, for them, Breton culture (see Elegoët, 1979). On the one hand, nineteenth-century school inspectors urged more and more schools for girls in Brittany, both to combat this clerical hold, and to get French and 'civilisation' into Breton families. On the other hand, Breton linguistic scholars, who had come to join the nobles and clerics, protested angrily as more and more Breton women and their children were turning to French, an evaluation they saw as imposed from Paris, and encouraged by the then proliferating 'maternal' or nursery schools (see Anon., 1895).[2] In 1886, there were an estimated 1 300 000 Breton-speakers; today there are an estimated 500 000 (cf. Galv, 1969, p. 10). Against this overall drop of over 60 per cent in the number of Breton-speakers, the population of Brittany has increased by over 4 per cent over the same period, and the population of Finistère has similarly risen, by an overall 13.6 per cent. It is not simply a matter then of life-long Breton-speakers having died off. It is more a question of a significant switch to French. And it is not the case that this adoption of French has been any straightforward imposition from Paris.

In the departmental archives of Finistère, there is evidence that, as early as 1831 for example, the local Breton education committee, with Breton-speaking members, was refusing a larger space to Breton in Finistère's schools, even though the government was offering it. Later on, local Breton republicans were actively complaining of still too much Breton in the schools. Significantly, in 1846, a Breton municipal education committee happily reported that a woman teacher had begun educating their local girls; they reported that the girls were introducing into the families a 'healthy morality' and 'the habit of using French' – and that all this had brought '. . . a certain polish which softens the savagery and natural roughness of the peasants' (cited in Ogès, 1934, p. 143).

Travelling tradesmen and relatively wealthy and well-respected horse-dealers helped to bring new ideas, republicanism and a smattering of French to even the most isolated, upland areas of Brittany – including Plounéour-Ménez – from the Revolutionary period onwards (Ariès 1948, pp. 54–55). The Léon, a former diocese, has traditionally been the most clerical and the most Breton-speaking area of Finistère. Plounéour-Ménez has been part of the Léon. Just after the Revolution, one Léon commune was already wanting a government girls' school, however, but complained: 'we have no female teacher; no woman yet dares to show herself as a republican' (Year VI; cited in Ogès 1942, p. 133). Things have changed since.

During my first summer living in rural Finistère, I went to a Breton-language Mass in the old Cistercian Abbey of Le Relecq, a hamlet near Kerguz, and also in Plounéour-Ménez. Apart from the occasional Breton hymns, Mass is usually celebrated in French. This once-a-year Breton Mass has been mounted by a section of the diminishing Léon clergy, more out of Catholic nostalgia and devotion than any radical language militantism; and they also have an eye on the possible attraction of newcomers and tourists. In a commune which, like so many others in France, has been actively involved in its own versions of national church/state battles, church buildings have been neglected by the municipal council, and any funding, from collections at services, is very welcome to the priest. The bishop of the diocese came along for this Breton Mass: he delivered an impassioned sermon, in Breton, to a full congregation, mostly women, and many of them no longer practising Catholics, but there for this special occasion. The bishop complained that Brittany was no longer producing its traditionally high quota of boys and girls for Holy Orders. He blamed it on the mothers: they were not bringing up their children properly. Quiet smiles appeared on several faces, and I afterwards had coffee with a group of local women, who spent some time ridiculing the sermon, and doing so in French. Amongst these women was the wife of a former mayor of the commune, whose own father had been mayor before him, and the conversation involved some self-consciously republican family pride. The mayors and municipal council of Plounéour-Ménez have long boasted their own form of political radicalism (a 'red' politics), which is best defined as anti-clericalism, and the commune has seen well over a hundred years of willing education of its girls in French.

Related evidence of local sentiment and ambition was offered when a new priest took up office in the parish. This new priest had just returned to Brittany after many years' mission abroad. Unlike his predecessor, he had, in an earlier era, been actively involved in the Breton movement. One of his first actions now was to increase the number of Breton hymns at weekly Mass. The local faithful quite liked this, noting at the same time that he had also re-introduced the old Latin *credo*. However, this priest then tried to deliver his weekly sermons in Breton, and was met with swift reaction. Notes were delivered to his presbytery, from local women, expressly asking him not to speak Breton. With sadness, he explained to me that: 'It is almost as if Breton smells of cow-shit (*kaoc'h saout*, Breton) to them. They think they are ladies (*Mesdames*, French).'

From cow-shit to finery

Any isolated, Breton, un-French world has long since gone, if it can be said ever to have existed. Certainly, however, aristocratic and bourgeois notions of ideal femininity had no obvious popular hold amongst the early nineteenth-century peasantry. In the 1830s, educated travellers to Brittany, including to the Plounéour-Ménez area, reported that women there seemed to be less valued by men than their animals, and were, they said, the 'submissive vassals' of the peasant men (see Brousmiche (1829–31) 1977, vol. 2, p. 205; Ariès 1948, Chapter 1). Although we might grant the peasant world its own unacknowledged, autonomous metaphoric of male/female difference here, we can certainly allow that life on the land was hard and very different from the life of town ladies. Peasant women would barely have recognised the symbolism of femininity that was opposing them and their men to France.

By the end of the nineteenth century, however, the production of crude, home-spun, home-woven cloth, for local use or the linen trade, had virtually gone, and had given way in some areas to the making of lace for the delicate garments of elegant Parisian ladies (Ariès, 1948, p. 34). Breton women were not slow in making new fashions part of their own world. In the 1920s, a visitor to Saint-Pol-de-Léon, the Cathedral town of the old Léon diocese, near the north coast, noticed that the women there had abandoned the dark, traditional costume of their mothers, with its apron and discreet white *coiffe*, and they were, he said:

> . . . all flaunting themselves in lavish, city attire; their legs, pinkened by flesh-coloured stockings, are perched on high-heeled shoes. (Cited in Ariès 1948, p. 59)

It is perhaps no coincidence that such fashionableness should have been evident in a town near the coast. The coastal areas and the towns, in general, had long been a pole of attraction away from the land and the interior, creating a demographic density around the edge of Brittany and a relative sparsity inland. Since the eighteenth century especially, government finance had helped to create a relative wealth and security nearer the coast, in maritime and administrative interests. A popular scorn for the land was progressively manifest in the nineteenth century, in migrations to the coast, and sometimes outside Brittany, too, including to Paris (Ariès, 1948, pp. 31, 61–62). Migrations became permanent emigrations in the second half of the century, with visits home that increasingly framed the towns, the coast, security, finery, and French as a single powerful pole of all that the peasant condition was not.

The flight of both men and women from the land was well under way in the 1930s, but it was overtaken by a predominantly female exodus from agriculture after the Second World War. Since the end of the nineteenth century, there had been a growing aspiration to be a housewife, or a town lady, or anything but a peasant's wife (cf. Weber 1977, p. 174). This trend was now accentuated, and particularly as the length of girls' schooling was beginning to catch up with that of boys. From the mid-1950s to the mid-1970s, the rate of female emigration from the land rose steadily, surpassing the figure for men, for Brittany overall, and for Finistère alone (see Trégouët

1978). Plounéour-Ménez is still an agricultural commune, in land-use and in external image and self-image, and agriculture is still by far the largest single occupational sector. By the mid-1970s, however, only 18 per cent of the total population, or 46 per cent of the active population, was actually working farms, whereas a little over a decade earlier these proportions had been 37.5 per cent and 72.3 per cent, respectively. Over the same period, there was an overall drop of almost 18.6 per cent in the population of the commune, and yet significant increases in nearby and less agricultural communes all the way up to the nearest town of Morlaix, near the north coast. Of the young aged 15–24 years in Plounéour-Ménez in 1962, one and a half times as many of the girls as the boys had left by 1968. The economic area of the *pays de Morlaix*, which includes Plounéour, shows an increase, over the same period of almost 11 per cent of women working in the tertiary sector (and 1.7 per cent of men; SEMENF, 1976, p. 49). In the village of Kerguz itself, villagers can conjure up a time in living memory when over one hundred people were still living off small plots of land; there are now only three farms, and two active peasants' wives. Each has sisters who have moved away and married salaried men. Another woman recently persuaded her husband to give up their farm and take a job in Morlaix. She is now a proud housewife, working part-time in a shop, and has elegant clothes and a new house with modern furniture, amenities, and general organisation of space that peasant homes lack. She would frequently show off her new home to visitors, and point out, in careful French, the welcome difference between her new life-style and the 'hard, dirty' life she had previously known on a farm, and which she so hated.

Femininity and French have arrived, and together they can speak a sophistication that is other than peasant work. The comment of the new priest which I cited earlier is already suggestive of the reality of these values in local life; such values do not necessarily manifest themselves in overt action of the kind involved in actually taking variously plaintive or hostile notes to the presbytery. Rather, they present themselves through the unreflecting proprieties of daily behaviour.

Women can define their femininity, and men their masculinity, through the language they use, and language-use has it correlates in social space. The fields and certain bars tend to be male domains, and, in all-male company of a certain age, Breton is the usual language of communication. Sanctions against the use of French here include a fear of being thought 'stuck-up' (*fier*, Breton). Contrasting with this world of rough and ready masculinity are certain female domains such as the special *salon* or parlour set aside in many farmhouses for guests. Sanctions against the use of Breton here are tacit but still forceful; Breton is not used at polite tea-parties.

In the militant world, the choice of language is a self-consciously political act, and the Breton/French linguistic difference is, for the movement, a political opposition. At the local level, amongst native-speakers of Breton, language choice is not, in daily life, a political statement and the Breton/French difference is not a political opposition. Local speakers could choose to make these things explicitly political, of course, and especially so in the context of a country in which language, identity and politics have been so strongly associated. However, in the daily round, language choice has more to do with local and familiar structures of identity or social status – including gender, age, occupation, etc. – than with any self-consciously political statement of French or Breton identity.

Village women in Kerguz commonly speak Breton to their husbands and other men, and both Breton and French when helping the men in the fields. One locally born woman has returned to the village with her husband after a working life as a domestic in Paris; her husband, from a nearby village, worked on the railways there. Anna speaks Breton to her husband, but likes to speak French as the voice of sophistication in the village, including when helping out in the fields. Whatever her life was like in Paris, Anna is glamour in the village. She soon installed a bathroom, toilet and central heating in her house – none of which the other local women had. When the men are out drinking rough, red wine, playing *boules*, or working with the machines, women like to visit each other for coffee and sweet cakes in the afternoon. This has long been a rather special, and now distinctly feminine, thing to do. Anna prefers tea to coffee, and often declines the cakes, as she is slimming. She prefers dainty savouries anyway. The other women admire her sense of refinement, and allow her to conjure up, in French, a world of fashion and ladylike good taste that the female Breton world has fully a space for.

Such afternoon conversations over tea and coffee move between

Breton and French. When the men are present at evening gatherings of the whole village, such as occurs at New Year, the women sit together at one end of a long table with their sweet cakes and sweet wine and speak predominantly French, and the men pack together at the other end in a haze of cigarette smoke, eating cheap *pâté*, drinking hard liquor, playing dominoes or cards, and speaking predominantly Breton. While Anna at one end speaks French to the women, her husband at the other speaks Breton to the men.

A sense of finery and fashion as the prerogative of the woman is well-established. Peasant women still often buy all the clothes for their husbands and unmarried sons, including their 'best Sunday shoes'. Peasant men take some pride in saying that they 'couldn't care less' about what they wear, not because they do not dress up when appropriate, but because men can, symbolically and actually, leave such things to women. Such a male/female distinction extends also to what is, in local self-perception at least, the relatively novel notion of romantic love: 'The women like that sort of thing,' they say. In order to halt the exodus of women from the rural areas in the 1950s and 1960s, Catholic groups worked hard in Brittany, as elsewhere in France, to try to publicise the idea that love and romance could exist in a peasant setting (see, for example, JAC – MRJC, 1979, pp. 72–73; here one sees somewhat unlikely pictures, produced in the 1950s and 1960s, of peasant men giving bouquets to their women). Marriage, traditionally an alliance between families, and arranged by parents or a go-between with a keen sense of social status and an eye on landed wealth, had become, especially for the women, a matter of individual choice that could operate with rather different criteria. French terms had already come in: for example, an *akord* (/akɔrd/ cf. French *accord*) was an initial agreement after which a couple became *fianset* (fi:a^{n}sɛd/cf. French *fiancé(e)*), or 'engaged'. A girlfriend or boyfriend, a relatively new status, is a *bon ami* (/bɔn ami:/; cf. French *bon(ne) ami(e)*). There is a more live and obvious Frenchness in this area, too. I was one day talking, in Breton, with a rather drunken group of ageing bachelor peasants that I know; suddenly, one took hold of my hand, much to the amusement of his mates, and kissed it, and said '*Enchanté, Mademoiselle*'. Everyone laughed. 'Be quiet', he said, back in Breton now, 'just shut up – you're jealous. *Je fais la cour.*' It was generally agreed that he was 'a one for the girls.'

Feminism

In the meantime, feminism has appeared with some force in French educated circles. Simone de Beauvoir's work, *Le Deuxième Sexe*, published in 1949, has been keenly taken up after the wide protests and upheavals of May 1968. Femininity has been denaturalised, declared to be arbitrary, and a myth for the definition and pleasure of men, whereby woman had become man's own incorporated 'half' (Beauvoir 1949, vol. 1, pp. 205–238, 313). Well-known feminist writers in France have since explicitly elided their 'struggle' with that of the 'oppressed' and 'ethnic minorities' everywhere, including that of the Bretons in France (see, for example, Halimi 1973; Groult 1975). Meanwhile, the Breton movement has itself espoused a more youthful and secular political radicalism since 1968, and has made feminism, the peasantry, and Breton synonymous in a vision of a new 'alternative' society.

Feminism has also been felt within the ranks of the movement itself. Female student militants in Rennes refused to do any more typing for their male counterparts, and Breton Women's Groups were briefly set up in the towns. These groups disbanded largely because the cause of Breton language and culture, and the cause of female liberation, whilst united in common opposition to the 'system', began to conflict when the definition was required to be positive rather than negative, and practical priorities had to be asserted. In the next section, we shall see other aspects of this internal conflict in the militant world. Different values of what it means to be 'Breton' – in this instance, Breton-speaking and feminist – which might unite the movement externally, in its appropriation of the popular world in opposition to all things 'French', can also come into conflict within the militant world when the context of definition, or just what is 'Breton' and what 'French', is unclear. There have been militant women who have firmly declared that they wanted more front-line roles, and would no longer be content just to marry a male militant (*un emsaver*) and breed Breton-speaking children (see 'War-du an istorekadur' in *Emsav*, 1975, no. 106, pp. 335–363). This has not been an easy objective to realise, and it is noticeable that those few female militants who do have prominent roles in the movement have first done their duty as Breton-speaking wives and mothers. One of the leading Breton-learning manuals has been strongly criticised in

Breton-learning courses for its tendency to present women in traditional feminine roles: the women characters in the book are often engaged in housewifely duties, cleaning, cooking and mothering for their menfolk, and they sometimes show great interest in the feminine frills of urban finery and fashion (for the manual concerned: Denez 1972). Thc author's main defence has been that his book is simply describing life as it is lived. At the same time, all the characters in the book, of whatever age, gender and milieu, speak Breton and only Breton and are clearly committed to doing so.

To many female militants, learning and speaking Breton is liberation enough, but there are others who have gone a stage further in pursuit of Breton authenticity. A number of young women, sometimes with their boy-friends or husbands, have moved back to the Breton countryside, in a general back-to-the-land trend in France, and have become 'peasants' or 'artisans', in their own image of this popular world as an unconstrained, unbourgeois, and un-French naturality; they feel they have shed intellectuality and the 'system', they have learnt Breton, and they are living in studied and rugged 'ecological' simplicity.

I know of 25 or more such couples, and sundry individuals, who now live in the area in and around Plounéour, some of them now working individual farms after having tried to set up a collective commune (or *communauté*) in the mountains. One young couple in Kerguz, keen on wholemeal foods and home-weaving, work a tiny vegetable plot, live in a tumble-down house, collect social security, and have set up a windmill to generate electricity. Anna, their nearest neighbour, complains that the windmill is noisy and unnecessary, and regards all their bits of metal and old crocks as a sheer 'mess' that is marring the view of the smart, renovated frontage and garden of her 'modern' home. What Anna regards as 'mess', the young couple regarded as 'recycling'.

Another back-to-the-country, militant couple in Kerguz, Albert and Soazig, hold a little more respect. He is a psychologist commuting daily to a clinic in Morlaix; she is a teacher-turned-artisan, having taken a course in carpentry. Next door to them live a lively 67-year-old local widow, called Thérèse, and her 42-year-old unmarried son, called Iffig. Thérèse and Iffig still have some livestock and wood-holdings, but rent out most of their farmland since Thérèse's husband has died, and her son now commutes daily to a job as a railway workman further North. Thérèse has often shown me her hands: 'Look at them, all red, swollen and ugly,' she would say. Years of farmwork and helping her husband and then their son on their wood-holdings, have taken their toll. Many of the local women, including Thérèse, would often admire my hands: 'so white and delicate', they would say, 'like the hands of a town lady.' At first, I was sceptical of such comments, which might easily be made in mockery; such scepticism, however, whilst not wholly inappropriate, was, I came to see, born of another world. When helping out in the fields or in the woods, I was often urged to put on gloves: 'Don't spoil those hands,' I was warned. Meanwhile, Soazig, next door to Thérèse, was gaining splinters, blisters and callouses from her carpentry – and yet she could, in her own Breton world, display her hands with a certain pride.

Such apparently diverse examples as old crocks and hands, might serve to underline the simple point that the same mundane objects can have very different definitions and meanings when placed in different value systems (see also McDonald, 1982). Certain mundane acts which, within the female militant world, are perceived and lived as displays of naturality and liberation are often, within the local world, lived as rude and embarrassing in polite female company. Local Breton women are felt to live an already feminist existence, and much about them, their life, their work, their language, is willingly taken up by the militant world as confirmation of this view. For example, the fact that local women in the rural world have usually continued to be known by their maiden name after marriage, has been seen as evidence of the already feminist, liberated nature of the native-speaking, female Breton population. However, the use of the maiden name does not conflict with or contest the civil use of the husband's name, and it is usually by the title of *Madame*, plus the married name, that village women like to be publicly presented, particularly to people from elsewhere, or whom they do not know well. Outside the contexts of kinship and locality, the use of the maiden name easily feels, to these women themselves, parochial and old-fashioned.

Such different evaluation, in the militant world and in the local world, of what might appear to be the 'same' objects, titles, acts or gestures clearly has linguistic or sociolinguistic correlates. Very different evaluations of the Breton and French languages, and of the Breton/French language difference, are involved. However, local women can incorporate new enthusiasms, including enthusiasm for speaking Breton, without this assimilation of new evaluations being, for them, the political stand and the 'liberation' that militant epistemology and politics requires it to be, and would publicly present it as. This point will become clearer, I hope, through further illustration, and it is a point I wish to stress. Whilst enthusiasm for speaking Breton is, within the militant world, a political enthusiasm, any response to this enthusiasm by local women which involves them actually complying and speaking Breton rather than French, as the educated outsiders now require, is not, in their own terms, a political act. It is a compliance which, in their own world, follows other channels, other structures of identity and evaluation. Nevertheless, whatever the women do can be subsumed within the powerful discourse of the movement, and they can become unwitting political referents, confirming and justifying the militants' stand.

For those in the towns, the inland, mountain area of Brittany has long been a metaphor of true, surviving Bretonness, and when I left the regional capital of Rennes to go to the tiny village of Kerguz, up in the mountains, the militants assured me that this was a place where I would be sure to find straightforward, empirical evidence of Brittany's truly 'Breton culture'. In later conversations with militant friends, I was warned not to be distracted by 'superficial' discrepancies, such as consumer goods and French, which can be explained, and to persist with Breton in order to find the 'real' Breton culture to which they themselves aspire. Militant discourse often stacks the world in layers in this way, and there is a common assumption that a pure and wholly Breton world might surface, and would have been manifest all along, if it were not for an overlay of French oppression. If people do not speak Breton in all contexts, this is, in the militant view, because they are oppressed and ashamed of their language and culture. This view takes no account of the very particular contexts in which it might be 'wrong' or odd for local people to use French in their own world; any such instances are merely taken as simple confirmation of the right and natural way for Bretons to behave. If it is accepted, however, that there may be popular sanctions against French, it has to be accepted that there are also strong popular sanctions against Breton. The contextual proprieties involved in each case cannot be understood independently, and together form a coherent system of values. But the militant view of ethnic identity is one that demands the identification of a people with a particular language and culture, and their historicist and essentialist view is common enough as a view of what ethnic identity involves. The minority identity has, it is assumed, been historically overlain with external accretions that have brought false consciousness. Such accretions include femininity, finery and French.

Such a viewpoint is not peculiar to the Breton militants, of course. The increased, general interest in modern France in its rural areas is linked to a decline in the agricultural population, and, coinciding as it does with feminist sensibilities and peasant riots alike, it is perhaps not surprising that there has been a fast growth of social science studies focusing on rural, peasant women (cf. Lagrave 1983). These studies tend to assert either that rural women are particularly dominated and oppressed, or that they have a power and authority that other women do not have. Whichever view is required, rural women are, and have been, called on to support it: either they are the proper focus of feminist concern because particularly oppressed, or they are the proper object of feminist attention because they are already feminist, liberated, untouched by the femininity that modern feminism rejects.

These theses are not necessarily contradictory, and, in the hands of the Breton movement, it can all become a question of women in Brittany being properly liberated, and Breton as they should be, once such external accretions as I have mentioned are absent or are taken away. Whether the women use French (=oppressed) or Breton (=liberated) can easily appear to the militants to be confirmation and justification of their own world and cause. The movement has a discourse which, no doubt well-intentionedly, invokes local women, but which these women are, in any case, powerless to contest. There is little space in the militant world for accepting that the Bretons have themselves valued and opted for French. In pointing this out, I am not seeking to challenge the authenticity of the militants' world, which is quite authentically Breton in its own way. It is clear, however, that the Breton movement's interest in Breton language and culture has its own focus, momentum and persuasiveness, but does not include an interest in the manners, proprieties, values and aspirations of the culture and people it would seem to be claiming to defend. If we talk of a popular Breton culture, then it contains, especially for the women, a peculiar Frenchness, that the militant world self-consciously rejects.

The popular world values French, and also values education highly, and the women are particularly implicated here. Maternal responsibilities demand a special sensitivity to education, and a childless woman risks low esteem on a number of counts. When a woman is childless, her womanhood is suspect, and when, on top of this, she is herself uneducated, social respect can be hard to attain. Local evaluations that village women in Kerguz have of one another fully suggest this complex of values. Thérèse herself, for example, is highly esteemed amongst local village women, and this in spite of the thrifty simplicity in which she lives. She has a hard-working son, and, for her age-group, is regarded as relatively educated by local standards: she stayed on at school until thirteen years of age, and she continues to read a good deal and takes a wide interest in current affairs. She regards one of the other local women as particularly stupid, however; this woman has had relatively few years of schooling. It is said of her in the village, with some amusement, that, when told of Kennedy's assassination, she simply asked: 'Kennedy? Is he from Plounéour?' This same woman is childless, and also readily speaks Breton to me, and has problems with French. She is rarely invited to coffee by the other women (only once a year, it seems, at Christmas time); indeed, the other women often pointed out to me that they found her fat and uncouth, and, on one occasion, my attention was drawn to the fact that she has a moustache. One of her redeeming features, however, as far as the other village women are concerned, is that she keeps a pretty flower-garden. The fields are an ideally male domain now, and gardening of this kind is very feminine. Much to militant regret, the popular Breton terms for garden and flowers – *jardin* (/ʒa:rdin/) and *fleur* (/flør/) – are, as in so many areas of ornateness and finery, taken from the French; literary and militant 'standard' Breton prefers *liorzh* (/li:ɔrs/) and *bleuniou* (blønju/), which, to the women of Kerguz, signify untended or overgrown land and wild blossom, respectively.

It would seem that just when the militants are aspiring to a certain ruggedness and naturality, to the countryside, the Breton language, and to some grass-roots Breton authenticity, the Breton women are looking to femininity, the towns, and French. We might pause to recall here that 'femininity' was used by the early Breton movement to cast the whole of Brittany in opposition to France, and to declare it distinctly un-French. The modern discourse of feminism might, revealingly, see this as the definition of Breton culture into a self-limiting and self-denigrating 'half' of an overall, French world. Indeed, this has been pointed out for the Scottish Gaels, defined into a 'half-world' by very similar structures (Chapman, 1978). The Breton militants, however, prefer to see the phenomenon as part of a general 'colonisation' of Brittany and of women, by France and by men. It is striking, and equally revealing, that the imagery of femininity that cast the 'Breton' world in studious opposition to things French, has once translated into the popular, peasant world, been a powerful motor of Frenchness. Further, women's double 'colonisation', in the militants' terms, by both French and by men, has given them now a greater competence in, and access to, a world of refinement. Pursuit of this refinement has virtually emptied the countryside of young women, and, in their own terms, this was a form of liberation. For local women, liberation has not been measured against some male-dominated, bourgeois life, but against the rigours and insecurities of the peasant life – that 'hard, dirty' life.

The mother-tongue

All this has left a striking toll of unmarried men in the rural areas, and male celibacy is matched by a high rate of alcoholism amongst the peasants – and especially amongst those men with smaller, unmodernised farms, and who have been brought up in Breton (Bertrand and Caro, 1977, pp. 191–195, 231, 259). It is perhaps significant that a very common New Year greeting in the mountain areas is '*Bloavezh mat hag ur bourgeoise a-raok fin ar bloaz*,' which might translate as: 'I wish you a Happy New Year and a ladywife before it's out.' Sometimes, the only apparently available women are back-to-the-land enthusiasts, who would like to speak Breton to their children. However, the local ageing bachelors tend to be in awe of these women's education, and it is common sentiment amongst them that they would, in any case, be strongly opposed to any wife of theirs speaking Breton to their children.

The notion of the 'mother-tongue' is a widely evocative metaphor; from early philology to many modern educational policies there has been some image of primitive primacy and primordial cultural attachment, and the notion has gathered an increasing moral imperativeness associated with the relationship of mother to child. Although in the complex Breton bilingual world, the concept has no easy translation, the Breton militants have invented a Breton term for it (*yezh mamm*) and have pleaded, for almost 100 years, for Breton in the schools on the grounds of its being the 'mother-tongue' of Breton children. In the late 1960s and 1970s, they were still pleading this but had been overtaken by local evaluations of French, with Breton-speaking mothers speaking French to their children. The generational gymnastics that can seem to be involved here, within any one family, usually have a wholly unreflecting symbolic rectitude of their own. Rather than give any specific examples here, I can only schematise and summarise.[3] Militants now speak of a 'break in the chain' of generations, and by this they mean particularly the use of French by Breton-speakers of the generations that might include their own parents or grandparents. A few militants have been brought up in Breton by parents who were themselves members of the Breton movement. It is often the case that other militants who had, in their own childhood, occasion to hear and understand any Breton will have done so through close contact with their grandparents.

Breton-speaking children are now rare, and mothers now speaking Breton to their small children are usually militants who have themselves learnt or re-learnt the language. In 1975, an influential Breton militant manual stated quite simply that if Breton was no longer the mother-tongue, then they would have to make it so, and have Breton in nursery or 'maternal' schools (*écoles maternelles* in French), and get mothers to use it, too (Gwegen, 1975, pp. 267–73). In May 1977, a new militant organisation called *Diwan* ('seed') began setting up independent Breton-language nursery schools, with a strong sense of power of 'maternal' schools (*skolioù mamm* in 'standard' Breton) to realise the image of a rightfully Breton-speaking childhood and a properly Breton-speaking motherhood. However, it was later calculated that, of the 119 young *Diwan* mothers involved in 1979–80, under 23 per cent felt they knew enough Breton to speak it to their children at home, and only 6.7 per cent were actually doing so, along with their husbands; none of these latter few mothers (eight in all) had themselves been brought up to speak Breton by their own mothers, and half of them came from outside Brittany. Moreover, their own little children were happily speaking French amongst themselves in the *Diwan* schools. With an intuition of the scale of the problem, a 1980 Congress of all *Diwan* members urgently discussed the question (in a special 'Bretonisation' commission) of how to get more of the mothers to learn Breton, and more to speak it to their children at home. Mothers present, however, objected that they had jobs and no time to learn Breton, and there was a general female protest, too, that it was a chauvinist argument to expect militant mothers to bear the load: it could, perhaps, be the fathers' responsibility. Some hesitation and confusion followed. Proportionately more of the fathers, in fact, knew or were still learning some Breton, and it was gradually agreed that the fathers could help out. However, it was felt then, and still is, that the mother's language is all-important; the idea of '*langue paternelle*' caused some chuckles: 'father-language', it seems, does not replace one's 'mother-tongue'.

There are very many more men than women in the Breton movement, and the fluent Breton-speaking male militant has great problems finding a mate who will match his Breton fluency. The few female militants who have been brought up in Breton in older families of the movement (sometimes known, in the movement itself, as *ar mafia* – 'the mafia') have little trouble finding a mate or spouse within the movement's ranks, or they recruit from outside. However, their brothers, and male militants generally, have greater difficulty and cannot easily recruit into the core of the movement. As I have already indicated, the demands are far greater on the women, expected as they are to become fluent Breton-speaking mothers. Relationships can break up over this issue, with the women leaving home and, in some instances, taking up a stand of freedom in disaffected hostility to all things Breton. There are also male militants, born of militant families, who have themselves decided to join the disaffected fringe and to remain with their predominantly French-speaking partners. In such cases, the men have commonly been accused, from within the core ranks of the movement, of being 'traitors' for taking up with such women. Militants have generally agreed (and re-affirmed more widely, in Inter-Celtic Congresses, for example) that the future of the Celtic languages lies with the women. It is the women, it seems, who were important agents in the advance of the majority tongue and they it must be who are to remedy the situation. As several women in rural Brittany have said to me: 'First they wanted us to speak French, now they want us to speak Breton.' This is, I think, an apt comment on a situation in which power and the centre of definition are always elsewhere.

In a curious and interesting way, the structural values of

femininity, feminism, the peasant, and French and Breton have met and crossed. Such a crossing, or apparent contradiction, of values need not, however, cause conflict at the local level. In a relatively undramatic way, and without great upheaval, women in rural Brittany have been able first to take on French, and now the new image of Breton, and to incorporate in their lives issues which elsewhere have been a matter of great political debate and conflict. Different values may simply be incorporated into existing structures, and gather their own contextual properties. Jeanne is in her forties and a hard-working, Breton-speaking peasant's wife on the largest, most modern farm in Kerguz. She keeps her home spotlessly clean, visits a hairdresser nearer the coast when she can, tries hard to slim, and has held great ambitions for her five sons, aged from seven to twenty. Paul, her eldest son, failed his studies, did his military service, and then 'dropped out' – doing odd jobs elsewhere. In Plounéour, however, he met a very wealthy newcomer named Katrin, who had dropped out of her own higher education to come and live in Brittany, where she joined up with the Breton militants. Katrin feels she is a liberated woman. One afternoon, Jeanne, well-groomed and in a smart dress, came to my door. She spontaneously spoke some Breton to me for the first time, and invited me to coffee: Paul, her son, and Katrin, his girlfriend, were there. I went to coffee, still somewhat puzzled as to why Jeanne had spoken some Breton to me like that. Katrin talked, over coffee, of glamorous trips to America, and how she would show Paul the world. There were some hints of marriage. Jeanne looked proud at this prospect for her son. Katrin had a Breton-learning manual with her; 'Tell her how you learnt Breton', said Jeanne to me excitedly. 'She wants to learn it too.' As if by way of explanation, Katrin then talked inspiredly of Atlantis, the Incas, the Indians, of strange mysteries, of Woman, of Babylon, the Celts, and the Beginning of the World. She smiled at her boyfriend and said what wonderful, natural people these were, and there were suggestions that her parents might buy him a farm. Katrin was ready to be a peasant's wife. Paul, the 'peasant' now of his girlfriend's world, then tried, for the first time in his life, to stammer out a few Breton words. 'I never learnt it,' he said, 'my mother never spoke it to me.' Jeanne looked embarrassed, self-consciously tidied her hair, and busied herself with the coffee and cakes. 'I can help you learn some now,' she volunteered finally, as the dutiful mother who had always tried to do the best for her son. Katrin smiled, tossed her long, untidy locks aside, rolled a cigarette, and wiped her hands on her kaftan and fashionable dungarees. 'You must speak some Breton to Paul,' she said to Jeanne, 'so he can teach me.' Jeanne obligingly uttered a few Breton phrases, and then changed into old trousers and overalls, and went off to milk her cows. Outside in the gathering dark, her hair-do was slowly wrecked in the wind and rain, and I later heard her shouting a few words at the cows in Breton, as she usually did, when taking them back to the fields – in a totally different Breton world.

This is a world where a good mother, by definition, speaks nicely to children, but this can involve a structure of values so strong that in a peasant family up near a town on the coast, where I stayed for a week during my research, the mother spoke French to her own two teenage daughters – and then Breton to cows, but French to calves, and Breton to hens, but French to their chicks, and Breton to pigs and sows, but French to piglets. My stay with this family had been arranged for me by a militant group who like to send Breton learners from the towns to 'Breton-speaking' peasant families where Breton can be learnt in exchange for helping on the farms. However, all the families always, it seems, have great difficulty speaking Breton to unknown 'outsiders', and particularly the mothers, and especially so when the outsider is younger and female. The mother on the farm continually had to check herself in mid-French, and make a conscious effort to speak Breton to me. She would laugh, say how odd and tiring it was – but add she had been asked to do it by a nice, young local teacher; it seemed the young and educated were doing this sort of thing now. Towards the end of the course, however, she and other peasant women were shocked and upset to find that, at a special dinner given by the militant organisers, they were expected to stand for a Breton national anthem. The militant press cameras clicked furiously. This is just one obvious example of the general point that local women are summoned, metaphorically and actually, in the militant world into a political role which, in their own terms, they are not performing at all. Putting it more extremely, we might say that local women can, and do, find themselves standing as radical feminists and Breton nationalists when, in their own terms, they might have imagined they were behaving in a way more evocative of sophisticated French ladies.

Abbreviations

AD	Archives Départementales (Finistère).
AEB	*Amañ Emgleo Breiz* (a Breton militant journal)
BSAF	*Bulletin de la Société Archéologique du Finistère.*
CIRREES	Centre Interdisciplinaire de Recherche et de Réflexion sur les Ensembles Economiques et Sociaux (Rennes).
CRDP	Centre Régional de Recherche et de Documentation Pédagogiques (Bretagne).
INSEE	Institut National de la Statistique et des Etudes Economiques.
JAC–MRJC	Jeunesse Agricole Chrétienne – Mouvement Rural de la Jeunesse Chrétienne.
MA and DA	Maïte Albistur and Daniel Armogathe (1977, below).
SEMENF	Société d'économie mixte d'étude du Nord Finistère.
SV	*Skol Vreiz* (a militant journal for the teaching of Breton).

Notes

1. See MA and DA, 1977, vol. 2, pp. 364–6, 368, 406–8.
2. This 'anonymous' pamphlet was written by the respected Celto-Breton scholar, Vallée (see Taldir, 1935).
3. Generational differences in language-use could perhaps be summed up schematically in the following way:

		Age
Generation 1	great-grandmother	c.80 years
Generation 2	grandmother and grandfather	c.50 years
Generation 3	mother and father	c.25 years
Generation 4	child	c.5 years

This might be in itself a fictional, but nonetheless typical, agricultural family inhabiting rural Finistère. Nearer the coast, French may intervene earlier. (I am grateful to Malcolm Chapman, Institute of Social Anthropology, Oxford, for confirming this general picture from his own research experience on the southern Breton coast.)

Generation 1 Great-grandmother feels more at home in Breton than French, and Breton is usually a more appropriate language, in any case, for much of her daily round. She knows that her French is not as good as that of her decendants, and she also knows that French is the polite language to speak to strangers or to important visitors. However, she does tend to use Breton more than she did, as her grasp of sociolinguistic proprieties begins to wane with age. Usually, she speaks Breton to her daughter and her son-in-law (generation 2), and they commonly respond in Breton.

Generation 2 Grandmother and grandfather use both Breton and French amongst themselves. Breton is often used when they are alone together, and talking privately or of private adult matters, (and do not want the children to hear), or when they are in informal situations with friends or relatives of their own age. They normally speak French to their children and to their children's generation (generation 3). They use only French to their young grandchildren (generation 4).

Generation 3 Mother and father speak French between themselves, and to grandmother and grandfather (generation 2). They have heard a good deal of Breton spoken around them over the years, but it has not usually been spoken to them. Their parents (generation 2) have made every effort to bring them up as French-speakers, and have never wanted or expected them to speak anything but French. This generation (generation 3) is, therefore, able passively to understand much Breton, but does not really speak it. They might, however use a limited amount of Breton in communication with great-grandmother (generation 1).

Generation 4 The child, and the brothers and sisters if there are any, do not speak anything other than French. They are normally addressed by everyone in French. Should great-grandmother (generation 1) forgetfully address them in Breton, they might just, if alone with her, muster some sense from her words, and respond in French. Their confusion is usually enough to jolt great-grandmother back into French, and propriety, herself. If parents (generation 3) or grandparents (generation 2) are present (a presence more likely to cause, or contribute to, great-grandmother's own confusion in the first place) then the children are likely to look to them for help. The children will reply through these older generations.

There are several qualifying factors and complications that one could introduce here – including, for example, the fact that generations 1 and 2 will usually have cohabited whilst generations 2 and 3 will not; and if generation 2 is living in the family home of the male partner (the 'grandfather' here) then the different uses of Breton and French between generations 2 and 3 may well have an extra edge of rivalry and exclusion, and affect also the language used within generation 2. It is not uncommon for mothers-in-law to use Breton to exclude daughters-in-law, for instance, and it has also been known in the past for daughters-in-law to use French, and only French, with everyone in the household to mark themselves off from mothers-in-law with whom they do not get on.

The kinship terms used here are, obviously, those of a British system. The appropriate Breton system is one in which both gender and educational level are important, and age more important than generation, in determining the terms used in kinship designation and, especially, address. Significantly, where the female gender is involved, and also when one moves nearer the coast, there is less lateral generalisation of terms and a more obviously 'French' terminology (see, on some of these points, Izard (1965), although he finds 'impoverishment' and a disappointing unCelticness here – where local women would, no doubt, find sophistication).

References and further reading

Albistur, M. and Armogathe, D. (1977) *Histoire du feminisme français*, 2 vols (Paris: Editions des Femmes).

Anon. (1985) *La Langue Bretonne et Les Ecoles* (St. Brieuc: Prud'Homme).

Ardener, E. 1973 (1971) 'Social Anthropology and the Historicity of Historical Linguistics', in *Social Anthropology and Language*, ed., Ardener, E., ASA Monographs 10 (London: Tavistock).

Ariès, P. (1948) *Histoire des Populations Françaises* (Paris: Editions Self).

Beauvoir, S. de (1949) *Le Deuxième Sexe*, 2 vols (Paris: Gallimard).

Beer, W. R. (1977) 'The Social Class of Ethnic Activists in Contemporary France' in Esman, M. J., ed., *Ethnic Conflict in the Western World* (Cornell University Press).

Bertrand, Y. and Caro, G. (1977) *Alcoolisme et Bretagne* (Rennes: CIRREES).

Boucheron and Nonus 1890 (1889) 'Compte-rendu des Conférences d'Octobre 1889' (Carré), in *Bulletin Officiel et Spécial de l'Instruction Primaire* (Académie de Rennes: département du Finistère).

Brousmiche, J. F. 1977 (1829–31) *Voyage dans le Finistère en 1829, 1830 et 1831*, 2 vols (Morvran).

Carré, I. (1888) 'De la manière d'enseigner les premiers éléments du français dans les écoles de la Basse-Bretagne', in *Revue Pédagogique*: 12: 3, 15 March 1888.

Chapman, M. (1978) *The Gaelic Vision in Scottish Culture* (London: Croom Helm).

Charpy, J. (1972) 'Dénombrements de la population des communes du Finistère', in *BSAF*, no. 99.

Chervel, A. (1977) *. . . et il fallut apprendre à ecrire à tous les petits français. Histoire de la grammaire scolaire* (Paris: Payot).

CRDP (1976) *Le Finistère 1800–1914 (les hommes)* (Rennes: CRDP).

Daumer, Y. (1977) 'Les Champions du Monde de L'Alcoolisme', in *Le Peuple Breton*, no. 168, November.

Denez, P. (1972) *Brezhoneg . . . Buan hag Aes* (Paris: Omnivox).

Droixhe, D. (1978) *La Linguistique et l'appel de l'histoire (1600–1800)* (Geneva: Droz).

Elegoët, F. (1979) 'Prêtres, Nobles et Paysans en Léon au début du XXe siècle. Notes sur un nationalisme breton: *Feiz ha Breiz*: 1900–1914.' in *Pluriel*, no. 18 (Rennes).

Galv (1969) *Livre Noir et Blanc de la Langue Bretonne* (Brest: Ar Falz 9).

Gazier, A. 1969 (1880) (ed.) *Lettres à Gregoire sur les patois de France, 1790–1794* (Geneva: Slatkine Reprints).

Groult, B. (1975) *Ainsi soit-elle* (Paris: Grasset).

Gwegen, J. (1975) *La Langue Bretonne Face à Ses Oppresseurs* (Quimper: Nature et Bretagne).

Halimi, G. (1973) *La Cause des Femmes* (Paris: Grasset).

INSEE (1980) *Annuaire Statistique Régional: Bretagne* (Rennes: INSEE).

Izard, M. (1965) 'La terminologie de parenté bretonne' in *L'Homme*, vol. 5, nos. 3–4, pp. 88–100.

JAC–MRJC (1979) *50 ans d'animation rural* (Paris: Promo).

Lagrave, R.-M. (1983) 'Bilan critique des recherches sur les agricultrices en France' in *Etudes Rurales* 92.

La Villemarqué, Th.-C.-H. H. de 1963 (1867) *Barzaz Breiz* (Librairie Académique Perrin).

Markale, J. (1976) *La Femme Celte* (Paris: Payot).

McDonald, M. (1982) 'Social Aspects of Language and Education in Brittany, France', D.Phil thesis, University of Oxford (Forthcoming, London: Tavistock).

Ogès, L. (1934) 'L'instruction primaire dans le Finistère sous le régime de la loi Guizot (1833–1850)', in *BSAF*, no. 61.

Ogès, L. (1937) 'L'instruction sous l'ancien régime dans les limites du Finistère actuel (suite)', in *BSAF*, no. 64.

Ogès, L. (1942) 'L'instruction dans le Finistère pendant la Révolution (suite et fin)', in *BSAF*, no. 69.

Prost, A. (1968) *L'Enseignement Primaire en France 1800–1967* (Paris: Colin).

SEMENF (1976) *Le Pays de Morlaix: évolution et perspectives* (Morlaix: SEMENF).

Souvestre, E. 1971 (1835–37) *Les Derniers Bretons*, vol. 1 (Brest: Le Portulan).

Taldir (1935) 'Genèse de la campagne en faveur de l'enseignement du breton', in *Le Foyer Breton* 52.

Tanguy, B. 1977 *Aux origines du nationalisme breton* vol 1 (Paris: 10/18).

Tregouët, B. (1978) 'Agriculteurs: le dépeuplement des campagnes', in *Octant* 3, Rennes, September.

Weber, E. (1977) *Peasants into Frenchmen* (London: Chatto and Windus).

9 Refusing to be Invisible: Turkish Women in Berlin

CLARE KROJZL

Aysel Özakin, a Turkish writer and broadcaster in her late thirties, has made a name for herself in political and literary circles in West Berlin. Articles about her have appeared in German newspapers. As a writer who dresses in jeans and sweaters, she is seen as atypical; Berlin women express astonishment that although she had been living in Berlin for only a few years, her ideas are so 'modern' and her dress style so fashionable. Aysel finds this unacceptable. She dislikes being patronised in ways which reinforce German stereotypes of Turkish women. Similarly, although she has written on both feminist and migrant worker themes, she rejects these categories as too limited for characterising her work: 'Nobody expected that Henry Miller would only write about the problems of being a foreigner in France' (*Berliner Tageszeitung*, 20 April 84).

As a migrant, first from rural to urban Turkey and then from Turkey to Germany, Aysel has gained her strong political stance from the migrant community within which she lives and works. While regretting some of the social effects of ghettoisation, she sees the separation of the Turks from the host population not as an inability to adapt itself to Western ways but as a political act, a deliberate resistance to Germany's policy of integrating its migrant workers into its own population where they will become inconspicuous and no longer a 'problem'. For the migrants this policy of integration is where the problem begins. It means their incorporation at the lowest social status and economic level, where they can be tapped to perform unpleasant work avoided by the host population. By strengthening their ethnic identity, these migrants retain their code of dignity and personhood. Among Germany's immigrant groups, the Turks are the poorest and the most culturally conspicuous, but while the men have been forced to make compromises with German practices, albeit with a minimum of capitulation to German social values in order to preserve their sense of honour, the women affirm their ethnicity as a statement of cultural difference from the Germans and of mutual support among Turks.

The Turks are undoubtedly the most disdained of the foreign groups in the city. Hostility towards them has both increased and become more overt during the 1980s. Women are often insulted in the street and described as vermin, as well as being the target of abusive wall slogans and poison pen letters. They are conspicuous by their physical appearance and style of dress – their *şalvar* trousers, and their colourful dresses and headscarves – although they are still less numerous than Turkish men and are more confined to their homes and workplaces.

Media coverage of the community is generally unsympathetic, or when it appears sympathetic (as did the articles on Aysel Özakin), it in fact reinforces German stereotypes, especially those relating to gender. The image of the Turkish 'pasha' as an autocratic male figure has been prevalent since well before the Turkish community was established in Berlin and probably hails from as far back as the Ottoman Empire, which received a number of Prussian officers in Istanbul for military reform. While the image of the Turkish male is seen as harsh, autocratic and aggressive, the Turkish female is characterised as helpless, ignorant, passive and a prisoner of her male relatives. A documentary on the Turks in Berlin, shown during my stay, concentrated almost exclusively on the ill-treatment of women.

These images were constantly being challenged by Turkish women I met in Berlin. Many of them were illiterate and spoke little or no German even if they had been living in the city for years. They faced constant humiliation as they endeavoured to find and keep paid employment, many of them for the first time in their lives, and to negotiate with the authorities for permits, kindergarten places and social security allowances. As others have commented, notably Abadan-Unat (1976, pp. 2–8), women are in many respects ill-equipped and vulnerable in the migrant environment and yet also receptive to the positive aspects of a strange society, in ways not matched by Turkish men. The very turbulence and uncertainty of their new circumstances appears to force them into action to retain control of the sphere of relationships which is their domain. By asserting themselves in marriage and family life, divorce, and against unfair dismissal from work, Turkish women are refusing to be invisible or to be manipulated.

Where women are politically aware, they are seldom involved in the public sphere of activity, so that in this sense their politics might easily be overlooked. We may thus pay attention to Turkish students reading Islamic fundamentalist literature published by Khomeini supporters among the Iranian student population, or to the Marxist lobby in the second generation of Turks, while neglecting the political implications of changes taking place in lives of illiterate women from Eastern Turkey as they attempt to grapple with an incomprehensible bureaucratic structure in the course of applying for social security, or divorcing a husband or finding a nursery place for a child. This chapter attempts to place women's activities within the framework of social institutions in West Berlin, to show how their personal acts oriented to specific situations can be viewed as political statements within the particular cultural context of migration. The refusal of Turkish women to adopt German customs and styles of dress is best understood in terms of the Turkish concept of honour, and thus as a conscious and deliberate resistance to acculturation, rather than as their inability to adapt – an interpretation often offered (e.g. Elsas, 1980, p. 6).

Turkish migration to West Berlin

The city of Berlin is situated about two hours' drive inside East Germany (the GDR) from the West German border, and is in fact closer to Poland. Road and railway access to Berlin is controlled by the border guards and People's Police of the GDR, and air access is restricted to the Berlin air corridor. Since August 1961, West Berlin and its population of two million has been entirely surrounded by the Berlin Wall, which divides it from East Berlin with a population of one million. The international political status of Berlin remains ambiguous: on the one hand, East Berlin is recognised by Western powers as a capital city, with appropriate diplomatic representations, while West Berlin is no longer a capital and has only consulate status. Although West Berlin is treated as a *Land* of the Federal

Republic of Germany, the entire city is still technically under Allied military rule by the four powers, so that military personnel have freedom of movement between the two parts.

Turkish migration to West Germany began in 1961, the year of the Berlin Wall, when East Germany curtailed the accelerating flow of emigrants (which in that year had reached the rate of 1000 per day). The buoyant West German economy which had absorbed unskilled labour from East Germany now attracted immigrants from other parts of Europe, mainly from Italy, Yugoslavia, Greece and Turkey. Based on low oil prices, the economy continued to expand, providing upward mobility and higher living standards for the indigenous population and lower-paid jobs for migrants. While the native Berliners have moved towards higher qualified posts and greater prestige in the administrative occupations or the technical level in manufacturing and industrial activity, foreigners take the less skilled jobs in industrial production, such as the metal industry, or as cleaners, the case for the majority of Turkish women. Migrants also predominate in shift and night work.

With the oil crisis of 1973, however, the steady growth of the preceding decade could no longer be sustained, even in the relatively affluent economic climate of West Germany and West Berlin. When production declined and workers were laid off, Turkish workers in Berlin were among those made redundant. Some returned to Turkey; others sought employment elsewhere in West Germany and further afield in Belgium and the Netherlands. The crisis brought a review of Federal and Berlin policy towards migrant workers, resulting in the Act known as *Anwerbestopp* passed on 30 November 1973, which stopped all applications for permits from new 'guest workers' from non-European Economic Community countries. Turks living in Berlin at that time risked losing their work permits and the right of reentry if they left the country for more than a few weeks in a year; those who have arrived in Berlin since 1973 are either relatives or dependants of people already in possession of permits. This ban is still in effect.

Before 1973, Turkish migrants had been free to come and go. Most were men who left their families behind and put up with minimal living conditions in order to save for future enterprise in Turkey. With the new regulations, however, as well as a labour market more favourable to the employment of women, Turks began to send for their families and to remain in Germany for longer periods. This did not mean that they regarded themselves as permanent or even semi-permanent residents of Germany; they have been the least willing of all foreign migrants to accept this eventuality. The next decade brought an influx of Turkish women and children to Berlin. Many Turkish children were born there, but they have no political or citizenship rights. Government policy, in its insistence on retaining these Turks in an actual or potential *Arbeiter* status, at once denies full citizenship to migrant families and rejects cultural pluralism.

Changes in Federal policy were followed by decisions on the part of the cities of West Berlin, Frankfurt and others to close certain of their more populous boroughs to new foreign residents in order to disperse the foreign population and prevent what was seen as the harmful effects of ghettos. The strong inclination of Turks to congregate residentially, where housing was cheap and where they had personal and business networks, was seen at the policy level as an obstacle to integration. The Federal Government's reluctance to accept migrants as citizens was thus contradicted at the local level by attempts to 'integrate' foreigners into the community. This overt policy affected these migrants in various ways: educational policy did not allow Islamic instruction in state schools and discouraged the use of headscarves by schoolgirls; advisory centres and refuges for Turkish women organised their activities in terms of 'integration'.

By 1981, the time of my fieldwork, approximately 120 000 Turks lived in West Berlin, 6 per cent of the city's population. Turks formed the largest group of migrants in both West Germany and West Berlin, in the latter case outnumbering the second largest group, the Yugoslavs, by over three to one. In spite of the policy of 'integration', the Turkish population in Berlin remained relatively concentrated in a few central inner city boroughs, especially Kreuzberg, nicknamed 'little Istanbul', and Wedding, with 'spill-over' populations in the neighbouring boroughs of Neukolln and Tiergarten.

Patterns of migrant response

The response of the Turkish community towards migration varies between first or second generation migrants and also according to sex. Those most reluctant to become involved with the host society are males of the first generation, although even here there are exceptions where, for example, businessmen need to establish associations. The majority of first generation males see their migration as temporary, undertaken to improve their material and social status on return to the homeland. For them, involvement with the host society beyond the most cursory contact with the place of work is seen not only as inappropriate but dishonouring. Honour depends on maintaining, and preferably improving, one's status. The concept of honour for Turkish migrants relates to their identification with economic goals in their home village and their determination eventually to return. Since German society defines the migrant as *Arbeiter*, worker with the lowest possible status, Turks cannot participate without dishonour. Such migrants tend to save at least half their income, either by saving in Germany or by sending remittances home through Turkish banks under special rates of exchange. By not becoming involved in the life of the Berliner community, they also avoid the extra expense of becoming attracted to the consumer society. While Turks do acquire consumer goods and take pride in doing so, they are reluctant to spend money in this way before having saved enough for building their house or setting up their own business in Turkey.

This type of response is often characterised by an increased emphasis on the control of women and girls by male relatives and the social segregation of the sexes. In the Turkish village the segregation of the sexes is balanced and women have separate living quarters; with men absent for a large part of the day. women enjoy not only a wide network of support from female kin and neighbours but also an important position in the control of information. Women are required to make the first moves in match-making negotiations and to take responsible decisions such as the choice of brides for their sons. These practices are closely related to the organisation of the rural economy in terms of household production rather than wage-labour. As the basis to the household economy has changed through urban migration and wage incomes, men have gained greater control and women have often been left helpless and without any effective means of sanction.

Kandiyoti *et al.* (1978, p. 25) note how industrial development in Turkey has decreased the spheres of women's influence, particularly in the control they appear to have had over domestic finances and the arrangement of marriages. When daughters-in-law lived with the groom and his parents, mothers exercised a prerogative of choice over brides for their sons, while the bride and her mother would make the initial moves. Now, however, fathers and brothers are more likely to control daughters and sisters, almost a reversal of the former arrangement. Some authors, however, view the present relative helplessness of women not as a result of industrial growth but as 'traditional' (Kündig-Steiner, 1974, chapter 1; Kudat and Gürel, 1978, pp. 4–6).

These developments have also been evident in the migrant community of West Berlin, with marriages being arranged by fathers rather than mothers and an increased concern on the part of men to be seen to control their women, by locking them in the apartments and by punishing daughters and younger sisters as well as wives who try to establish links on their own. This may be seen as an attempt in the migrant context to make the honour code explicit; for Turks in Berlin, honour becomes a more consciously maintained precept than in their villages. In this case, moreover, women lose the benefits of segregation because of the impossibility of establishing separate female quarters; they no longer have control over domestic information and affairs. The greater control exercised by men also effectively cuts off the networks of female support enjoyed by women at home. Working wives, on the other hand, have been able to retrieve some of their former influence over family affairs and decisions by means of their independent wage-earning and, if necessary, a separate bank account.

Where Turkish women have control over household matters, it is important not to characterise such signs as evidence of 'Europeanisation'. The willingness and ability of Turkish women to use their influence over decisions in this way is not related to how 'modern' or 'Europeanised' they perceive themselves to be. One of the most financially competent Turkish women I met was a traditional village woman who never left her apartment without covering her head; she was scrupulously religious and believed in sending her children to the Qur'anic school.

The position of first generation Turkish women in relation to the host community shows greater complexity than that of men. Turkish men are given worker status (which, as we have seen, the majority of Turks do not accept) but Turkish women are considered anomalous. Although the majority of women choose to work if they can, they are not seen as workers in the same way as men; while the worker status conferred on men may be low, it represents at least some status. Women, however, are perceived as dependants and, in terms of the worker identity, not a legitimate presence. German reaction to Turkish women ranges between pity and contempt.

Media attention to the 'problem' of Turkish women emphasises almost exclusively the negative aspects of their situation, focusing on their alleged passivity and helplessness in the face of violence and oppression. Changes in their outlook or behaviour are attributed to their adaptation to Berlin life with no regard to the inherent institutions and resources which Turkish women have to draw on within their own community and culture.

While the response of men to migrant life may be clear cut, particularly if they choose to reject the host society as far as possible, women who might wish to align themselves with their own Turkish community cannot help but be drawn to the German benefits of maternity, health care and welfare, as well as to the social attractions of the women's advisory centres when their familiar support network is either reduced or non-existent. Turkish man are seldom aware of the central importance of the women's own support networks. Being insecure themselves, they feel threatened when women act independently and often mistakenly interpret this behaviour as rejection of the Turkish community.

The second generation presents a different response. Although these young people have grown up in Germany, they are not German citizens and most have left school with no qualifications or training. The proportion of Turkish adolescent males who are neither working nor attending an educational course is very high throughout Berlin and West Germany: for example, an estimated two-thirds of Turkish youth in Baden-Württemburg fit into this category. They have little alternative but to make a living in the informal or even underground sectors of the Berlin economy. Many are said to have turned to criminal and semi-criminal activities; Berliners allege, for example that 90 per cent of the drug traffic in the city is controlled by Turks. Such allegations are impossible to prove. It is significant, however, that Turks are rarely the victims of the drug trade. For Berliners who resent Turks, the increased drug abuse among German youth is blamed on the Turkish group as 'corrupters of German youth', as one angry German woman wrote in an anonymous letter sent to a woman's advisory centre in southwest Berlin.

As Turks, these young men feel dishonoured by their lack of status and are obliged to engage in lavish material display and conspicuous behaviour. Having little control over their own circumstances, they often assume exaggerated control over their younger sisters in an effort to reaffirm their own dignity. Brothers may thus be fiercely repressive towards their sisters, sometimes denying them basic school equipment such as pencils and exercise books while themselves dressing in the latest fashions. For German Berliners, these Turkish youth are at once an epitome of the stereotyped characteristics of aggressiveness, volatility and male-domination, while representing the opposite of Turks as workers. Whereas the Turkish worker is unobtrusive, silent and obedient, the Turkish adolescent male is seen as voluble, conspicuous and anything but passive.

The younger generation of Turkish women, while under the strict control of their male kin, are potentially at the same time the ones most open to change, both in terms of their reappraisal of 'traditional' gender roles and in the opportunities presented by Berlin society. Their position is clearly shown in the ambivalence of Turkish males in regard to marriage. On the one hand, Turkish women with residence and work permits in Berlin represent desirable brides for men coming from Turkey, since marriage is now one of the few legitimate ways for a young male Turk to enter Berlin. On the other hand, both for these men and for Turkish men in Berlin, these young women are viewed as potentially dishonourable brides because they have been exposed to foreign influences. Teenage girls and young women thus represent a highly emotive subject for the Turkish community.

These young women not only come under the rigid control of their fathers, brothers and husbands, including veiling, physical confinement and violence as punishment, but they also receive, as will be seen, considerable mishandling and ideological coercion from paternalistic German institutions. These pressures impinge on individual lives in different ways and varying degrees: a girl may have numerous restrictions placed on her by male members of her household, but nevertheless be earning her own living or attending an educational course and at the same time engaging in the activities of a community or advisory centre. These young women are forced to divide their lives into separate compartments or, in extreme cases, to opt out of the Turkish community and to live as single women or as 'outcasts' with Turkish or German husbands or partners.

Turkish women are prepared for social adaptation from an early age, particularly in the area of family relationships (Kandiyoti *et al.*, 1978, p. 22). While adaptation to life as a migrant undoubtedly brings emotional crisis for women, for men this means in addition a crisis of identity and morale. Their low status as workers threatens their personal sense of honour; acceptance of that status would incur humiliation. Berlin employers prize their Turkish workers for their diligence, obedience, punctuality and willingness to perform hard and unpleasant tasks. Many Turks who do these things in Germany, however, would not have dreamed of doing them in Turkey and have no intention of doing them when they return. Migration for men represents a loss of control over their lives, but for women it often offers more options to them as individuals. Wage labour gives women the opportunity for independent incomes and to open separate bank accounts; in cases where marriages fail, a wife thus has a means of supporting herself and is not dependent upon male relatives to take her back. She may also turn to female networks outside the exclusive boundaries of the Turkish community.

Much of the activity engaged in by Turkish women in what may be called the political sphere may thus be seen in terms of the attempt to re-establish networks lost in the process of migration itself. Conflicts within the family are apt to arise out of conflicting perceptions of the proper goals of migration and the best means of achieving them. For men the aim is to stay in Berlin for the shortest possible time in order to save enough money to go back to Turkey and live honourably without the need for industrial labour.

Turkish men may resent the presence of their wives and children in Berlin for a number of reasons. Increased living expenses lengthen the period of stay. Added to this, the presence of wives and kin is potentially dishonouring to a man in terms of their being able to see the facts of his low status in the eyes of the Berliners. As long as a man's family remains in Turkey, he can tolerate discomfort and loneliness in the knowledge that he counts as 'somebody' in the view of his family at home. Faced with the double humiliation of his low status and the knowledge that members of his family are aware of it, Turkish men may assert dominance over their kin and particularly over women. The struggles within the family can be deeply emotional as women try to exercise choices and men attempt to retain control in the name of honour.

Resistance to education policy

In Berlin, education is seen as a means of 'helping' Turks to integrate themselves into Berlin society. This stated goal shows itself at variance with the aims of many Turks, who have no intention of becoming integrated, and they react to education in much the same way as Polish-speaking workers from Silesia did in the last century, regarding educational policy as an attempt to eradicate ethnic and religious identity. Much of the political debate in recent years over the education of Turks has arisen from the prevalence of veiling among Turkish girls and the spread of religious education.

A growing number of Qur'anic schools have appeared in Berlin; these give instruction to children in the afternoons and at weekends, outside the secular school hours. These schools encourage girls, even as young as five or six, to wear headscarves completely covering the head and hair, a practice commonly reserved for rural areas of Turkey, for married women only, and legally forbidden for girls going to school there. Attendance at a Qur'anic school in Berlin is substantially more prevalent among children whose families have been living in Berlin for some years than among families who have recently arrived. Girls who wear a headscarf at school in the secular system are always told to remove it and are often the butt of derisory jokes by their German teachers about defective hearing and so on. Many girls compromise by wearing their scarf when travelling to and from school, but not in class.

It is often suggested that the Qur'anic schools are supported by the right-wing Turkish group, the 'Grey Wolves', and even hinted that right-wing German groups support such methods of dividing the Turkish population against itself. Many Turks point out that, by 'outlawing' Islamic education in the state schools, the German authorities leave it in the hands of those Muslim clergy who are ideologically the least representative of the majority. Turkish families are thus faced with a choice between no religious and cultural education for their children or Islamic fundamentalism.

The situation is further complicated by the fact that a number of Turkish teachers in the secular system are employed by the Turkish Ministry of Education and are sometimes accused of spying on the migrant community. As in Turkey itself, political opinion among Turkish teachers in Berlin ranges from extreme right-wing to extreme left-wing views, complicated by varying degrees of commitment to Europeanisation or retention of Turkish ethnic identity. These teachers in this new environment find themselves under pressure to preserve ideological respectability among their German peers and in the eyes of the authorities. Because parents sense that these Turkish teachers serve two masters, they suspect their motives.

In their confusion, children look to their Turkish teachers for guidance but are frequently disappointed, while many German teachers in schools for Turkish children are not motivated towards their work and are perceived by Turks as unruly and undignified. Given this lack of clear direction within the secular system itself, and the animosity between the secular and religious schools, it is not surprising that many children give up their education almost before it has begun. Resistance to German education arises both from the ideological requirement to maintain family honour in the migrant environment and the practical need for children to act as child-minders in families where both parents go out to work.

The personal becomes political

The unstructured approach of Turkish women gives a flexibility and resourcefulness to their activities which may not be accessible to men. Yet, the importance of women's political activities in Berlin may be obscured by the tendency to view politics in relation to trade unions or to party membership and support. More attention is given in the media to male political groups and to party politics than to women's groups. Again, among the politicised groups of Turks in Berlin there is a tendency to regard specifically female issues as self-indulgent or superfluous when compared with the 'real' issues; they perceive no connection between the character of political oppression in Turkish migrant experience and the conflicts of gender relations within family life.

In the most practical and sustained efforts to establish dialogue between the Turkish and Berlin communities, the younger women predominate. Those involved in projects with Turks come from both the German and Turkish communities and from all walks of life and social backgrounds. During the process of working together, both Turks and Germans have shown significant changes in outlook; they have also developed a strong call to articulate the everyday problems of Turkish women in alternative ways, in particular to go beyond the heavily depersonalised and 'disinfected' style of analysis which has often dominated mainstream discourse. The experience of these women working politically thus echoes the desire of Turkish novelists, poets and playwrights to rehumanise the migrant condition by retrieving the personal elements of their lives.

German research on migrant issues is heavily biased in favour of the collection and analysis of statistics with little reflection on the concepts of the host society and almost entirely devoid of the Turks' own view of their situation or their personal experiences. This one-way communication is particularly evident in government publications, which are professionally produced but offer no framework for dialogue between the two communities (e.g. Elsas, 1980; Senatskanzlei, 1979). Turkish writing, in contrast, has an affective quality which implies criticism of these institutions dealing with Turks in a depersonalised, quantitative manner. On occasion, this resistance to the dominant approach uses extremely provocative symbolism. In 1981, when the newly-elected government in Berlin tried to repatriate all young Turkish people not in full-time education or working, demonstrators appeared on the streets wearing the Jewish star on their sleeves. The issue here is not to what extent there is an actual parallel between Jewish and Turkish experience (the Jews, after all, were Germans), but rather the ability of Turks to draw on this evocative imagery for political strategies.

Berliners see Turkish women as being passive and inept, even invisible, while being physically the most conspicuous social group of Berlin. Welfare organisations attempting to advance their cause try to reduce this conceptual tension, as they perceive it, on the one hand by making Turkish women more socially and politically active, on the other by obliterating those Turkish characteristics, such as their style of dress and specifically Turkish habits, which make them physically noticeable. In consequence, Turkish women often find themselves removed from one area of dependence to another without any opportunity to formulate their own priorities or to use their own methods for achieving them.

The veil is a case in point (cf. Sharma, 1978). If Germans see the veiling of Turkish women as a sign of outmoded tradition and women's subordinance, Turkish women use it as a deliberate political act oriented towards the future and demonstrating control over their lives. Veiling asserts gender differentiation in a society which seems determined to break it down and at the same time provides a visible symbol of the separateness of the Turkish community as a whole. The veil thus affirms the female aspect of Turkish identity both by concealing it and making it conspicuous, while underlining the feelings of powerlessness of the Turkish community. As a political act, the practice of veiling can be seen as conservative in reinforcing traditional gender roles and radical in its conscious rejection of the ascribed status of Turks in Berlin.

Often women's power goes unrecognised even within their own community. In the case of one Turkish couple I knew from the Black Sea area, the wife had complete control over the family finances, to the extent that her husband had no idea how much money she saved on their behalf each month. Although she also earned wages, in many respects, especially observances related to religion, she was much more conservative than her husband. Whereas he held no strong views about girls and women covering their heads in public, for example, she believed this custom to be very important. In her own eyes, she was fulfilling the role expected of her as a wife and mother. Such conservatism cannot be understood to imply 'passivity' on her part. Her husband, far from objecting to her financial control, had great respect for her and regarded this arrangement as superior to that of husbands and wives with independent bank accounts, a system to him indicating a lack of trust between the partners.

Women's refuges and advisory centres

The debilitating effects of German liberalism on Turkish women are evident from the way refuges are run. The women's refuge I knew in Berlin, for example, had never had a Turkish speaker on its staff and appeared to have no intention of doing so, although there were literally thousands of Turkish women in Berlin who would gladly have done the job. This refuge had at times as high as a 40 per cent intake of Turkish women in their residential care, as well as their children. Hardly any of these women who passed through their hands spoke more than a few words of German. On numerous occasions I offered my help as interpreter or translator for Turkish women, but was turned down. When I recounted my experience to a Berlin woman who worked in a newly established advisory centre, she remarked that women who worked in the refuges in Berlin regarded themselves as an elite vanguard of the women's movement. Allowing for the staff's real concern for the privacy and safety of the women who took refuge with them, often from violent situations which necessarily entailed a careful questioning of anyone who expressed a wish to become involved, it was difficult not to find their lack of Turkish staff bafflingly counterproductive. Perhaps, as my Berliner friend pointed out, it was their intention 'to lead Turkish women about by the hand, as if they were small children.' In political terms, the irony was that group which claimed to be the most 'radical' displayed the most obviously 'liberal' characteristics.

A more positive approach to Turkish women is taken by the *Frauenläden*, or women's advisory centres. These are drop-in centres where staff and volunteers can help with filling in forms, making telephone calls, and putting women in touch with Turkish-speaking doctors and lawyers. The centres also offer a wide range of activities, including literacy and photography classes and day-trips to the Berlin lakes and forests. Usually open for about three or four hours a day for the working week, these centres are financed by the Berlin Senate and in some cases share facilities with other community-based projects. Women who use these centres often stumble upon them by chance, when they notice the 'shop' as they walk past or hear about it from a neighbour or friend. A core group of women call in regularly, sometimes long after they have any specific problem to deal with. They are keen to help with the running of activities and in the discussion of future plans, and they often volunteer to organise cleaning rotas.

The staff and volunteers in advisory centres are both Turkish and German with differing philosophies about how the job should be done. All staff I met were active feminists, but their political views ranged from 'Green' through to socialist and Marxist. In general, however, the existence of Turkish staff prevented work in the advisory centres from becoming doctrinaire in its approach. By definition, the centres took their cues from the expressed needs of Turkish women in the community.

The value of the centres was widely recognised among those who had professional or personal contact with the Turkish community. When the centres were threatened with closure in 1981 as a result of cuts, doctors and psychiatrists protested along with the centre staffs that an indispensible service to the community would be lost if funds were stopped. They argued that the social isolation of Turkish women without access to such means of support was one of the major causes of mental and psychosomatic illness. Women who found themselves in a strange city, bereft of their familiar networks, unable to speak the language and thus often trapped within two or three streets were able to get help. Once involved with a centre and having gained some confidence and practical skills, women learned to travel from one side of the city to the other. One woman travelled two or three times a week from Spandau in the far west of the city to Kreuzberg, which adjoins the Berlin wall, a journey the full length of the West Berlin underground line.

Another visitor to a centre in Kreuzberg had a circulatory illness which caused her to feel giddy if she climbed ladders in the course of her work. Afer producing a certificate to this effect at the union building where she worked, she was subsequently dismissed from her job. With the centre's assistance, as well as that of a lawyer they had found for her, she claimed compensation from her employers for unfair dismissal; they were legally obliged to offer her alternative employment, and could not in any case dismiss her on the grounds of an illness. Although she had been working in Berlin for a number of years with her husband, neither of them spoke sufficient German to be able to cope with a lawyer; the centre sent me along to interpret for her.

Apart from offering practical assistance such as this, the centres offered company for women who would otherwise have no social contact outside the home. Toys would be brought out for the children, someone would start tea brewing in the samovar, and we would sit chatting for hours. In another room, a class would be going on in literacy or German. Conversation was relaxed and any business conducted in an informal manner. Women were encouraged to make their own phone calls and participate as much as possible in what concerned them. Many women would wander in and out to say hello during the course of an afternoon; relationships were very affectionate and women formed close bonds – the social workers, volunteers and women from all social backgrounds.

Experiences of this kind made Turkish women reassess the importance of personal contact and support from other women. They often had to fight to keep any form of contact outside the home, particularly if they were without employment, as was becoming more common in the recession. Women in Berlin had to make an effort to establish and maintain networks which would have been automatic in their home environment. In making this effort, they were in a sense making a political statement and asserting, or reasserting, control over this aspect of their lives. The existence of the women's centres thus expressed two aspects of the situation of migrant women. On the one hand Turkish women were forced outside the home in order to live 'normal' lives in the company and support of other women. While in Turkey male kin had almost no control over female networks, given the kin and neighbourhood networks which existed and the pattern of labour division and living quarters, in Berlin, women's re-creation of 'traditional' networks is seen as a loss of control by many men, who are able to sanction the movements of women by virtue of their control over living quarters and the relative helplessness of women in a strange environment. In Berlin, therefore, the 'traditional' behaviour of Turkish women becomes political. This is first because they have to assert what they were previously able to take for granted, and second because in making this assertion they often unintentionally became involved in the political struggles of the Berliners who work alongside them. Once again, what was conservative in Turkey becomes radical in the Berlin context.

Here, and in the women's refuges, they are introduced to radical politics concerned with feminist questions, the squatter's movement and other issues of importance to the Turkish community. Some women find themselves ill-equipped to deal with active politics, not only because they perceive these issues in different ways but because of the danger that politically engaged groups in Berlin take up the problems of Turkish women and articulate them in their own way and to a large extent for their own ends. This often leads to Turkish women yet again being cast in the role of helpless victim, with no serious attempts to examine their strengths or take their views seriously.

Conflicting perceptions

As my fieldwork went on, I became more aware of the discrepancy between the German view of the Turks and the way in which Turks were coming to see themselves in the migrant context. In the absence of social and political status, and the voice that goes with them, Turks increasingly articulated their concerns through personal relationships and emotional values, in their social groups and their artistic and creative activities. It is perhaps ironic that Turks are collectively identified in the minds of Berliners with emotional volatility and unpredictability, qualities taken to be signs of inferiority and inadequacy, when Berlin society itself frequently becomes intensely emotional, especially in the political sphere when issues of order and principle are discussed. This suggests that emotional life is *controlled* in Berlin culture: emotional responses have to be contained within an area considered legitimate, such as debates primarily concerned with overall rational issues; the direct expression of emotion is regarded as dangerous and identified with outsiders and foreigners. This relates to the way information regarding migrants is presented: in a detached and remote style, devoid of personal perceptions.

Berlin culture continues to uphold the social virtues of orderliness, obedience, duty and cleanliness, virtues which had their roots in pre-industrial Germany but which now support the rational technological life of an industrialised city. For the Turkish community, the implicitly masculine and military imagery of these virtues is problematic in more than one sense. The Turks themselves have a strongly masculine warrior imagery and uphold two extremes of gender identity; as we have seen, the perceived masculine role often becomes exaggerated almost to the point of caricature and certainly to the point of conflict, both within the Turkish community and between Turks and Germans. In performing this culturally prescribed masculine role, Turkish men see themselves as protecting the principle of a precious and distinct feminine identity for Turkish women and, by extension, of a valued and different culture – the Turkish community as a whole.

In comparing themselves with German women, many Turkish women perceive them as oppressed by their domestic routine at the expense of human relationships. Although, for example, Turkish women pride themselves on cleanliness in the home, they perceive Berliner notions of cleanliness as being of a different order. One woman described the furniture in a German apartment as 'all lined up and gleaming like soldiers,' a clear allusion to military imagery and implying strong criticism. Turkish women draw a direct connection between this German lack of feeling and their own low social and political status. Aysel Özakin views her relationship with her German boyfriend as symbolic of relations between Turks and Germans in general. She believes that people in present industrial society are unable to express emotion and have no real conception of what relationships are possible between people. She regards the preoccupation of many Berliners with sex as an indication of 'emotional poverty', in the sense that the sexual act seemed to be the only legitimate form of intimate relationship. These perceptions colour much of her writing.

Turkish writing – poetry, short stories, novels and plays – now flourishes in Germany and is read by Germans as well as Turks, in translation and in bilingual Turkish-German editions. Literary publications include work by children and amateurs as well as by professional writers (Jugend Schreibt, 1980; Ören, 1978; Özakin, 1982). Joint German and Turkish publishing groups and companies are becoming commonplace and indicate one of the most important areas of cooperation between the two communities. Theatrical and performing arts groups, supported by community centres, have also burgeoned in West Berlin. These groups encourage bilingual productions, street fairs and cultural events with Turkish dancing, puppet theatres and children's events, designed to bring Turkish and German groups together and to offer Turkish culture to a wider audience. In this shared cultural enterprise, understanding is fostered at the personal and the collective levels; on both sides, the attitudes based on stereotypes begin to disappear.

Until this kind of activity becomes widespread, the depersonalised discourse on migrants can be used as a screen to prevent serious consideration of Turkish-German relations as a dynamic process, rather than one in which, in its crudest form, Turkishness is viewed as an impediment to becoming German. In this latter perspective, responsibility for 'integration' is placed with the Turks themselves; the host society's own social institutions are not open to discussion – or to plurality of vision.

The political situation of Turkish women in Berlin can thus be defined as the conflict between their own gender and family roles, already in a state of transition prior to migration, and the 'double message' of local government policy which aims to integrate Turks into Berlin society by eliminating their distinguishing characteristics.

From this discussion of Turkish women in Berlin, we may distinguish three main political trends in the approach of the host society. Government and city policies attempts to deprive migrant groups of their ethnic visibility and to integrate them economically into the lowest levels of society. The liberal approach of the media and certain welfare organisations, while at odds with the main economic imperatives, remains ethnocentric in its refusal to face the possibility of plurality. This manifests itself in the treatment of Turkish women as backward and helpless and the attempt to obliterate their Turkish identity in the name of helping them. Within this approach an element of radical thinking may be discerned which perceives social and economic policy towards migrants as hypocritical and exploitative, but still seems unable to break the mould of treating Turks as backward and without resources. In practice, the women's centres, considered in terms of Berlin politics to be liberal in comparison to the leftist women's refuges, display more understanding in their genuine attempts to leave control and direction in the hands of Turkish women themselves.

It is in this context that my Turkish friend Aysel resents Berliner attempts to categorise her as atypical and to patronise her with their approval, simply because she dresses as they do. Aysel's concern with the migrant community, and especially its women, has a dual element in its desire to free Turkish women from the control of its men exercised in the name of honour and to free them also from the trap of German liberalism to enable them to determine for themselves what to think and how to live.

References

Abadan-Unat, Nermin (ed.) (1976) *Turkish Workers in Germany* (Leiden: Brill).

Elsas, Christoph (1980) *Einflüsse der Islamischen Religion auf die Integrationsfähigkeit der Ausländischen Arbeitnehmer und ihrer Familienangehörigen* (West Berlin: Senatskanzlei).
Jugend Schreibt, Förderzentrum (1980) *Täglich eine Reise von der Türkei nach Deutschland* (Fischerhude: Verlag Atellier im Bauernhaus).
Kandiyoti, Deniz *et al.* (1978) *Women in Turkish Society* (Istanbul: Turkish Social Science Association).
Kudat, Ayse and Gurel, Seval (1978) *Personal, Familial and Societal Impacts of Turkish Women's Migration to Europe* (Paris: UNESCO).
Kündig-Steiner, Werner (1974) *Die Türkei* (Tübingen, Basel).
Ören, Aras (1978) *Deutschland ein Türkisches Marchen* (Düsseldorf: Claassen Verlag).
Özakin, Aysel (1982) *Soll Ich Hier Alt Werden?* (Hamburg: Buntbuch Verlag).
Senatskanzlei-Planungsleitstelle (1979) *Leitlinien und Neue Massnahmen zur Ausländerintegration in Berlin* (West Berlin: Senatskanzlei).
Sharma, Ursula (1978) 'Women and their Affines: the Veil as a Symbol of Separation', *Man*, vol. 13, no. 2.

10 Survival and Support: Women's Forms of Political Action

HELEN CALLAWAY

The women whose voices come through these pages lead ordinary lives in their societies. They perceive themselves as powerless and, in terms of the wider political systems, must be seen as relatively so. In all of these cases, they were caught up in political conflict, sometimes with shattering violence. These chapters document their responses to situations varying from brutal war, experienced by Greek Cypriot women during the Turkish invasion of Cyprus and by Palestinian women in Beirut, to the relatively benign case (however fierce the local battles) of Breton women involved in issues of ethnicity and self-identification.

Many of these women responded to the immediate problems with practical efforts and found themselves stretching their capacities, forming organisations with other women, and exercising powers they had never before exerted. As their personal lives became projected onto the political plane, they reached new levels of activity and awareness. Some of these women experienced terrible losses and personal violence. In most cases, although not always fully recognised, their activities helped to shape the course and outcome of the conflict. And, by taking part in the political struggle, they themselves changed.

Did this experience empower these women to articulate women's issues and to participate more fully in the public policies of their society? While many sensed and probed the limitations of their conventional gender roles, in most cases they did not attempt to change them but deliberately gave priority to their children, their menfolk and the wider goals of their society. These chapters show clearly how women's roles during a time of war or heightened tension cannot be analysed separately from their specific context of class and ethnic differences, of national history and purpose, and of cultural tradition. Gender relations are deeply embedded within wider power structures.

Women's active involvement

In the studies included in this collection, women have little participation in formal political and military institutions, but when conflict erupted they developed their own modes of survival and support. The authors show how 'ordinary' women took up all sorts of practical and innovative ways to exert pressure on the political scene. When Catholic women in Northern Ireland devised a warning system against army raids by 'bin lid bashing', as Lynda Edgerton describes, they became involved in political activity. Similarly, Palestinian women in Beirut, in the account by Rosemary Sayigh and Julie Peteet, volunteered as silent sentinels outside meeting places to warn of approaching army agents. Women formed support groups, organised the welfare needs of their communities, carried out public demonstrations. They also drew on symbolic resources, as in the case of Turkish women in Berlin analysed by Clare Krojzl, who veiled themselves to assert Turkish cultural identity and to refuse assimilation into Berlin society on German terms. In situations of strife, women's daily lives became politicised. Their forms of political action grew out of their experience as women and developed to meet the exigencies of their world at risk.

These diverse examples show how political conflict itself calls forth women's active involvement. If these women are observed as powerless and think of themselves in this way, as soon as they take part in the most minor action to aid their group, they enter into the 'negotiations' of power. Some of these examples, particularly in Iran and Cyprus, reveal women losing ground as a result of the conflict. Others show women gaining considerable strength through collective action and playing a significant part in the struggle itself. Palestinian women, as Sayigh and Pateet point out, have played an important part in the Resistance. Moiram Ali's study of British miners' wives demonstrates their role as the driving force behind the 1984–85 coal strike.

In recent years, feminist scholars (among them, Janeway, 1981; Rendel, 1981; Stacey and Price, 1981; O'Barr, 1982; Randall, 1982; Hirschon, 1984) have extended the scope of political studies by setting out new questions about women in the political domain and by analysing the complex relations of gender and power. Others (including Berkin and Lovett, 1980; Stiehm, 1982a; O'Barr, 1985) have focused on women in times of war and liberation struggles. When women during a time of conflict come to the front as a vital force in the political strength of their group, are they able afterwards to enter formal political institutions and take a greater role in the policies and decisions of their society? Do they gain more equitable gender roles? From these diverse chapters on women in specific situations of political conflict, certain issues emerge which help to extend our understanding of these questions: how conflict sets the stage for specific sexual violence against women, the way classifications are imposed to circumscribe women's lives, the varied forms of political action that women take up to meet particular emergencies, and how ideology often promotes gender polarity in order to assert cultural identity.

Violence against women

In some of the cases described in these chapters, political conflict has brought great physical risk to all members of the society. Bombs erupt indiscriminately, bullets hit those without weapons. When war or civil turbulence prevails, men generally carry out the main military operations and account for the highest proportion of the dead and wounded, yet women and children are also engulfed in the bloodshed. Moreover, women become the targets of specific sexual violence, not only brutal rape from enemy forces, as 'spoils of war' in the manner recorded throughout history, but rape and beatings from men of their own society and even from their own husbands in the heightened aggression of a time of hostility. In the situations described in these chapters, however, the most extreme violence against women comes from the forces of the state itself, which officially prescribes and legitimates such violence, as exemplified in Khomeini's Iran.

The new legal codes put into effect in Iran, as Homa Nategh writes, make it not only possible but mandatory for the Revolutionary Guards to 'marry' young girls arrested for committing counter-revolutionary acts and to rape them before putting them to death. These codes also stipulate that a woman can be accused by her husband or father of adultery and, without any recourse, be turned over to the Islamic tribunal for public execution by stoning. If in many countries domestic violence is condoned as belonging to the private sphere, in Iran it has been authorised by the theocratic regime: the Qur'an is interpreted as saying that good husbands should on occasion beat their wives and Khomeini has personally directed that a man must correct his disobedient wife by corporal punishment.

While some Greek Cypriot women experienced savage rape from invading Turkish soldiers, as the evidence presented by Maria Roussou shows, they were metaphorically violated a second time by the official line of the church allowing husbands and fiancés to gain divorce or dissolution of the engagement contract. These women were victims first of the enemy and then of their own society, which failed to protect them and then, through no fault of their own, expelled them to the margins of social life. This case shows clearly the dangers for women in a society which designates men as 'protectors' and women as 'protected'. In her probing analysis of the complexities of this symbiotic relation, Judith Hicks Stiehm (1982b, pp. 367–76) suggests that women and men should share the risk and responsibility as defenders of their society. Her reasons do not include the idea that women might well be better able to defend themselves (in such cases as the Greek Cypriot women during the Turkish invasion), although this is a possible result, but emerge from the asymmetrical relation of the male 'protector' to the female 'protected' and the ideology of violence this permits. She considers that women's direct participation might reduce the murderous and unforgivable acts of violence carried out by the male military with an 'on behalf of' justification.

In a number of these cases, political conflict has created a continuing situation of war or near-war. For many families in Northern Ireland, as Edgerton states, violence has become part of daily living. Here excessive coercive force against women is seen by many women's organisations to come from the state in its 'strip searches' of female prisoners. Although no statistics are available, Edgerton considers the likelihood to be strong that both sexual and domestic violence have increased with the militarisation of the

Province. Individual men of the paramilitary organisations have been able to commit rape without being apprehended by calling on their military connections for support. Moreover, the power of the military outside the home also increases the possibility of this power being used within the home: some men attempt to control their wives by beating them and use their position to prevent the injured women from getting assistance. In times of strife, as this chapter also illustrates, women show themselves capable of acting brutally against other women to enforce conformity to social norms.

Of all these situations, the Palestinian women in Beirut have sustained the longest and most physical insecurity, as shown by Sayigh and Peteet; in their account, however, this has not included rape by enemy forces or increased domestic violence by their own men. During their long years of exile, these women have been directly in the line of enemy fire through various wars and more recently have experienced successive massacres within their own refugee camps. Many have been casualties of war. One of the most poignant images of life-affirming womanhood in this book is that of the Palestinian woman during a siege who went to fetch water to keep her children alive: hit fatally by a sniper's bullet, she continued to balance the water container on her head as she sank slowly to the ground.

Classifications and control

Political conflict often involves redefinitions of social reality. The authors of these chapters show how cultural concepts operate to control women's lives, but also in some cases how women act against imposed classifications to assert their own definitions of themselves and their society.

The most radical example of gender reclassification in this collection occurred in the Islamic Republic of Iran. Here, as Nategh writes, the *lex talionis* introduced in 1980 not only disinherits and debases women, but inscribes her legally as less than human. This law states that Islam considers a woman to be 'half a man' and thus denies her any rights as a mother or wife or even as a human being. If she is attacked or raped, she cannot bring any charge against the wrongdoer. Should she be arrested for an offence, she cannot prove her innocence because a 'just' man can classify her as an 'unsound person' whose testimony along with that of a lunatic, an intoxicated person or a minor is not admissible. Through this law, men are awarded the active power of defining social situations to their advantage.

The legal repression of Iranian women became visible in everyday life with the compulsory requirement for women to wear Islamic habit in dark colours of a chador, a headscarf completely covering the hair, long sleeves and thick stockings. When the war with Iraq and the resulting economic crisis brought added sufferings, Nategh tells us, women began to rebel. The same women who became so massively involved in the religious demonstrations which helped to overthrow the Shah and bring in the Ayatollah are today the most open enemies of the Khomeini regime. They show their opposition by discarding the prescribed Islamic dress and, above all, by daily protests against the war and the economic recession.

The control of Greek Cypriot women, as the study by Roussou shows, comes more subtly in the constant evocation of the myth of Penelope. The women, known as 'false widows', whose husbands disappeared at the time of the Turkish invasion in 1974, are counselled to wait patiently for their husbands' return. In this state of uncertainty and loneliness, not only do they encounter numerous legal and economic problems but they are denied any social identity. Legal measures to redefine these women as 'widows' have not been taken; these women would then be free to remarry and again take a full part in social life. Roussou argues that such measures would undermine the existing male-oriented social order which depends on the strict control of women for maintaining its structures of honour and prestige. Despite their difficulties in this anomalous position of 'not wife/not widow', these women themselves hold the traditional values of their culture and have not organised to press collectively for a change in status.

In the case of Israeli kibbutz women, both the internal classifications of work and the national conflict inhibits women's moves for advancement. Alison Bowes analyses how the pioneer women colluded in their own subordination. While they sought to take on men's work of manual labour in the fields and on the roads, termed as 'productive work', the men had no inclination to reciprocate by carrying out the traditional tasks of women. With the birth of children and the improvement of living standards, kibbutz women involved themselves in the new work of collective childcare and housekeeping, but this was now classified as 'unproductive work'. These categories, Bowes points out, used in ordinary kibbutz talk and in official language, devalue women's work. Although contemporary kibbutz women are now excluded from 'productive work' and from important areas of politics, they are not united in any effort to recover the lost ideals of equality; many fight for improvements, a few call on the resources of modern feminism. Bowes cogently argues that change in the position of kibbutz women requires change in Israeli society as a whole, and this can only come with peace.

Turkish women in Berlin actively resist the categories imposed on their migrant group by the German hosts. As Krojzl explains, the political significance of their veiling relates to the Turkish community as a whole, as a conspicuous symbol of cultural separation from German society and a rejection of the '*Arbeiter*' classification which places them at the lowest social status and economic level. The German media characterise the Turkish male as aggressive and authoritarian and the Turkish female as helpless, ignorant and ill-treated by her menfolk. Turkish migrant women reject these stereotypes. They refuse to adopt German customs and styles of dress not because they are unable to adapt, the interpretation so often given by the host population, but because by strengthening their ethnic identity they sustain their dignity and personhood. However powerless these migrant women may feel in the difficulties of their daily lives in Berlin, they are taking upon themselves 'the power to define' (Sutton, 1976), the demonstration of their group identity. They are engaged in the politics of classification.

Breton women, too, are involved in the politics of self-identification, although as Maryon MacDonald shows in precise details which are sometimes amusing, the educated militant women and the relatively unschooled peasant women hold opposed models of Breton female identity. Militant women endorse feminism, the Breton language, the ruggedness of an artisan life in the countryside and an ideal of Breton authenticity. Meanwhile, peasant women aspire to conventional femininity and a dash of finery, the French language, and life away from the hardships of work in the fields. If militant women frame the idea of 'liberation' in opposition to the male-dominated, bourgeois life of French cities, peasant women measure their advancement in terms of entering a world of greater refinement and leaving behind the harshness and insecurity of Breton farm life.

Women's forms of action

These chapters are particularly interesting in revealing both how the conflict came into women's homes, politicising their daily lives, and how women's forms of actions to meet the new situations grew out of their traditional patterns of organisation and their gender roles as providers and nurturers. While in some cases women moved into the political spotlight, as for example the miners' wives who took part in national and international speaking tours, they presented their arguments as women. They did not see themselves, nor were they perceived by others, as moving into men's domains.

The role of mother and housewife acquired new emphasis and a political dimension: for individual women when men took on greater political and military duties outside the home, leaving them to provide for families on their own; and for women collectively when their maternal role was extended to provide food and welfare for the community, as miners' wives did during the strike. The soup kitchen became their political base.

Physical reproduction has become explicitly political for Palestinian women, who consider themselves to have a 'military womb', giving birth to fighters for the resistance. As a result of their exile, motherhood has become transformed from the family level to a national act and duty. For them as well, the ideal of the 'active housewife' illustrates how women in the camp setting expand their traditional domestic and social duties to include new political activities. This may involve the 'triple burden' of managing a large household, holding a salaried job and undertaking political work. Again, the 'martyr's mother' attains a special role; as Sayigh and Peteet point out, she may never have been politically active, but her maternal sacrifice is exalted as a supreme political act. Privileged to gain the ear of resistance leaders, these mothers have been able to perform a political function in the camp as intermediaries.

In the Palestinian context, women are accorded special powers because of their 'natural' role. Those whose sons or husbands were in prison, for example, confronted leading politicians, even demanding an audience with the Prime Minister. The authors of this study trace this action of women on behalf of their male kinsfolk to ancient Semitic roots; because they are *women*, they have the right of access to the powerful to seek compassion. Here women draw on symbolic resources, the imagery of female powers in their cultural heritage, as the basis for political action.

Some of these chapters show how women are able to create and use an information network in the subtle dynamics of informal decision-making. While women in the Israeli kibbutz, for example, do not participate in the formal governing institutions, as Bowes explains, they exert considerable influence in the affairs of the kibbutz 'by passing on the right kind of information to just the right people'. They are able to build reputations of individual kibbutz members and mobilise support for particular enterprises because their work in the service sections brings them into regular contact with a wide network of people throughout the community.

In the diverse situations covered by these chapters, women's organisations show a wide range in their purpose, structures, cohesion and strength. For the Turkish women in Berlin, the women's advisory centres financed by the Berlin Senate provide a meeting place where these women, who have lost their familiar networks through migration, find sympathetic company and support for managing specific problems. In the informal classes, they are able to learn the German language and a variety of practical skills; they also plan day trips to Berlin's scenic spots. Once these women become involved in a centre, they take part in its planning and daily running. While these women do not initiate these centres and their gatherings represent a relatively loose form of organisation, they often have to assert themselves with their menfolk to attend, and by doing so, as Krojzl analyses, they make a political assertion of control over this part of their lives. They are also introduced to radical politics concerning feminist issues, squatters' rights and other questions of importance to Turkish immigrants.

In the Beirut camps of the Palestinian refugees, the weekly women's seminars became an effective form of mobilisation for busy housewives. Set up by the women cadres of the resistance, they covered a wide range of topics from child health to current events. Here women who did not usually speak up in public found their voices by taking part in the discussion, raising questions, setting out complaints. These seminars, again a flexible and loosely structured meeting, served as a node linking the problems of women's daily lives to the wider aspects of the resistance.

If these ordinary Palestinian housewives were relatively unorganised, as Sayigh and Peteet describe, they were able to sustain political action. The example cited of the older woman with a son in prison, who rose to the occasion in the midst of danger when asked by a woman cadre to spread the news of a sit-in against kidnappings and arrest, makes clear how the inspiration for women's political mobilisation often arises from personal experience. To gain support for the protest, she had only to say: 'Today it's my son in prison, tomorrow it may be yours. Who will march with you tomorrow if you don't march with us today? Isn't every young man in this camp the son of all of us?'

In some situations, women spontaneously joined together in informal local groups as a practical way to meet the emergency at hand. During the miners' strike, women in pit villages all over Britain formed women's support groups to work together on the common problem of feeding and clothing a community deprived of its income. These support groups, started under a variety of local names, banded together to form the national body called Women Against Pit Closures; this provides a fascinating example of 'organisation from below', to paraphrase a concept from development vocabulary. While these groups started as an extension of women's work as mothers and housewives, as Ali describes, some of them initiated action well beyond women's traditional roles. They sponsored women to join the men on the picket line. Here, confronted by the massive strength of the police, the miners' wives developed new tactics of wit, ridicule and diversion – occasionally leaving the police in embarrassed confusion (Bloomfield, 1985, p. 16). Gaining self-confidence and political awareness in these support groups, a few individual women rose as representatives to speak on women's perspectives of the coal war; some who had hardly been out of their mining villages before now travelled throughout Britain and abroad. Both during and after the strike, the women's support groups were widely acknowledged by the men of the National Union of Mineworkers for the strength of their action.

Across the Irish Sea, women in 1967 were among the founders of the Northern Ireland Civil Rights Association, which became a mass movement for extending democracy and ending sectarian rule. Before long, as Edgerton records, the pressure of political events had reached such a heightened state of hostility that all-women demonstrations were sparked off to meet specific situations. Similar to the women's support groups in the miners' strike, and to women's historical prominence in food riots of Britain and France (Randall, 1982, p. 41), the first all-women demonstration formed on the issue of food – the shortage of fresh milk and bread – for the families cut off by the Falls Road curfew. Gradually women became organisers in NICRA, and it was mainly women who planned the Rents and Rates Strike as a protest against internment; this involved more than 30 000 households at its height. Again, these women felt it to be their family duty to protest about the imprisonment and ill treatment of their fathers, husbands, brothers and sons. Out of women's traditional roles grew strong public campaigns.

Some women's campaigns in Northern Ireland reached across the religious divide. The Milk Campaign, for example, in protest over the stopping of milk for school children over the age of seven, began with both Protestant and Catholic support as the 'Mothers of Belfast' set out their agenda to gain mass support. Although this campaign achieved considerable success, the decision to stop school milk was not rescinded and the campaign itself lost momentum in August 1971 when the announcement of internment without trial brought more impassioned political concerns.

The chapter on Northern Ireland presents the only example in this collection of women as peacemakers to end the political conflict. In August 1976, when three small children were killed and the mother seriously injured, two women sparked off a spontaneous and massive movement for peace. Within a few weeks, despite the opposition of extremist groups on both sides, over 100 000 people had come out on the streets in sympathetic marches. At its height, this movement – known as the Peace People, with men having joined as well – caught the imagination of the world's press and in 1977 the two founders, Betty Williams and Mairead Corrigan, were awarded the Nobel Peace Prize. Whatever the disputed aftermath and their defeat in bringing an end to the conflict, their achievement was notable. It was through this movement, Scilla McLean writes, 'that people were able to *begin* to imagine a different way of solving conflict' (1982, p. 324). She continues:

> Individuals, women particularly, whose lives until the movement began had never led them to articulate their opinions and desires publicly, learned to assert themselves, express their wishes, and taste active involvement; there are many such cases. However reduced, in numbers and scope, it is a living exercise in community democracy, in the midst of a situation of extraordinary violence, renowned for entrenched positions and pathological refusal to negotiate.

This example, while unsuccessful in overcoming the historical conflict, suggests sources of power that women (whether or not working with men) have not as yet fully developed.

Again within the purview of this book, one of the few organisations formed specifically to promote women's issues was the Northern Ireland Women's Rights Movement. Set up in 1975 as an 'umbrella' for various interested organisations in a united women's movement, it brought together those from both Protestant and Catholic areas to work for such common demands as nursery facilities, equal opportunities in education and work, equal pay and so on. This organisation established the first women's centre in Belfast and through its debates and campaigns has created a forum for women's issues. As cases of sexual and domestic violence became cited, the Northern Ireland Women's Aid Federation and the Rape Crisis Association were formed to give assistance. Despite the prevailing political conflict, Women's Aid has been able to provide women's refuges in 'neutral' areas, where both Catholic and Protestant women have been able to come for protection.

These chapters show the fluidity of women's political action, how they formed organisations structured formally or informally according to their immediate and long-term purposes, how they improvised and used their energies to enlist support for their community. Women gave their strongest commitment, understandably, to the political cause of their own group, but also, in the examples shown, they organised a movement for peace and for women's rights. These studies from Western Europe and the Middle East make clear how the political action of 'ordinary' women arises from the domain of their everyday reality and is exerted towards their life-affirming concerns for the safety of their families and the sustenance of their communities.

Gender polarity and cultural identity

Political conflict by its very nature creates changes in society, often unpredicted and sometimes devastating. When it continues for many years, as the women of Palestine and Northern Ireland have experienced, the effects on the population can be particularly damaging and demoralising. In Iran, women have become so disillusioned by the regime they themselves helped to bring about, Nategh writes, that their queues during the long hours of waiting for an item of food have become 'women's political parties'.

The chapters in this collection delineate women's political action in times of conflict; they show, as well, how this experience changed women. Of women in Northern Ireland, Melanie McFadyean has written:

> The great irony is that the war of the last fifteen years has made the women stronger, more independent, braver and more determined. The war has politicized people; these years have inspired the debate between feminism and nationalism, have made women question the institutions that generations before them had taken for granted – marriage, the church, birth control, the law. (1984, p. viii)

In her contribution, Edgerton describes the political awakening, the courage, and the sense of new identity these women gained as they joined in protests and mounted demonstrations against the injustices they felt so strongly. Although these new experiences helped them to discern women's issues, they have not given them priority; fighting for women's rights would mean going against the entrenched attitudes of their own society. Women have taken on new public political activities on behalf of their men, Edgerton concludes, but on the domestic scene they are still awaiting reciprocity.

Ali's chapter on the women of the British mining community brings out their resourcefulness, humour and dedication as they became more and more involved in supporting the strike. If the soup kitchens meant their familiar domestic work writ large, some women moved into the public arena by joining the picket line and others by going on speaking tours abroad. They gained self-confidence through the work of their women's support groups, shared experiences with women from many other areas and became more aware of common interests. An Oxford woman who welcomed the women from Maerdy wrote, 'Involvement in struggle has changed us all' (Sweeney, 1985, p. 70). And the voice of a miner's wife echoes many others: 'I became a totally different person.' Yet, as Ali convincingly argues, they did not see their commitment to the miners' strike as a feminist struggle; on the contrary, they challenged middle-class feminists to reappraise *their* attitudes about working with men and about the links between the feminist movement and the lives of working class women. During the long year of the strike, these women from mining community became politicised to broader national issues and pledged themselves to go on fighting. The women in Sherbern-in-Elmet, for example, have continued their political activities by raising money for sacked miners and, at the same time, campaigning against the closure of a hospital, an issue which particularly concerns their own lives.

Do women make any lasting gains from their intensified economic and political activity during a period of conflict? In her introduction to Muthoni Likimani's vivid fictional documentation of women's activities in the Mau Mau movement, Jean O'Barr (1985, pp. 23—35) questions the view sometimes put forward that wars, revolutions and nationalist movements are 'watersheds' resulting in significant advances for women. Reviewing the various nationalist movements in Africa, she traces how these gave African women new opportunities to demonstrate their capacities and power, but how in most cases they were not able to consolidate these gains for full participation in the new governments arising after independence. She examines the effects of Kenyan women's strong participation in the nationalist cause. This was an empowering experience, she observes, but did not represent a 'watershed' for these women. Beliefs about women's place in the family and about how the mother role defines power and position were not altered; women did not take positions of leadership in the public sphere. O'Barr concludes:

> Without leaders and an ideology to articulate how women relate both to families and to the world of work and policy, the ability and strength women demonstrated during Mau Mau has yet to be fully tapped for Kenyan national purposes. (p. 35)

Her perceptive analysis has relevance to the studies in this collection. These diverse ethnographies of women's lives in the midst of conflict show them learning new skills, gaining political awareness and taking on new roles in the public arena. They give little evidence, however, that through their efforts women have gained any greater share in the making of public policy or even of decisions in areas which affect their own lives as women. Some individual women are shown examining their lack of equal rights, and the Northern Ireland Women's Rights Movement encouraged action on a range of issues concerning women's daily lives. In the main, however, these essays show women placing others – their children, husbands and community – ahead of themselves. The political conflict enlisted their energies but inhibited collective action to promote women's interests.

Arising from these varied studies is an area for further research and analysis: the ideology of gender in the affirmation of cultural identity. In times of political conflict, particularly when a military build-up is necessary, masculine values become heightened and enhanced. Bowes brings this out in her chapter on Israeli kibbutz women. Here the paradox arises of legislation giving women equal rights and women joining the army along with men, yet an ideology of the heroic male fighter pervades society while religion continually reinforces traditional gender roles. Her analysis shows how the multiple structures of contemporary Israeli society interconnect in the devaluation of women.

Other examples as well show the enhanced imagery of the male confronting the enemy, protecting the outer boundaries of the society – men at the frontline of battle, men on the picket line – while women are designated in the background to carry on the tasks of survival and support. Even when women join the 'lines' of men, they are considered exceptional; in this way, the stereotypes of male and female are reinforced. The roles of 'mother' and 'housewife' may be enlarged and praised, as the case of Palestinian women vividly brings out. Yet this presents a contradiction: the value given to female roles emphasises gender polarity, thus strengthening male roles as the dominant structure.

Aligned with this heightened ideology of gender difference, another factor comes into play during a time of conflict. To strengthen group mobilisation, cultural or class identity often becomes more sharply defined. This usually requires a return to 'tradition' – that cultural storehouse of historical events, mythical happenings, evocative symbols and elusive images which can be used to convey charged meaning in the present. In many societies women are designated as the 'bearers of the collective' (see Yuval-Davis, 1980) – physical and social reproducers of future subjects. On the ideological plane, cultural images of women are called forth to represent the timeless world of the past. The veiling of Turkish women in Berlin, as Krojzl indicates, provides an effective symbol of Turkish cultural identity and separation; this custom in urban Turkey has become almost obsolete. For women who are seeking social change, what is the effect of their performing a drama in historical dress in order to embody the present-day cultural identity of their group?

The contradictory implications for women of cultural evocations of the past are set out with particular clarity by Sayigh and Peteet in their analysis of the tensions faced by Palestinian women since their uprooting:

> On the one hand, they refused cultural changes imposed on them through expulsion from Palestine, clinging to an idealised vision of the past, and striving to preserve all forms of authenticity. On the other, as they became increasingly active in the struggle for the return to their homeland, they realised that this demanded radical social change.

These women represent the situation of many others caught in the tension between the symbols of tradition and the desire for social change, the demands of ideology and the reality of daily living. These chapters documenting women's involvement in political conflict provide rich data and add important perspectives to the growing literature on gender and power.

References

Berkin, Carol R. and Lovett, Clara M. (ed.) (1980) *Women, War and Revolution* (New York and London: Holmes and Meier).

Bloomfield, Barbara (1985) 'Maerdy Women's Support Group', unpublished thesis, Ruskin College, Oxford.

Hirshon, Renée (1984) 'Introduction: Property, Power and Gender

Relations', in Hirschon, Renée (ed.) *Women and Property – Women as Property* (Beckenham, Kent: Croom Helm).

Janeway, Elizabeth (1981) *Powers of the Weak* (New York: Morrow Quill).

McLean, Scilla (1982) 'Report on UNESCO's report: The Role of Women in Peace Movements' in Stiehm (1982a).

McFadyean, Melanie (1984) 'Introduction' to Fairweather, Eileen, McDonough, Roisin, and McFadyean, Melanie, *Only the Rivers Run Free. Northern Ireland: The Women's War* (London and Sydney: Pluto Press).

O'Barr, Jean (ed.) (1982) *Perspectives on Power: Women in Africa, Asia, and Latin America* (Durham, NC: Duke Center for International Studies).

O'Barr, Jean (1985) 'Introductory Essays' to Likimani, Muthoni *Passbook Number F.47927* (London: Macmillan).

Randall, Vicky (1982) *Women and Politics* (London: Macmillan).

Rendel, Margherita (ed.) (1981) *Women, Power and Political Systems* (London: Croom Helm).

Stacey, Margaret and Price, Marion (1981) *Women, Power and Politics* (London: Tavistock).

Stiehm, Judith H. (ed.) (1982a) 'Women and Men's War', *Women's Studies International Forum*, vol. 5, nos 3–4.

Stiehm, Judith H. (1982b) 'The Protected, the Protector, the Defender', in Stiehm (1982a).

Sutton, Constance R. (1976) 'The Power to Define: Women, Culture, and Consciousness', in Bryce-Laporte, Roy S. and Thomas, Claudewell S. (eds) *Alienation in Contemporary Society: A Multidisciplinary Examination* (New York: Praeger).

Sweeney, Anne-Marie (1985) 'The Oxford Women's Support Group' in Oxford Miners Support Group *The Miners Strike in Oxford*.

Yuval-Davis, Nira (1980) 'The Bearers of the Collective: Women and Religious Legislation in Israel', *Feminist Review* no. 4, pp. 15–27.

Index